Studies in Literacy, Family, Culture and the State

The interface between the written and the oral

Whilst the fundamental significance of the spoken language for human interaction is widely acknowledged, that of writing is less well known, and in this wide-ranging series of essays Jack Goody examines in depth the complex and often confused relationship between oral and literate modes of communication. He considers the interface between the written and the oral in three major contexts; that internal to given societies, that between cultures or societies with and without writing, and that within the linguistic life of an individual. Specific analyses of the sequence of historical change within writing systems, the historic impact of writing upon Eurasian cultures, and the interaction between distinct oral and literate cultures in West Africa, precede an extensive concluding examination of contemporary issues in the investigation, whether sociological or psychological, of literacy. A substantial corpus of anthropological, historical and linguistic evidence is produced in support of Goody's findings, which form a natural complement to his own recently-published study of *The Logic of Writing and the Organization of Society*.

Studies in Literacy, Family, Culture and the State

Literacy
Literacy in Traditional Societies (edited, 1968)
The Domestication of the Savage Mind (1977)
The Logic of Writing and the Organization of Society (1986)
The Interface between the Written and the Oral (1987)

Family
Production and Reproduction: A Comparative Study of the Domestic Domain (1977)
The Development of the Family and Marriage in Europe (1983)

Culture
Cooking, Cuisine and Class: A Study in Comparative Sociology (1982)

The State
Technology, Tradition and the State in Africa (1971)

The interface between
the written and
the oral

JACK GOODY

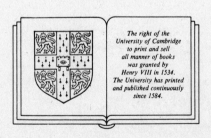

The right of the
University of Cambridge
to print and sell
all manner of books
was granted by
Henry VIII in 1534.
The University has printed
and published continuously
since 1584.

CAMBRIDGE UNIVERSITY PRESS

Cambridge

New York   New Rochelle

Melbourne   Sydney

Published by the Press Syndicate of the University of Cambridge
The Pitt Building, Trumpington Street, Cambridge CB2 1RP
32 East 57th Street, New York, NY 10022, USA
10 Stamford Road, Oakleigh, Melbourne 3166, Australia

First published 1987
Reprinted 1988

Printed in Great Britain at the University Press, Cambridge

British Library cataloguing in publication data

Goody, Jack
The interface between the written and the oral. –
(Studies in literacy, family, culture and the state)
1. Written communication. 2. Oral communication.
I. Title. II. Series
001.54   P221

Library of Congress cataloguing in publication data

Goody, Jack.
The interface between the written and the oral.
(Studies in Literacy, Family, Culture, and the State)
Bibliography.
Includes index.
1. Written communication. 2. Writing. 3. Oral communcation.
4. Sociolinguistics.
I. Title. II. Series.
P211.G66   1987   001.54   86-24428

ISBN 0 521 33268 0 hard covers
ISBN 0 521 33794 1 paperback

CE

Contents

Figures

Tables

Preface

This book deals with three aspects of the interface between the oral and the written which are often confused. There is the meeting of cultures with and without writing, historically and geographically. There is the interface of written and oral traditions in societies that employ writing to varying degrees in various contexts. And there is the interface between the use of writing and speech in the linguistic life of any individual. Chapter 11 takes up these problems specifically for language but the interest runs throughout the book.

The impact of the written channel upon cultural systems was never of course everywhere the same. It depended upon social circumstances and varied with the type of system employed for the visual representation of language. Such systems developed out of other forms of visual representation or graphic device – to put the notion yet more generally. They can be ordered morphologically and to some extent historically in a developmental sequence with a reasonable measure of precision.

There are many ambiguities in the use of the word literacy. In talking about its consequences, Watt and I (1963) referred to the presence of a system of writing, that is, not just to the written word as such but to the teaching of a system of writing; others use the term to indicate a specific level of accomplishment. Clearly there are a number of possible variations in the impact on culture, depending upon:

1 the nature of the script and its method of reproduction,
2 the numbers able to read and write at a specific level (for example, a signature),
3 whether individuals are learning to read and write their natural

tongue, a related language, a different living language, a dead
language or an invented language,
4 the width of use within the culture (e.g. whether or not that is
restricted to religion),
5 the content of the written tradition.
   Again, the question of literate (or non-literate) societies is
different from that of literate (or illiterate) individuals; in the first
case the term refers to the presence or absence of a written
tradition, in the second to the ability to read or write to a particular
level. It is in order to avoid some of these ambiguities that I have
tended to talk about societies with and without writing when
dealing with the first kind of interface, or with general comparisons.
   The opening section of the book deals with the sequence of
historical changes to and in writing systems, though it is one that
future evidence and subsequent reflection will certainly require us
to modify. The second part considers problems of the historical
impact of writing upon Eurasian cultures, while the third probes the
interaction between oral and written cultures (as distinct from the
co-existence of oral and literate channels within the same culture)
which is found in West African societies both in the recent past of
the historian and the yet more recent present of the fieldworker,
evidence for the latter coming largely from my own observations.
This is the situation I have earlier tried to describe for West Africa
(1968b). But in much of Asia and Indonesia such interaction is a yet
more salient feature of cultural systems; for example, the commentary of the Balinese puppeteer is strongly influenced by the themes
of Indian sacred writing contained in the *Mahabharata* and the
Ramayana, as is so much of the art and architecture. Here we are
dealing with the interface between oral and written cultures and my
general approach is to use the study of historical processes to
interpret the here and now, and the analysis of present observations
to understand what happened in the past. Comparative history and
comparative sociology are part of a single process of understanding
and explanation. Since I am also writing from an anthropological
background, the process of understanding and explanation has an
'ethnographic' dimension; that is to say, a dimension relating to
intensive studies (my own and those of others) and incorporating
the notions of the people whose behaviour is being studied. In

other words, I do not distinguish a separate domain of cultural studies concerned with meaning, since this must be one element in most social analyses but especially in those dealing with communication.

There are a number of general questions that need to be clarified at the start. First of all there is the question of the transmission of what I call 'standardized oral forms' rather than 'oral literature', in order to avoid the implication of 'letters' that is embedded in the concept 'literary'. In this we must include transmission from the oral register to the written form in which we know the oral product. The transmission of such forms (SOF) may occur:

1 in performance (before a local audience),
2 in rehearsal, where there is a different kind of interaction between speaker and listener which may involve a limited alternation of roles in the process of teaching and learning,
3 in performance out of context, e.g. in making a written record, which entails a shift of the poem or tale from one register to another.

It is the analysis of this last process that is critical in assessing the status of verbal forms such as the Bagre, the long 'myth' of the LoDagaa of northern Ghana, to which I refer throughout the book. 'Oral literature' is usually presented to non-participants in the form of the written word. In assessing the status of these versions, we have to remember that until recently their recording was necessarily undertaken *outside* the normal context of performance. Before the coming of the transistorized tape recorder (and to a limited extent the earlier gramophone), our knowledge of any except the shortest oral communication was confined to those produced under the third type of situation, when an outsider was usually involved as the audience and transcriber. The position was slightly different when an individual belonging to a society that had just acquired writing wrote down oral material in his own language, if that material formed part of his very own corpus of knowledge; in theory certain Near Eastern myths could have been written down in this way. But in virtually all these cases writing down, whether by dictation, or even from one's own memory in the case of long standardized oral forms, entails a 'constructed' performance, since the very deliberate process of spelling out (dictation) and writing down (transcription) often produces significant differences.

From the problem of transmission, I turn to that of the registers or channels available within any particular culture, and how this second level of interface is affected by changes such as the introduction of particular forms of writing, printing or of other channels, all of which must be seen as additions to oral communication. For while writing may replace oral interaction in certain contexts, it does not diminish the basically oral–aural nature of linguistic acts. Strictly speaking, therefore, it is a mistake to divide 'cultures' into the oral and the written: it is rather the oral and the oral plus the written, printed, etc. This being the case, for the individual there is always the problem of the interaction between the registers and the uses, between the so-called oral and the written traditions, that is, at the third level of interface which I consider in the fourth and final section.

The complexities of the second level of interaction between registers in the same culture come out when we consider the process of writing a 'paper' or 'speech' for a conference. In composing such a talk, which is not a 'talk' at all but a 'lecture', a reading, I may first sketch out a rough outline, either in my head or on paper; more probably this phase will be implicit rather than explicit. I then construct and rehearse the sentences (or at least the constituent phrases of those sentences) before committing them to paper. I do so 'sub-orally', monitoring them through the 'inner ear'. The words, phrases, sentences are then written down, altered or rearranged, and finally read through before they are delivered to the audience. I may store the words and the structure more or less verbatim so that I can speak without 'script', without 'notes', without immediate visual reference. What a good 'speaker', you may exclaim; or what a terrible 'talk'. Although the work was first formulated 'orally', by mouth or silently in the mind, it was not communicated directly to the ears of the other, the hearer, that is, aurally. Between formulation and communication, the recording (recoding) and reading (decoding) of the message by the use of writing has intervened, involving the transfer from sound to sight, from ear to eye. This transfer to a graphic medium enables me to recast sentences, change the order, alter the structure. Nor do I have to do this all at one time, the time of composition; the production of the text or score, as distinct from the utterance or performance, can be a continuing process, subject to review.

One can of course 'review' the words when composing a song in the head. One can and does. With longer constructions, especially those without the strong rhythmic character of song or verse (and virtually all verse in oral culture is song, that is, accompanied by music or given a musical form through the voice), the process is obviously more difficult. On the other hand, writing necessitates some measure of reconsideration since it involves the transfer of linguistic material from one channel to another. The writer pauses, thinks what he is saying, as if he was dictating slowly to himself. I use the verb 'dictate' deliberately since, as we have seen, it is a process that has dominated the recording of oral forms and has mediated the transformation of utterance into text that has provided us with the raw material for scholarly study.

So when I compose orally (in my head) the sentences that I now write, I compose sentences for writing, ones that are adapted to the written channel. Some work has been done on the difference in the nature of linguistic communication in English depending on the channel employed and this is reviewed in chapter 11. Such research employs various psycholinguistic tests such as *cloze* procedures to distinguish kinds of verbal ability, written as distinct from spoken *usage*, within the context of written and spoken communicative *acts*. Other methods have been used to differentiate between the frequency of nominalization and verbalization, of nouns and verbs – one is reminded of Bateson's cry 'down with nouns' – taken as indicators of literature influences in sentence structure, in speech or writing. Then there is work on repetition, formulaic expressions and parataxis (the way of joining clauses). These differences of expression vary between individuals within a particular literate culture, but they also mark the products of the written and the oral traditions respectively.

In the present discussion the term 'tradition' usually refers to specific aspects of the content composed in or transmitted through the oral (spoken) and written registers in a particular culture. But as we have seen, we make a mistake if we think of these 'traditions' as totally distinct one from another. There is bound to be constant interaction for reasons that are too obvious to mention. Even where a large proportion of the population neither reads nor writes, they often partake indirectly of both 'traditions'. Hindu India is a case in point. In the distant past reading and writing has at times been deliberately restricted to the Brahmin or other higher castes; until recently this was the case with the reading of religious texts. Nevertheless in all regions of that vast country a literate religion pervaded the world view of every caste from top to bottom, whether or not the believers could read or write. Some wanted to modify it, some broke away altogether, but the products of the written religion dominated much of their social and cultural life. Not only the content but in many cases the very presence of writing itself structures religious practice, providing a source of truth (the Bible grasped in the right hand, the Jewish phylactery on the wrist, the Muslim verses sewn on the fighting smock). But the written word often has to become the spoken word in order to communicate fully with spiritual beings as with human ones; and so it was frequently considered essential for the literates not only to read aloud but even to internalize the text and then to recite it from memory. Only in this way was full understanding possible, for understanding involved overt, public, communication, often without direct recourse to the Book.

Moreover, even where some pluralistic societies do have something one can describe as distinct 'traditions', one oral, one written, the 'oral' differs in certain basic respects from the structure of tradition in a *purely oral* society. Firstly there is a constant dialectic between written and oral activities. Each literary work that is accorded high status, whether it is the Bible, the Qu'ran or the works of Marx, gives rise to commentaries that take shape in both the spoken and the written registers. From the historical point of view, we know of these commentaries only when they are written down and become the *Torah*, the *Hadith* or the *Smirti*, that is, when they themselves are subsequently incorporated into the written corpus. The Religions of the Book provide particularly vivid examples of such incorporation, the learned written tradition constantly drawing upon such commentaries. Secondly, major topics of human concern are largely defined and appropriated by the written tradition and its commentaries; that is where we find discussion of Heaven and Hell, of morality and taboo, of God and his prophets. Hence the oral is left to fill in the interstices, to pick up the residue, to deal with less central issues. The 'myth' is developed in writing while folktales continue to have an oral half-life around the winter hearth; religion is the Church, magic the marginal; Easter services are conducted by the priest, the spring rituals are a matter of parade and display, of jest and irony. One of the problems inherent in the work of the folkloric, anthropological nationalists of Europe in the nineteenth century was their failure to appreciate the partial nature of the 'oral tradition' to be found in a society with writing, anyhow one with long and extensive literacy.

In most of this book I will concentrate upon 'literary' material in the usual sense of this word as referring to 'art forms'. But other important cultural items are intimately affected by the use of writing. I was recently enquiring into certain rural protests in northern Ghana which were closely linked to the use of literate mechanisms (that is, registration, mortgages, courts) for acquiring land (1980). Some of the difficulties arose from the deliberate manipulation of the power of the word by the literate, the educated, the schooled. Others resulted from a general over-valuation of the 'truth' of the written word, while yet another element was the inevitable consequence of literacy, its role as a reductive instrument, in this case reducing the multiplicity of human rights in a plot of land to a simple, one-line statement, 'X owns Y'. All over the world, the techniques of writing have been used to acquire, that is, to alienate, the land of 'oral' peoples. It is a most powerful instrument, the use of which is rarely devoid of social, economic and political significance, especially since its introduction usually involves the domination of the non-literate segment of the population by the literate one, or even the less literate by the more. Where writing is, 'class' cannot be far away.

I have used as a testing ground for my discussion of oral cultures and oral traditions my own fieldwork among the LoDagaa and Gonja of northern Ghana. I spent two years with both of these groups (in the latter case working with Esther Goody) and have exchanged visits with both peoples up to the moment of writing. When I first stayed with the LoDagaa of Birifu in 1950, a European school had just been established in the settlement. Some young men had already been sent to school elsewhere and had returned as teachers. The Gonja had for long been influenced directly by Islam and writing had played a peripheral role in the society even before the advent of the new education, resisted by the Muslims but accepted more readily by other groups. Writing had begun to make its mark in a 'restricted' way, although modern schooling has altered the situation dramatically over the past thirty years. Nevertheless, the oral tradition continued within a changing context and I recorded versions of the Bagre 'myth' of the LoDagaa over a thirty year period (Goody 1972; Goody and Gandah 1981).

In discussing some aspects of the interface and the nature of 'logical' reasoning, I have continually referred to the 'syllogism'. This is partly because a seminal study of Vygotsky and Luria focussed on this activity, which therefore became central to subsequent psychological experiments, partly because it is a paradigm of Aristotelian logic, and partly because I do not find it profitable to discuss logic, reasoning or rationality except in terms of specifics of this kind. For me, too, the syllogism serves as a paradigm.

I should add that what I am trying to explain is not logical operation on a day to day level, since it never occurred to me that this was absent in oral cultures, but why they do not have the 'logic' of the philosophers. Not why they cannot add (they can) but why they do not have mathematicians and mathematics, not whether or not they analyze language (they do) but whether they have grammars and grammarians (*in sensu strictu*), not whether they have poetry, but whether they have literature (that is, written literature).

Since writing is so closely associated with schools, it is inevitable that I return to this subject on several occasions. In Chapter 6 I touch upon some effects on African society of European schools; in Chapter 7 I discuss forms of knowledge and refer to the kinds taught in schools in Ancient Egypt; in the following chapter I consider the question of memory in oral reproduction and compare the procedures with that of early Sumerian schools; in Chapter 10 schooling forms an important variable in the psychological experiments bearing on cognitive abilities and skills, and I return to consider the connection of writing with schooling (as distinct from education) from the earliest times.

It has been suggested to me that I should use the introduction to this volume to offer 'a reply to critics' of what some see as the oralist (Maxwell 1983), some as the literacy, thesis (Street 1985). If I do not do so, it is partly because I often find such exercises picayune when carried out by others, more suited to an article than a book. Partly too, because I prefer to try and advance the analysis in other ways. In any case I do not have an overall theory that determines each particular hypothesis but simply a topic for enquiry, which seems to produce answers, perhaps partial, to intellectual questions. Watt and I considered calling our original article 'A Theory of Literacy', but rejected it in favour of 'consequences'. By 1968 I had preferred 'implications' for the first term and more recently 'writing' for the second, in order to try and avoid some of the ambiguities. In more substantive ways earlier contentions have been changed in favour of new ones. The 'alphabetic' writing of the Greeks is no longer seen as so unique an achievement, while its dates seem to require revising in an earlier direction. Logographic scripts like the Chinese contain many phonetic components and the division between these, syllabaries and alphabets is less pronounced in certain ways. The result of these reassessments is not to abandon the idea that the invention and development of writing were important events for humanity but to elaborate the argument in the light of new information or informed criticism.

A revaluation of the original statement of the hypothesis was necessary not only because of the longer history of what was, in most respects, an alphabetic script; but also because it was clear that certain of the features attributed to alphabetic writing were to be found in other systems. Backward in time this meant the Ancient Near East, for which some aspects of the relation between writing and cognition were discussed in *The Domestication of the Savage Mind* (1977) while others are considered in the second chapter of the present study.

But it also meant reconsidering the effects of writing in India and China, a topic to which some attention was given in a volume of essays, *Literacy in Traditional Societies* (1968), more specifically by Gough. Our initial emphasis had been too much on the tradition of western humanism and the problems to which it gave rise. We certainly gave greater weight than we should to the 'uniqueness of the West' in terms of modes of communication, a failing in which we were not alone; it has been at least an implicit assumption, not only of many classical historians and those who have studied the rise of industrial capitalism, but also of some of the valuable studies of literacy in Western Europe that have appeared since we first wrote. One of the best antidotes to such ethnocentrism is Rawski's book, *Education and Popular Literacy in Ch'ing China* (1979). While recognizing the difficulties that logograms present for learning to read and especially for learning to write, she points to the widespread existence of schools and of the elements of literacy in Ch'ing China. The notion of literacy as a level of attainment carries other implications than with an alphabetic or syllabic script because individuals can recognize anything from 1 to 30,000 characters. The script gives access to the reading and composition of written works in a very different way. Despite these qualifications, the general trend of this research is to strengthen rather than lessen the case for emphasizing the social and cognitive effects of writing.

I have made one exception to this resolution not to offer an 'answer to critics' in the present context, that is, in the discussion of the major work of Scribner and Cole (1981) on the Vai in chapter 10. I needed to resolve for myself what appeared to be a divergence between the import of the work we had carried out jointly, which is reported in chapter 9, and the results of their extensive, carefully-planned and scrupulously administered tests undertaken over a period of years. The outcome includes a consideration of the costs and benefits of using psychological tests to explain cultural–historical data. Or to rephrase the problem, since I have a general commitment to the unity of the social sciences (at least in terms of their results making sense to one another), to the limits of a too narrowly defined concept of cognition. Both discussions go back to Vygotsky but my own solution lies in being less mentalistic and more 'historical' than his experiments allowed for.

Finally this book represents another kind of interface. When I originally studied social anthropology, it was not only because I was interested in other cultures of a traditional kind, but because I wanted to see what light their situation threw on the modern world,

not only 'ours'. For those we were studying all of course existed in
the contemporary scene. The rapid change they were undergoing
and the nature of the adjustment was of the greatest importance not
only practically but also in a theoretical perspective. In the social
sciences change often has to take the place of experiment in order
to investigate causal implications.

Since I was interested in this interface, I have not hesitated to
draw together aspects of my experience of two particular 'simple'
societies in the broader context of Africa and of Europe, historically as well as regionally. Such an approach may cause discomfort
to those scholars who, either for reasons of temperament or theory,
prefer to concentrate on one group or on one situation at a time.
But it seems to me that, as among the LoDagaa, there is room for
more than one approach to knowledge.

Most of the chapters presented here have been published before
as work in progress but in somewhat different forms; I thank the
publishers concerned for permission to include them in the present
volume. A version of chapter 1 appeared as "Alphabets and
Writing" in *Contact: human communication and its history*, ed.
R. Williams, published by Thames & Hudson, London, 1981. A
form of Chapter 2 was given at a conference in Bielefeld and
published in F. Coulmas and K. Ehlich (eds.), *Writing in Focus*,
Berlin, 1983. Chapter 4 was presented as a paper for an Urbino
Symposium, published under the title, *Oralità: Cultura, Lettera-
tura, Discorso* (B. Gentili and G. Paioni, eds.), Edizioni dell'
Ateneo. Chapter 5 appeared as "The impact of Islamic writing on
the oral cultures of West Africa" in *Cahiers d'études africains*
(1971): 455–66. Chapter 6 was printed in the *Times Literary
Supplement*, May 12 (1972), pp. 539–40 as "Literacy and the
non-literate". Parts of Chapter 7 appeared in French as "Les
chemins du savoir oral' in *Critiques*, Dec.-Jan. 1979–80, and a fuller
version in D. Tanner (ed.) *Spoken and Written Language: exploring orality and literacy*, published by Abex, Norwood, N.J., 1982.
Chapter 8 was published in French in *L'Homme* 17 (1977): 29–52,
as 'Mémoire et apprentissage dans les sociétés avec et sans écriture;
la transmission du Bagré'. Chapter 9 was written with Michael Cole
and Sylvia Scribner and published in *Africa* 47 (1977): 289–304. A
very different version of chapter 11 appeared in *Soviet & Western*

Anthropology edited by Ernest Gellner, Duckworth, London (1980), pp. 119–33.

Finally I would like to acknowledge the help received from the many scholars who have at one time or another read and commented upon parts of this manuscript, including J. Alexander, R. Allchin, V. Allerton, M. Bernal, J. Bottéro, D. and T. Carraher, M. Cole, R. Finnegan, E. Goody, R. Horton, P. Johnson-Laird, S. Levinson, G. E. R. Lloyd, J. Oates, D. Olson, J. Ray, T. Turner, and a host of others over the years (especially S.-Hugh-Jones and G. A. Lewis). For help with word-processing and research on the final version I am indebted to Antonia Lovelace, Janet Reynolds and Carolyn Wyndham.

St Johns College
Cambridge

Acknowledgements

The author and publisher are grateful to the following for permission to reproduce illustrative material:

Figure 1 (p. 9) Cambridge University Museum of Archaeology and Anthropology
Figure 2 (p. 11) Egyptian Museum, Cairo
Figure 5 (p. 23) Staatliche Museenzu, Berlin
Figure 6 (p. 24) Musée de Louvre, Paris
Figure 7 (p. 29) Trustees of the British Museum
Figure 11 and Table 3 (pp. 248 and 223) Harvard University Press. Reproduced from S. Scribner and M. Cole, *The Psychology of Literacy*, 1981, pp. 253 and 17

I

Writing and the alphabet

1

The historical development of writing

Systems of communication are clearly related to what man can make of his world both internally in terms of thought and externally in terms of his social and cultural organization. So changes in the means of communication are linked in direct as well as indirect ways to changes in the patterns of human interaction. Language is the specific human attribute, the critical means of interaction between individuals, the foundation of the development of what we call 'culture' and of the way in which learned behaviour is transmitted from one generation to the next. But if language is inextricably associated with 'culture', it is writing that is linked with 'civilization', with the culture of cities, with complex social formations, though perhaps not quite in so direct a manner. Nor is this only a matter of the implications for social organization, radical as these were in the long run. It is not just a question of providing the means by which trade and administration can be extended, but of changes in the cognitive processes that man is heir to, that is, the ways in which he understands his universe.

Writing and design

The physical basis of writing is clearly the same as drawing, engraving and painting – the so-called graphic arts. It depends ultimately on man's ability to manipulate tools by means of his unique hand with its opposable thumb, coordinated of course by eye, ear and brain. There is little evidence of such activities in the early phases of man's history, during the Early and Middle Old Stone Age. But with the coming of the later Old Stone Age (the Upper Palaeolithic, c. 30,000 – 10,000 BC) we find an outburst of graphic forms in the caves of south-western France, then later on in the rock shelters of Southern Africa and much later still, on the birch bark scrolls of the Ojibway of North America.

Writing, then, has its roots in the graphic arts, in significant design. To use distinctions that sometimes overlap and are not always very helpful, both the intention and the consequences of these designs can be described as either *communicative* or *expressive*. Expression can be seen as an incomplete communication, and on one level as self-communion, a kind of graphic monologue, the aim of which is the externalization of thoughts and feelings or simply the creation of design itself (as in a doodle or some more regular pattern) without any immediate communication taking place; in this case the encoder and decoder are one and the same person, since no others are involved, although expression in a long-lasting medium may mean that after a lapse of time another person can receive and interpret the message, whatever the intention of the originator of the design. In terms of reception as distinct from emission, even a non-significant design, for example, a pattern, may, like a natural object, be endowed with meaning, or with a more precise meaning, by the perceiver, even though communication, in the strict sense, has not taken place (that is to say, where intention is absent). Nevertheless, the prior existence of a system of interactive communication appears to be a prerequisite for these reflexive forms of meaningful act.

The designs in their turn range from the *iconographic* (which we can also refer to as the pictorial, the figurative or the eidetic, as for example when a picture of a 'horse' stands for a horse) to the *arbitrary* (the non-pictorial or abstract). In speaking of writing systems, iconographic designs are often referred to as pictographs (or pictograms, if they are isolated signs rather than extensive systems), abstract ones as ideograms; however these terms are somewhat misleading and in any case tend to be used inconsistently. In between these two poles we have quasi-pictorial designs, which may be

1 *metonymic*, as when a part stands for the whole, a picture of a saddle for a horse; or
2 *associational*, as when hay stands for horses. In some aristocratic

societies a horse may stand for a knight, as three-dimensionally in chess; this latter variety of sign is sometimes called 'ideographic', for example by Diringer (1962:102); or

3 *formalized*, as when four dots :: stand for a horse (the feet looked at from below), or the sign $\boxed{: : :}$ from the Vai (West African) syllabary for a case of gin (the bottles looked at from above). Non-pictorial designs are (i) *phonological*, for example, H for horse, (ii) *purely conventional*, for example, the sign ? to indicate that a 'question' has been asked.

Once again the categories are neither exclusive nor unchanging: the peacock or elephant in a North Indian embroidery may develop over time into a highly formal design whose reference is partly extrinsic to its form, that is to say, the reference has to be supplied by convention rather than by observation. Indeed the process may go yet further so that the specific relation between signifier and signified is totally lost (that is, cannot be reconstructed) and disappears into 'pattern'. But loss of meaning is not the only way we arrive at this point; in many cases such a relationship may have been absent from the outset, for there is no evidence, in the graphic arts at least, of a general progression from representation to abstraction (Boas 1927:352), indeed, if anything the reverse is true (Leroi-Gourhan 1964:262).

Such designs or patterns are purely abstract, geometrical, falling into the category of non-significant design.[1] Equally a non-pictorial design, such as the swastika, may acquire significance (that is to say, become meaningful in the 'symbolic' sense of standing for something else) in the specific context in which it is found, whether this be Hindu India or Nazi Germany.

In other words, whether the graphic design lies towards the pictorial pole (the pole of 'natural indices'), or the formal or arbitrary pole, its form affects the relationship between the signifier (the graphic design) and the signified. At one level, a pictorial or natural design 'means what it says'. At another level it may not; the early alphabet took an iconographic form, a hang-over from an earlier script since the individual signs themselves were semantically meaningless. Equally an arbitrary design is often 'non-significant' (as in many patterns) but it may mean what people agree it should say; the relationship is arbitrary both in terms of whether it has a meaning (for the individual or the collectivity) and in terms of what that meaning should be.

This distinction within significant design between pictorial and arbitrary roughly corresponds to the wider (semiotic) distinction some authors make between 'natural indices' and '*signa*'. The former are self-explanatory, but in the case of *signa*, "A stands for B as the result of arbitrary human choice" (Leach 1976:12; Mulder and Hervey 1972). Early graphic systems (e.g. North American pictographs) are clearly not totally arbitrary since the association is often (partly at least) 'by nature'; one kind of object (a drawing) indicates another kind of object (as well as indicating a morpheme for or a more extended verbal description of that object) by graphic representation. That representation may sometimes be pictorial, sometimes of a metonymic kind ('part for whole'), but it is more usually of a stylized, simplifying variety (for example, stick figures in action, corresponding to verbs). In these cases the representations lean towards the realm of 'natural indices'. But any graphic repertoire (especially for a full writing system) must certainly introduce arbitrary indices, i.e. *signa*, if only because language itself has no one-to-one link with objects or actions in the outside world, so the system cannot be purely pictorial. Since language, as de Saussure insisted, is arbitrary, so too is writing, though a direct 'pictographic' link is possible in the case of some logographic signs (i.e. signs for words, for morphemes), just as a similar link is possible with sounds by means of onomatopoeia in the case of the spoken language. However, the point must be made that even the simplest forerunner of writing includes some non-pictorial signs.

The further subdivision of *signa* into *symbols* and *signs* also applies to graphic systems. Symbols are defined by Mulder and Hervey as "*signa* dependent on a separate (occasional) definition for their correct interpretation – e.g. x, y, z in an algebraic equation" and signs are "*signa* with wholly fixed conventional denotation, e.g. $\pm$, $=$, $\equiv$, in an algebraic equation" (Leach 1976:13). The difference is related by Leach to the fact that signs (e.g. $+/-$) do not occur in isolation, but only convey information when combined with other signs. "*Signs* are always *contiguous* to other signs which are members of the same set" (1976:13). Whether this formulation makes for an adequate contrast with 'symbols'

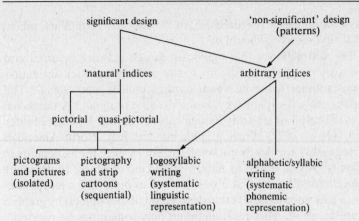

Table 1. Variations in graphic representation.

seems open to doubt but the structural context of all signa, indeed all indices, is undoubtedly important, and certainly critical in discussing particular graphic systems. In terms of 'natural indices', pictograms (isolated natural indices) and pictographs (systems of such indices) are to be distinguished in just this way; in terms of *signa*, ownership marks need to be distinguished from the letters of the alphabet. However it seems preferable to treat this distinction as a variable displaying a number of discontinuities (and a variable that constitutes one of the differences among systems of writing and proto-writing), not simply as a binary contrast. For all *signa* occur in a structural context; none stand completely alone. But some sets are more tightly structured than others. Clearly the alphabet, as an approximate system of signs for phonemes, is very highly structured; a syllabic system slightly less so and a logographic system, which provides signs for words, is structured yet more loosely – and in a similar way to language itself. Other graphic systems (including the highly developed variety used by the Maya, whose status is subject to much disagreement) lie further down the continuum, at the end of which we find the non-pictorial forms (largely isolated signs) painted about cavern walls as well as the pictures of the strip cartoon or those of the individual variety that decorate the studio wall. Even at this end of the continuum the idea of a 'set' is still present, though in a very limited sense and hardly to the degree supposed by Leroi-Gourhan for the Aurignacian cave-art of South-western France, which he tries to interpret as a highly structured semiotic system.

Proto-writing

The use of pictorial representations in sequential form, found mainly in North America, has been called picture-writing. The early authority on 'pictography', Garrick Mallery, described it as conveying and recording an idea or occurrence by graphic means without the use of words or letters (1886:13), constituting one form of "thought-writing directly addressed to the sight", the other form of such communication being gesture language.

Two comments need to be made about this view. First, we need to maintain a distinction between the single and the sequential use of graphic design. An example of a 'pictogram' would be a zig-zag sign to indicate 'electricity' or 'lightning'; it stands by itself both physically and morphologically, that is to say, it does not necessarily form part of a wider semiotic system; it does not need to stand in opposition to or in conjunction with other such signs. It is similar, in some respects, to a single picture on a wall. A sequential system of 'pictographs' such as we find in embryonic writing, in attempts to reproduce the flow of speech or of linguistically dominated 'thought', is closer to the 'strip cartoon'; the kind of sequence we find in the pictorial representations of the national myth of the establishment of the Ethiopian crown, which incorporates the famous visit of the Queen of Sheba to Solomon, a visit that resulted in the birth of Menelik, first ruler in the line of Judah, which was held to continue until the deposition of Haile Selassie in 1972 (Fig. 1). By sequential design I refer to a succession of distinct elements, which may of course be pictorial, for example in a rose-pattern. Picture-writing involves a systematic, sequential relationship between designs, although the degree of systemization may be low.

Secondly, while Mallery, like many others, speaks of pictographs as 'thought-writing' (or even as 'ideographic' systems) that represents objects or events, concepts or thoughts, without the intervention of language, it is difficult to accept the absence of a linguistic element, even for gesture. For animals, gesture can be

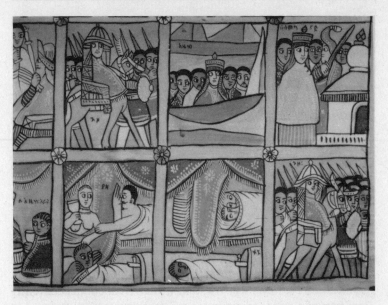

Fig. 1. The national myth of Ethiopia, celebrating the visit of the Queen of
Sheba to Jerusalem and her meeting with Solomon, was recorded
throughout the country in a series of 'strip' paintings.

described as non-verbal communication. But for human beings, the
coding and decoding of gesture must include a linguistic component, as in all processes of thinking or of conceptualization.
Indeed, one important definition of symbolic gestures, 'emblems',
sees them as acts which have a "direct verbal translation usually
consisting of a word or two" (Ekman 1976:14), though of course
other forms of gesture exist (facial expressions of emotion, regula-
tors, adaptors and illustrators) where there is neither the same
precise meaning nor the same mutually perceived intention to
communicate. How much more deeply is language embedded in
the specifically human activity involved in graphic design, where
language appears as an intrinsic intermediary? As Leroi-Gourhan
maintains, figurative art is "inseparable from language"
(1964:269); the whole development of graphic forms is linked to
speech. Leaving aside the notion of a possible line of historical
development, it is clear that one is never engaged simply in making

an icon of an object as such; a horse standing in a field is a horse viewed in terms of a language that places the animal in a system of categories, as well as in the more widely embracing context of discourse that attributes to the animal certain general characteristics of speed, diet, and links it with various mythological, political and economic notions. Neither in the mind's eye nor on the spread of canvas can a representation of the outside world be independent of linguistic usage, that is, independent not simply of categories but of the accumulated experience embodied in discourse. Equally, as Rosch has insisted (1977), category systems themselves are clearly not independent of the nature of objects in the outside world. There is, as the phrase goes, 'feedback'.

After these preliminary comments on the spread of types of graphic design, let us return to the historical question. It is presumably not by accident that we find the conjunction of the emergence of *Homo sapiens* with a greatly increased brain capacity on the one hand, and with, on the other, the first appearance of graphic art together with what have been called the "striking innovations . . . in the psychic sphere" as evidenced by the careful burial of the dead, clothed and wearing personal ornaments (J. G. D. Clark 1977:104–5). These graphic forms begin with the engraved and painted materials of the Aurignacian deposits (*c*. 30,000 BC), but the major flowering of art occurred between 25,000 and 10,000 BC and consisted mainly of cave paintings. Graphic art seems to have come into being in the late Old Stone Age, that is to say, at the time the present species of mankind became the dominant, indeed the only, hominid species. The larger brain size may be directly connected with the dominance man achieved, but speech may already have been present. So too may have been the enlarged vocal cords (Lieberman *et al*. 1972). Although, as we have seen, graphics and language are often viewed as alternative modes of communication (and so in some ways they are), any elaborate use of visual 'representation' requires the advanced conceptual system intrinsic to language use. It is true that the simplest painting on pebbles (such as are found in the earlier Azilian cultures), or the imprinting of hands and feet on cavern walls, may not involve a high degree of conceptual elaboration. Even though elementary graphic signs are thought by some authors

Fig. 2. The Narmer Palette. One of the first examples of writing in Egypt, bringing out the link between graphic forms, pictures and writing.

to be part of a more elaborate system, a true semiotic, such a degree of structuring seems unlikely; the 'communicative' or 'expressive' aspects of such art appear to be general rather than specific, loosely rather than tightly structured. Nor did they lead to any formal semiotic that could be described as embryonic writing. It is generally agreed that this gap is filled morphologically in quite another part of the world, by the so-called 'picture-writing' of the North American Indians.

Both being forms of graphic representation, the connection between art and writing is close not only in the early stages but in later calligraphy, illumination and illustration. Early writing in the Near East often has a figurative (sometimes a sculptural) counter-part; word and picture are complementary (Fig. 2). In Egypt the Narmer palette represents the beginning of both writing and monumental art, and the same conjunction seems to occur in Mesopotamia. Even when found singly or in small groups, early graphic forms, pictorial or arbitrary, are sometimes taken to be communicating 'messages', implicitly or explicitly, and as such are assumed to be forerunners of writing. At the explicit level of interpretation, the message content may not be very different in a representation of a hand with pointed finger or of a bison with an arrow in its flank, though one may be a standardized index (a grapheme), the other a unique or isolated picture. In North America single indices, depicting a man's 'totem', the emblem of his clan or of himself, are sometimes found located in quarries or at water holes to show that a particular group or person had visited the place. Similar designs are commonly used as signs of the owners or makers of property, like the marks of Near Eastern potters or the five arrows of the Brothers Rothschild.

An important step is taken when these pictures or *signa* are strung together in sequential form, most notably in the great scrolls of the Ojibway *Midéwewin* society, since the possibility of syntax, as distinct from a 'path expression', now arises. While such picture-writing is often placed in contrast to later systems of writing because of its reliance on visual communication largely "independent of the spoken language" (Gelb 1974:1034), I have argued that the assumption of a direct link between cue and brain seems misleading. Language is always involved and linguistic translations are made of the graphic sequences. Indeed a variety of first-level translations are possible, a fact indicating that the sequences do not transcribe language but suggest it. There is no systematic, one-to-one relationship between the graphic and the linguistic codes as such. Hence the developed picture-writing of the Ojibway can be described as mnemonic, that is to say, it can only be understood by someone who, in the case of the records of chants, has learnt the specific linguistic acts which the signs signify. In the case of records of legends and myths, however, it is not so much a mnemonic as a prompt, or rather a peg on which to hang a variety of possible versions. This is a question to which we shall return after looking in more detail at the proto-writing of the Ojibway and of their neighbours, the Dakota (or Sioux) of the Northern American plains. The Dakota invented a calendrical system of Winter Counts, the best example of which is that painted on a buffalo robe by Lone Dog (Fig. 3). Commencing in the winter of 1800–01, every

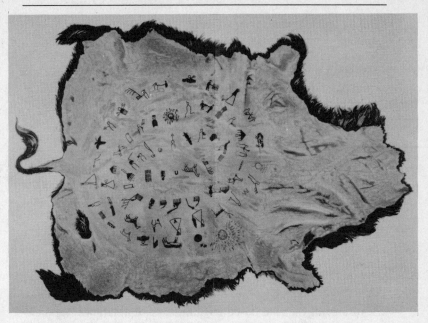

Fig. 3. Buffalo robe by Lone Dog. A restricted system of pictorial signs used by the Dakota Indians recorded the passage of time by counting winters, each sign representing an event of the year that had passed.

year is represented by a sign referring to an incident, often trivial,
that had occurred during the past twelve months (Mallery 1893).[2]

Among the Ojibway, the use of 'pictographs' inscribed on
birchbark scrolls centred upon the cult of the Midéwewin, marked
by a type of 'tutorial shamanism' which in many areas replaced the
earlier forms of 'visionary shamanism'. In tutorial shamanism an
individual became a pupil of a senior member of the society and
handed over a large amount of wealth in exchange for instruction
involving the scrolls.

It was by means of these birchbark scrolls that the "complex rituals
of oral traditions of the southern Ojibway were transmitted by the
Midé shamans to their disciples or candidates for initiation"
(Dewdney 1975:13). Consequently the scrolls were secret documents, meant to act as a mnemonic for the initiate but not as a means
of communicating information to the world at large. "Should the
secrecy of his information be uppermost in his mind he might employ
condensation, abstraction, atrophy, or even *amputation*. Or he
might go further, using symbolic conversion or the ultimate device
for misleading the uninitiated: substitution of the significant form by
another completely irrelevant one" (1975:18). The function was
always mnemonic. "It was not the written word, merely a means of
recalling the oral tradition and the details of the Midé master's
instruction ... even the oral tradition was not transmitted in any
rigid way from one generation to another. . . . it must be kept in mind
that behind the instruction scrolls were individuals for whom the
dream spoke with an authority equal to, and sometimes exceeding
that of the oral tradition. Interaction between the dream, the sacred
lore, and the mnemonic device of the scrolls produced, by a sort of
cross-fertilization, a richer and richer body of rites, variations on the
traditional themes, and birchbark pictography" (p. 22).

The Ojibway scrolls dealt with some of the main features of Midé
concern, that is, the creation of the world and of man, the origin of
death, the introduction of the Midéwewin, and the ancestral origins
of the Ojibway people. "For each and all of these purposes a scroll
could be devised as a mnemonic aid" but they would form the basis
of very different interpretations by the self-same person (p. 23–24).
Their role resembles that ascribed to the Australian *churinga*,
plaques of wood or stone engraved with abstract designs, spirals,

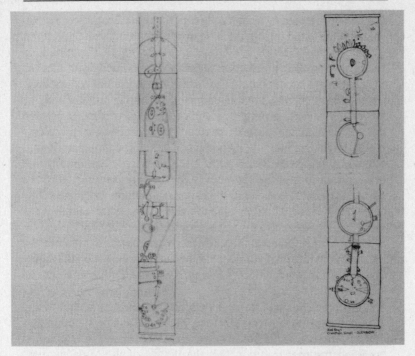

Fig. 4. North American Ojibway birch-bark scrolls, redrawn by Mallery. Mnemonic devices recalling tales of their origin (left) and the creation of the world: the link with language is tenuous.

straight lines, groups of dots, that indicate the content of myth or the location of sacred places. It is the same function of 'mytho-gram' that Leroi-Gourhan has attributed to some paintings and engravings of the Late Stone Age in France, where 'mytho-graphy' is the visual equivalent of the verbal 'mytho-logy' (1964:268, 272). While this is not the only part played by North American pictographs – Mallery, who worked on them in the late nineteenth century, mentions the mnemonic recording of chants, calendars and chronology as well as the use of graphemes for notices of visits and direction, for warning signs, elementary topography and especially for the identification of individuals and clans by 'totemic' designs – it was clearly one of the main uses of sequential pictographs in general.

The scrolls, then, consist of origin tales or Medé migration stories, and of ritual charts showing the stages through which the neophyte progressed (Fig. 4). Each of these takes the form of a visual narrative, a more abstract, formalized version of the kind of strip cartoon used in the popular paintings of the Ethiopian myth. Each implies the idea of a journey, a coming or a going, of movement over space, although in fact the passage of an initiate through the stages of initiation does not necessarily imply any physical movement at all. The journey is the way in which time or passage is envisaged; hence the importance of narrative, of the journey through time and space. One's eye moves from part of the scroll to the next, unwinding the creation of the world or the origin of death, a different type of scanning to the decoding of language signs involved in reading, that is, in reading a text.

The Ojibway graphics are a form of what Kramer has called "literature writing" (1970:33); the system appears to be similar in general to that used by the Cuna Indians of Panama (Nordenskiöld 1938) which Kramer sees as emerging after the collapse of Spanish rule in the nineteenth century (1970:127) and which Nordenskiöld associates with Mexican writing. We find a functionally similar kind of mnemonic graphics among the Iban of Borneo, with signs carved on wooden staves.

The Cuna graphics were used mainly for learning and remembering songs and incantations. Nordenskiöld records an incantation and songs, in the first of which there is a symbol for every word, in the latter only for the most important words. "In both cases the picture writing serves as a support for the memory and is used mainly by those who want to learn the incantation and the song" (1938:422). In former times this 'writing' was carved on pieces of wood which were buried with the owner.

But such writing also had other uses. One Cuna Indian is supposed to have kept a diary for many years, noting down storms, the angle of the sun, visits by foreigners, and other events. Another used it to record the history of the tribe, reportedly writing English in picture-script. But in any case these uses were marginal and would presumably require the same 'encoder' to 'decode'; indeed, the notion of decoding may well be out of place since these signs appear to be prompts to the memory rather than a true writing system.

It is significant that while Kramer (1970) treats the Cuna as a written culture as far as literature is concerned, Sherzer (1983) analyzes it as an oral one. While the graphics may offer a few of the advantages of a full writing system, language is not encoded as such.

What is the nature of this proto-writing, often called pictographic, and seen as being a precursor of writing systems that use arbitrary signs? Clearly there is a strong pictorial element in the Ojibway scrolls. But the presence of this component is not the result of any inability to use or invent arbitrary signs. As Boas has insisted for art, there is no evidence that 'representative' (pictorial) art preceded the 'formal' (arbitrary) kind. The pictorial element dominates because of the mnemonic (or, better, suggestive) relationship between sign (or index) and signified (or signifieds, since there may be a considerable number of ways of interpreting a given text and even a given sign).

Gelb analyzes the forerunners of writing under two heads, descriptive–representational devices and identifying–mnemonic ones. The categories (let us call them descriptive and memory devices) are not exclusive, neither are they particularly helpful, but they will serve to emphasize the point about the pictorial element in these mnemonic systems. The first type of device was used by American Indians in making the peace treaties of wampum beadwork where an Indian may be represented as embracing or shaking hands with a White; in principle, understanding such signs does not depend upon understanding a particular language. Descriptive devices of this kind are basically natural indices of a static kind.

The identifying–mnemonic (memory) devices are used not to describe an event, but to record or identify the words of a song, the actions of an individual, the events of a year. They may be abstract or pictorial, and are 'signs' of a sequential kind. However they are not transcriptions of language, but rather a figurative shorthand, a mnemonic, which attempts to recall or prompt linguistic statements rather than to reproduce them. There is no systematic link between sign and sound until we reach true writing systems using word signs (logograms), where the shorthand disappears in favour of an exact transcription of a linguistic statement. For example, three cows are represented by two word signs, one for 'three', one for 'cow' (that is, linguistically), rather than by three similar signs (whether pictographic or abstract) for 'cow' (that is, non-linguistically, representing sight rather than sound). In some early systems of writing the use of such transcription is limited to simple administrative records, for example, among the Mycenaeans or the early Sumerians. But nevertheless there is a definite attempt to transcribe linguistic terms rather than simply to employ graphic signs as markers for recall. Because of the large number of signs needed, both transcription and recall may be facilitated if word signs contain a pictorial element, since an understanding of the graphic code is assisted by visual cues. The concrete nature of the referential system is a matter of its own internal logic rather than a feature of the constitution of the 'primitive' mind. Indeed Chinese, which is the only major logographic system still in use today, contains just such a pictorial element, though much of this appears to have been lost over time.

Early writing systems

It follows from what we have said about 'picture-writing' that the principles behind writing proper are not of a totally different kind. Objects, actions and persons cannot readily be separated from their linguistic symbols, so that even pictorial signs or symbols operate through a linguistic channel as well as a visual one. The main development lies in the degree to which the graphic system succeeds in duplicating the linguistic one, that is, in the extent, first, of word-to-sign (semantic) correspondence and, secondly, of phonetic correspondence.

The full implications of such a system have been developed only in the Old World, where it has been suggested, on little evidence, that all scripts, or at least the idea of writing, derived from the Mesopotamian of the fourth millennium BC (Gelb 1963:212–20; Powell 1981:431). Before discussing developments in the Ancient Near East, we need to consider the history of graphic systems of linguistic representation in Mesoamerica that begin around 600 BC. We have already noted the widespread use of pictograms in North America. In South America the Inca of immediately precolonial times employed an elaborate administrative system of record keeping, based on knots (Murra 1980; Zuidema 1982) in the organization of their complex "pyramidal mode of production" (to use Murra's phrase for the movement of goods and services up and down the mountains, the seat of the ruler). Records were kept by means of knotted cords called *quipu*, which were colour-coded and appear to have served, *inter alia*, as a way of recording transactions in tribute – and possibly treaties. A complex state exercises pressures in favour of the development of a recording system, especially if its central finances are based upon the collection of tax or tribute, as witness the Cretan records of such transactions in Linear A and B. Indeed even booty production leads in the same direction, as we see from the use of scribes in Egypt and Assyria to record the spoils of war.

Much earlier Central America developed a method of graphic representation in an area that had, in the Early Formative Period (1500–900 BC), especially among the Olmecs, experienced a period of "complex and elaborate iconography, with a variety of abstract symbols artistically expressed in stone sculpture, ceramics, and roller-stamps which may have been used for decorating textiles or human bodies" (Marcus 1976:42). Against the background of this proliferation of 'design' a form of 'hieroglyphic' writing arose around 600 BC associated with the Zapotec and emphasizing the connection between script and art. While Marcus maintains that writing began in a "pre-State evolutionary context, among societies with intensive agriculture and hereditary social ranking, but prior to true social stratification or political centralization" (p. 37), these are difficult distinctions to draw even when one has full ethnographic information. What is certain is that the major uses were different from those of writing in the Old World, taking the form of "*political information set in a calendrical framework*" (p. 43).

There are four major systems of writing in Mesoamerica:
1 the Maya in southern Mexico, Belize, Guatemala and Honduras
2 the Zapotec of southwestern Mexico, especially in Monte Alban (Oaxaca)
3 the Aztec in central Mexico (round Mexico City) and Teotihuacan
4 the Mixtec

The first two, the oldest (600 BC to AD 900), are described as hieroglyphic, at first on stone, the two later ones (AD 900) as 'pictographic', featuring pictorial manuscripts on hide and paper (Marcus 1980).

Of these the Zapotec is oldest, appearing in the Oaxaca valley as early as 600 BC. 'Writing' occurs primarily as inscriptions on stone and in paintings. In addition there is an extensive series of documents compiled by the Spanish conquerors in the late sixteenth century.

Zapotec society of this period was clearly stratified into the Coqui, who were hereditary rulers and nobles, and the Xoana, who were commoners and slaves. In the top group, elder sons became rulers, younger ones priests (a widespread phenomenon found elsewhere in the world).

Many Zapotec glyphs referred to the calendar of which there were two kinds, one secular, one ritual. The first (the Vague Year) comprised a cycle, obviously a solar one, of 365 days (18 'moons' of 20 days, plus one period of 5 'unlucky' days). The second was based on a cycle of 260 days, the Sacred Round, with 4 units of 65 days further divided into 5 units of 13 days. Each day was assigned one day name glyph out of a total of 20, plus one number out of 13, making up the cycle of 260 days. "Each day had its own ritual significance, and Zapotec rulers and nobles were named for the day on which they were born. Typical of the noble names that appear on Zapotec stone monuments are '1 Tiger,' '8 Deer,' '5 Flower' and '11 Monkey'" (Marcus 1980:50–2).

The Zapotec also used toponyms, that is, glyphic place names for landmarks and boundaries. These we find on a Zapotec painting from Santiago de Guevea, made nineteen years after the Spanish conquest. The same kind of toponym is found on the Zapotec inscriptions in Monte Alban which begin about 500 BC when the hill settlement emerged as the 'capital' of Oaxaca valley.

The defensive settlement of Monte Alban includes some 300 stone monuments. Many of these obviously celebrate the feats of the rulers, their conquests, the sacrifice of their captives, together with royal genealogies, marriages and the giving of names to important dependencies and tributary districts. "The names of many of the rulers are taken from the 260-day calendar, and their territories are defined by toponyms, usually the names of mountains" (Marcus 1980:52).

One section at Monte Alban is particularly interesting on account of its remarkable gallery on the east face of building L, where the four rows of stone plaques are known as Los Danzantes, the Dancers, because of the series of figures represented there – grotesquely sprawled naked human bodies with eyes closed. They have been variously described as dancers, swimmers, ecstatic priests, even medical anomalies. But in 1962 Coe identified them as slain or ritually sacrificed captives, and this interpretation has been largely accepted. "Of the shared conventions in Mesoamerican iconography some of the most widespread are those that depict captives. Prisoners are displayed in humiliation; they are stripped naked and bound, and their posture is awkward and distorted. Their captors, in contrast, are dressed in elegant regalia and are posed in rigid dignity" (Marcus 1980:53). There is a sharp contrast between the twisted captives and the rigid captors.

If a prisoner has been sacrificed, he is shown with his eyes closed and his mouth open, and in many instances with flowery scrolls, presumably representing blood, issuing from his wounds. The Maya later built many open galleries where prisoners were depicted in this way; the carvings were set into staircases so that the victors could figuratively "tread on the bodies" of the conquered when they were approaching the building at the head of the stairs, usually a temple. The Aztec built displays that served a similar purpose: the *tzompantli*, a rack or wall consisting of the skulls of enemy dead. (1980:53)

In the present case we have figurative representations of the same kind, more durable, more monumental, capable of being 'designed' in more flexible and more complex ways. The earliest known Zapotec carving of this type was found north of Monte Alban; between the legs of the naked figure appears an ornate dot, the number one, and the glyph *xoo* meaning earthquake or motion, possibly a name, in addition to the blood scrolls.

Thus in the early phase of Monte Alban we have a series of monumental scenes of captives and probably lists of conquered places. There are many monuments each giving a little information, essentially of a repetitive kind. When Monte Alban became a major urban centre, its monuments began to deal with diplomacy, as in the famous 'Visitor' inscriptions on the south platform of the main plaza.

Zapotec had a restricted sign system compared with later Maya writing of the Classic Period, between AD 292 and 909. Among the hundreds of Maya glyphs of this period are many which can be identified as verbs, nouns, adjectives, prepositions, and other parts of speech (Marcus 1976:56). Of all the Mesoamerican writing systems it most closely "corresponds to a spoken language" (p. 57). Fox and Justeson (1985) speak of logographic signs, of rebus phoneticism and of phonetic syllabic representation, though the script appears to have been interlingual, like Chinese, limiting the possible application of the phonetic principle. Its main use seem to have been "for the public glorification of the secular elite". But it was also employed for calendrical purposes, as well as for associated mathematical and astronomical ends, that is to say, in ways linked morphologically with the Dakota Winter Counts. One is struck by the extent to which the script was employed for writing down numbers (which constitute a self-contained sign system), a feature that also marks the early stages of Mesopotamian and Cretan writing. The emphasis is on numeracy as much as literacy.

Literacy waned and monumental Mayan inscriptions disappeared by AD 830. Later pictographic systems were developed by the Mixtec and Aztec (AD 900–1600), who created pictorial manuscripts on hide or paper. But the great Aztec urban centre of Teotihuacan in the Valley of Mexico gave little attention to writing or calendrics (Marcus 1976:64). This fact in itself indicates the less central part that writing played in the organization of Mesoamerican social life, its absence from broadly economic or administrative contexts, even after a millennium. The contrast with the extensive use of cuneiform even in distant Elba by 2500 BC is dramatic. Whether or not this contrast derived from aspects of social organization or culture external to the script will no doubt be impossible to disentangle. But it is worth considering that while we know the languages of the scripts we are still unable fully to decode them. To what extent could the script have been similar to that of the early pictorial tablets that preceded the cuneiform of Mesopotamia (Uruk IV–III) which Powell (and Diakonoff) regards as mnemonic in nature? "They contained the information necessary for the accountant to interpret the record, but there is nothing in them to suggest that they represent a systematic attempt to fix most or all of the language in a way that can be decoded by an outsider" (1981:421). Such a suggestion would be consistent with Diringer's contention that even the Mayan script was almost always in need of "supplementary oral description" (1982:102), and perhaps also with Marcus' claim that while Mesoamerica possessed "a true form of writing" consisting of "a series of hieroglyphs arranged in vertical columns and in many instances combined with numerals" (1980:50) – forms which resemble the lists and tables of much Mesopotamian writing – the glyphs are "at least *indirectly* related to the spoken language" (my italics). However this may be, and recent research is constantly bringing forward new evidence and new theories both for pre-Columbian Mesoamerica and for the Ancient Near East, let us now turn to the latter area where we find not only the main sequence of developments in early writing systems but also the application of literacy to an increasingly wide range of communicative contexts.

It is clear that pictorial signs were incorporated into all early writing systems. But they were certainly not the only source either of the signs themselves or of the developed system of graphic–linguistic correspondence that we call writing. Before this appeared, conventional signs clearly had meaning, just as isolated ones do in non-literate societies today. Conventional signs for numerical quantities are central to the development of any elaborate calendar or method of calculation, so that it is not surprising to find the recurrent use of numbers in early graphic systems such as the Mayan. Indeed the use of so-called pictographs and arbitrary signs were combined in many early writing systems, as when a pictorial sign for a container was accompanied by a number of marks or impressions to indicate the quantity of containers involved (Fig. 5).

Such a calculus involving record keeping by means of material representations and graphemes has been proposed as the basis of the oldest form of writing, namely cuneiform (Schmandt-Besserat 1977, 1978, 1981). A re-examination of the records of archaeological excavations in West Asia covering the ninth to the sixth millennia BC, pointed to the wide distribution of clay 'tokens' (in

Fig. 5. The early tablets from Uruk (IV) *c*. 3200–3100 BC provide evidence of the development of a systematic link between sign and sound; (right) for 'five four' and representational signs for cow and bull, read: 'fifty-four cows and bulls'.

effect, hand-made pebbles), consisting of fifteen basic shapes further divided into some 200 sub-classes by size, marking or fractional variation (such as half-spheres). It is suggested, not without contestation (Powell 1981, Le Brun and Vallat 1978; Lieberman 1980), that the meaning of some of these tokens, whose distribution and frequency varied over time and space, can be discovered by comparing them with the earliest writing on the tablets from Uruk in Mesopotamia (*c*. 3100 BC), with which the tokens found at Susa (in the Khuzistan region of Iran) were roughly contemporary, some of the early Uruk signs reproducing in two dimensions almost their exact form (Fig. 6).[3]

The distribution of these tokens around the Fertile Crescent running between Mesopotamia and Egypt, and their appearance at the beginning of the Neolithic period, provide a clue to their use. The shift to agricultural production based on cereals involved the storage of grain for use throughout the year and the possibility of a surplus over immediate nutritional and consumption needs, a surplus that could then be exchanged with other producers, of animals, crafts, or of other products. Equally, primary produce

Fig. 6. The shape of clay tokens from Susa shows some correspondences with the earliest writing on inscribed tablets from Uruk.

could then be collected as tribute or 'gift' in order to maintain an elaborate political or religious hierarchy of kings or priests. A significant change in this recording system, for such it appears to be, occurred between 3500 and 3100 BC. This period also saw the rise of cities whose economy was rooted in trade as well as in production, specifically that of Uruk, the largest urban centre in Mesopotamia (possibly the only true city) and the home of the earliest tablets (Powell 1981). Craft specialization and the beginnings of manufacture had already made their appearance; the invention of the wheel by the end of the fifth millennium meant a great potential increase in the production of pottery. Later, bronze metallurgy developed, trade expanded, cities were built. The increase both in production and in trade encouraged the elaboration of recording devices which were required for inventories, shipments, payments of wages, the calculation of the profit and loss. The system of tokens became more complex, particularly the graphic component of them, deep grooves being made with the end of a stylus. About one third of these new tokens were perforated, apparently so that they could be strung together to record a particular transaction. At the same time we begin to find clay envelopes or *bullae*, which also appear to have been used to separate off one exchange transaction. The envelopes could then be marked with the seals of the individuals involved. It has been suggested that those found at Susa were used as bills of lading; a rural producer of textiles might send a consignment of goods to the city merchant, together with an envelope containing the tokens indicating the kind and quantity.

Such a procedure would clearly open up the possibility that instead of sending three-dimensional tokens in an envelope on which seals had been stamped, the material representations themselves should be omitted and the outside of the envelope marked with the shape of the tokens, either by impressing them in the clay or by using a stylus to create a graphic form in two dimensions. The problem of reducing three-dimensional objects to a two-dimensional form is of course a central problem of the graphic arts (Boas 1927:351) and one that must lead to some measure of stylization. Thus the envelope became the writing tablet, the shapes became signs, tokens became writing, first the undeciphered pictorial cuneiform of Uruk IV and then the more abstract system of representation that was adopted throughout much of the area in which the tokens have been found.

That writing developed in some such way is also suggested by its history in Crete where the Minoan civilization began to reach a complex level around the twentieth century BC when the first signs of a script appear. Pictorial signs for commodities and decimal numbers were accompanied by the carving of seal-stones with patterns made up of a few, usually three or four, related pictorial signs. Chadwick (1976) doubts if these were a true script but rather sees them as a 'symbolic system' similar to the late medieval craft of heraldry that used pictorial (and other elements such as colours) to designate individuals, their status and their pedigree. The association of a numerical notation, signs for commodities and inscribed seals is what one would anticipate in a shift from tokens to script. The tablets in the early Cretan script known as Linear A, though they remain undeciphered, seem to contain a series of records of quantities of commodities (mainly agricultural, but including textiles) listed against names. As with Linear B, the tablets consist largely of tables.

The first writing system arose in West Asia around 3100 BC during the period that saw the development of the great urban centre of Uruk. Some regard the undeciphered pictorial system from Uruk IV–III (possibly Sumerian, Powell 1981) as the result of a long development (Lieberman 1980), others as "a sudden sign explosion" (Green 1981:367). Some see it as mnemonic (Powell 1981), others as logographic (or logo-syllabic) because of the systematic way in which it succeeded in representing the units of a language by means of signs.

Logographic writing

Logographic systems of writing clearly develop from simpler uses of graphic signs. But the full writing that came into being incorporated the systematic and comprehensive representation of words (and their referents) by individual graphic signs. Clearly many words have referents which are linked to 'the world outside', so that the written sign X, which we will take to signify 'cross', refers to the concept and to the object or the action, as well as to the sound. But the most immediate reference is to the sound, whereas in the pictorial devices of proto-writing, none of which, as we have argued, can be dissociated from the linguistic channel, the more immediate reference is to the object or the incident itself.

Systems which represent every word by a separate sign are unknown, although Chinese constitutes the closest approximation. Every developed type of writing possesses some signs that represent syllables and phonetic sounds as well as words and hence economizes on the number of signs needed. For example, the sign for 'man' plus the sign for 'drake' could read 'mandrake'. Because of this feature, these first complete systems are known as *logo-syllabic* since they use signs to express both words and syllables.

Their initial development seems to have been confined to adjacent parts of the African and Asiatic continents, to the exclusion of the areas where the use of "pictographs" was most developed. We know of seven such systems of writing in early human societies:

1 Sumerian-Akkadian in Mesopotamia, 3100 BC to AD 75
2 Proto-Elamite in Elam, Mesopotamia, 3000 BC to 2200 BC
3 Egyptian in Egypt, 3100 BC to second century AD
4 Proto-Indic (or Proto-Indian) in the Indus Basin, Indian sub-continent, around 2200 to 1000 BC
5 Cretan in Crete and Greece, 2000 BC to twelfth century BC (hieroglyphic, Linear A and Linear B)
6 Hittite and Luwian in Anatolia and Syria, 1500 BC to 700 BC (Anatolian hieroglyphic)
7 Chinese in China, 1500–1400 BC to the present day.

Of these systems, three, that is Proto-Elamite, Proto-Indic and Cretan Linear A remain undeciphered, despite many attempts to break the codes.

The earliest elaborated system of writing is the cuneiform (wedge-shaped) orthography which appeared at the end of the fourth millennium BC. This script was used to write down the language of the Sumerian people who inhabited the lower part of Mesopotamia, "the land between the two rivers" of the Tigris and Euphrates where they flowed into the Persian Gulf, and was later taken over by another people of this area, the Akkadians. It was written on moistened clay tablets on which the scribe stamped the triangular end of a reed to produce various combinations of the basic impression (Fig. 7). The clay dried and the tablet was either stored away or dispatched to its recipient.

The shape of these characters was mainly non-pictorial, 'abstract', arbitrary, though some displayed evidence of a pictorial origin (Fig. 8; see p. 45), deriving from the undeciphered script of Uruk (level IV). There is also evidence of a cuneiform

Fig. 7. Cuneiform signs. The way in which cuneiform signs were formed
from the triangular end of the reed in moistened clay can be seen in this
legal document and its envelope, bearing seals, from Atchana in south-east
Turkey, c. 1700 BC

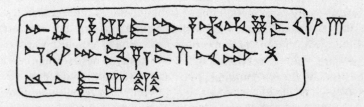

Fig. 8. Canaanite cuneiform: Proto-Canaanite inscription from Lachish,
thirteenth century BC. The cuneiform alphabet from Ugarit, displayed in
what is the earliest complete ABC extant (although it seems to have
followed the invention of a linear alphabetic script).

script, contemporary with Uruk III and very similar, used to write down the language of the proto-Elamites of Kish (Jamdet Nasr), in which the abstract element was stronger from the beginning. With the development of the form of writing known as Linear Elamite (Script B) we see the emergence of a script composed of syllables with periodic word signs. Both traditions existed side by side and may have had a common progenitor. But of this we know nothing and it is clear that the origins of Mesopotamian writing include non-pictorial signs such as those used on the earlier tokens.

Whatever the morphological similarities between the more developed graphic systems of North America and early writing in the Near East, the uses were vastly different. The former were primarily mnemonic and therefore elaborated for purposes where memory was considered important, for example in recalling mythico-ritual processes as in the Ojibway scrolls. Another use, not unrelated to the former, is the calendrical one found in the Dakota Winter Counts. Other uses are relatively minor, but few if any concern what we would usually describe as the economic life.

How different was the situation in Mesopotamia! According to Driver in *Semitic Writing*, the development of the cuneiform script was the result of 'economic necessity' (1948:2). The earliest Elamite and Sumerian records are not concerned with 'communication' in the usual sense of that word, and certainly not with writing down oral myth or composing poetry, that is, with 'literary' purposes. They were "mere lists of objects pictorially jotted down on clay-tablets with the numbers of each beside them, indicating by a simple system of strokes, circles and semicircles" (1948:2). Usually associated with ancient centres of cult or court, the records refer to the property and accounts of temples; however, they are "purely economic or administrative, never religious or historical". Such a situation appears to have continued for the first 500 years of the history of writing; the only exceptions were some scholastic texts, which were "mere lists of signs and words, required for the training of scribes" (1948:3).

The same was true of Egypt, though the economic context was different and monumental texts were more in evidence; later writing was used to keep a calendar for calculating the annual flood of the Nile and "to give permanent form to the spells and prayers necessary to ensure a plentiful harvest year after year and to transmit them in the correct form to future generations" (p. 3). While the stimulus was apparently economic in both countries, it was priests and administrators who devoted themselves to the leisured exploitation of this complex system of writing. The complexity of the writing confined its systematic use to a well-trained set of scribes, whose training was at times carried out by priests. In Mesopotamia the lexical texts of Uruk III provide evidence of the existence of schools for scribes who were probably members of a college of temple priest–administrators (Green 1981:367).

Let us recapitulate the sequence of developments. The earliest tablets come from a few sites in Southern Mesopotamia, the most important of which are Uruk (modern Warka; level IV, c. 3200–3100 BC and Jamdet Nasr or Kish (c. 3000 BC). These are inscribed in a pictorial script only partly deciphered, thanks either to the nature of the picture or to a relation with later cuneiform. The language of the script has not yet been agreed but may be Sumerian; the contents appear to be "lists of commodities, business transactions and land sales" (Oates 1980). Next come a few hundred tablets from archaic Ur (probably Early Dynastic 1, 2900–2500 BC), underlying the Royal Cemetery, which are still very difficult to read, consisting mostly of lists but containing a few descriptive phrases. The Royal Cemetery itself is probably some 300 years later (2600–2500 BC), then in the following century we have approximately 1,000 tablets from Fara (Shuruppak) in a form that enables us to see more clearly that we are dealing with an early form of Sumerian writing. The texts themselves consist almost exclusively of numbers, followed by depicted objects. But those from archaic Ur also deal with matters such as land and its products, agricultural implements and cattle, and in addition we find a certain number of school texts. More recent finds from Abu Salabikh, of the same period as Fara, even include some fragments of literary works as well as lists of words. The fundamental discoveries at Ebla (Tell Mardikh, in North Syria) have produced an extrordinary library from approximately the same period. Here the cuneiform script was used to write not only Sumerian and Akkadian but a language which appears to be West Semitic and, possibly, a form of Proto-Canaanite which was later to be used for the first alphabets. These largely unpublished texts include legends, state treaties and other written documents (Matthiae 1979; Pettinato 1981).

In terms of form, the texts from the lowest levels of Uruk (Uruk IV)] consist solely of numbers and pictured objects; those from Jamdet Nasr include the first sign with determinative value (i.e. a semantic indicator), while those from Ur have a few syllabic signs to indicate the cases of nouns and other grammatical features; and at Fara these same syllabic signs also come to be used to indicate the phonetic pronunciation of difficult words (i.e. phonetic indicators).

The early linear and pictorial signs were simplified into groups of characteristically wedge-shaped strokes, which pushed aside the earlier pictorial forms. In addition the direction of writing changed. It was no longer from right to left in vertical columns but switched through ninety degrees, and was written from left to right to avoid smudging. Thus the increasingly formalized pictograms were now laid on their backs.

The final development of a major kind occurred when the dynasty of Akkad (*c.* 2400–2250 BC), which was Semitic speaking, terminated the early dynastic period by seizing power and uniting the empire. Akkadian now became the dominant spoken language but not only did Sumerian cuneiform script continue to be used to write down Akkadian but the Sumerian language was also needed to get access to the older materials that it had preserved. There now emerged the notion of a 'dead' language, one that was used for written transactions alone, entailing a complete separation of the spoken and written at the linguistic level, a feature that, as we see in chapter 11, has dominated many phases of written cultures ever since.

At about the same time as the developments in Uruk, and possibly under some kind of stimulation from Sumeria, the Egyptians developed a 'hieroglyphic' system for writing their Afro–Asiatic language, a group that includes Semitic as well as Hausa. Egyptian hieroglyphic writing, so-called by the Greeks because they saw its basic use as religious, was, with Sumerian cuneiform, the main script in the ancient Levant for the first 2,000 years that writing was known. We have to separate very clearly the diffusion of specific *scripts* from the diffusion of the *idea* of writing, that is, stimulus diffusion. Both processes were at work in the Middle East.

The two main streams seem to have allocated a somewhat

different role to writing, as was the case in the Americas where the bureaucratic use of knots by the Incas was distinguished from the largely 'monumental' use of glyphs by the Zapotec and Maya. For in the Mesopotamian case, the employment of writing for accounting purposes seems very clear, while in Egypt, in the earliest phases, we find mainly stone inscriptions which obviously perform a different role from the widespread clay tablets of Mesopotamia. The problem here is partly that papyrus, even in Egypt, does not survive as well as clay tablets, so that we do not come across inscribed papyrus until the Fourth Dynasty (2600–2500 BC), though we know it was used earlier. However the original script does seem to be monumental in character, although it was later adapted for other purposes in the forms designed to be used with ink on papyrus, namely hieratic and later demotic, the reverse of the process in Mesopotamia.

The Egyptian script appears in a fairly advanced state at the time of the First Dynasty (*c.* 3000 BC), the finest example being the well-known 'Narmer Palette'. On the palettes and mace-heads, scenes of conquest are rendered symbolically, for example, with the King represented as the Falcon or other royal beast and the provinces by their emblems. As on seals, we find the use of the *rebus* principle (e.g. an eye standing for I), in other words we have a mixed system of design and writing. In the very first picture of a painter, that of Mereru-ka painting the seasons (Sakkara, *c.* 2300 BC), we find an interesting aspect of this trend, the tendency to equate graphic forms, words with non-verbal marks, for a drawing of the seasons is unfinished and appears to be completed with hieroglyphs. "Picture cycles and hieroglyphs, representations and inscriptions," comments Gombrich, "were more interchangeable in Egyptian eyes than they are for us" (1968:106), though the tradition does continue in the illustrated book, the caption to the joke, the ballooned speech of the comic strip.

Following these preliminary stages, a developed system of writing appears in the Early Dynastic surviving almost entirely in the form of tomb inscriptions on stone and other artefacts. The script appeared suddenly, as if the impetus was from outside. Certainly some internal characteristics resemble cuneiform, for example, the mixed logo-syllabic character and the class determinatives. For very soon the Egyptians added to their pictorial signs a set of phonograms (or phonetic indicators), which showed the way the word should sound, and then determinatives (or semantic indicators), which showed the category of the object or action. While such additions were sometimes needed to remove the ambiguity of polyphonic words, many were simply redundant, reflecting the elaborations of scribal practitioners added to the complexities of logographic decoding. Simpler forms of Egyptian writing emerged over the centuries, first hieratic, then demotic, and these were preferred for profane purposes. Nevertheless the basic principles remained unchanged and the simplifications were in style (i.e. in becoming more cursive) rather than in structure.

What are the characteristics of these early logo-syllabic systems? Whatever innovative processes they encouraged, they were themselves very conservative in form. Egyptian hieroglyphics remained much the same over three millennia, though it did develop alternative forms of script. The same was true of cuneiform. Early on both Egyptian hieroglyphics and Sumerian–Akkadian cuneiform were able to represent the sound as well as the meaning of words by means of glyphs and graphemes. For example, in the later Archaic tablets at Uruk III and Jemdet Nasr, we find an arrow, Sumerian TI, which was used to write the word for Live/Life, a homonym in Sumerian, namely TI(L). In this way it was possible to transcribe a name to be read EN.LIL-TI, (the god) Enlil (gives) life. Such rebus writing dissociates the sound from the meaning of the word, which is the basic principle of phonetic systems, whether syllabic or alphabetic.

While the possibility of phonetic development was open to them, the Sumerian scribes continued to complicate their lives with logograms and determinatives. We are faced not only with conservation as such but with a vested interest in the status quo which prevents others from gaining control of an important means of communication. As Hawkins remarks, "it is clear that ancient writing was in the hands of a small literate elite, the scribes, who manifested great conservatism in the practice of their craft, and, so far from being interested in its simplification, often chose to demonstrate their virtuosity by a proliferation of signs and values which border on the cryptophoric. Thus most ancient scripts retained a mixed logographic–syllabic character" (1979:132). Egyptian writing was especially conservative. It was never employed by any outside body, although cuneiform was adapted

for many other languages, for instance, at Ebla in the middle of the
third millennium where it was used for diplomatic and archival
purposes. Sometimes too, cuneiform was used for the transcription
of local languages in simplified forms. Nevertheless the major
scripts of the Near East remained complex throughout their existence, suggesting the presence of a scribal sub-culture that aimed to
retain control of the new technology.

Another major civilization of the third millennium BC, that of
the Indus Basin in the north of the Indian subcontinent (c. 2200
BC) also saw the development of writing. The Indus Basin script
may have had some connection with that of Sumer; there were
certainly links in the trade in semi-precious stones such as carnelian
and lapis lazuli from Afghanistan. One authority has suggested that
the language itself is also Sumerian (Kinnier Wilson 1974), but
others have considered it to be an early form of Dravidian, the
group of languages now spoken in South India (Parpola 1970;
Fairservis 1983); however both proposals are at present highly
conjectural. The seals on which the inscriptions, all very short, are
mainly found appear to have been used in mercantile operations,
and are similar to those from the Persian Gulf, an area with which
trade was taking place and where some of the seals have turned up.
Most of these seals seem to show the owners' names (in early
Sumeria the names were usually of scribes) and to have been used
for stamping goods and making tokens and amulets, while others
may have served a dedicatory purpose. According to one authority
(Fairservis 1983:52), they appear to provide evidence for the roles
of coppersmith, storehouse overseer, irrigation supervisor and
landowner, as well as attesting to "a class of scribes, to people in
charge of weights and measures and to supervisors of the distribution of stores, the grinding of flour ... There were also captains
of boats and custodians of fire" (p. 52).

In the East Mediterranean, another important system of writing
developed at roughly the same time. The scripts of the island of
Crete begin with pictorial devices on seals dating from 2800 BC
which showed some Egyptian influence. Subsequently, around
2000–1850 BC, these devices develop into pictorial (hieroglyphic)
inscriptions which lead through a cursive form into Minoan (Linear
A), a linear script dating from c. 1700 to 1550 BC and not yet
satisfactorily deciphered, though the American scholar, Cyrus

Gordon, has recently claimed that both Linear A and Eteo–Cretan (written in the Greek alphabet, 600–300 BC) are in a north-west Semitic language. This script contained a limited number of signs, between seventy-six and ninety, presumably constituting a simple syllabary, nearly half of which were adapted from earlier pictorial forms. Linear B, consisting of some eighty-nine characters partly derived from Linear A, seems to have been associated with the mainland Mycenaean civilization that took over from the Minoans about 1400 BC. Brilliantly deciphered by Ventris, it was shown to be a form of Greek, used mainly for economic and military account books and continuing in use until the invasions of the later Dorian Greeks around 1100 BC. From then until *c.* 750 BC, runs the accepted account, Greece passed through the Dark Ages and had to re-import writing from the Phoenicians, adapting it to a fully alphabetic form.

The Hittite script developed somewhat later than the Minoan in the middle of the second millennium BC. The Hittite empire occupied much of the area of the present day Turkey, lying between the Black Sea and the lands under Assyrian rule. It was the discovery of the royal archives of Hatti (Boğhazköy) that brought to light the way in which this kingdom used the cuneiform script of Mesopotamia, borrowed from a north Syrian source, to write down its Indo–European language (1650–1200 BC). In addition to the extensive series of cuneiform texts, there exist a number of inscriptions and other writing in a hieroglyphic type of script with pictorial signs (*c.* 1500 BC) and including some semantic indicators. While clearly stimulated in a general way by an acquaintance with Egyptian forms, this script was an independent invention. Both cuneiform and hieroglyphic forms were used for writing not only Hittite but also Luwian (1400–1200 BC and 1350–eighth century BC), a related Indo–European language.

The Chinese script is the most recent of the major logo-syllabic systems, both in its invention and in its use. The first evidence comes from divinatory records dating from the fifteenth century BC. This use of writing appears at a time when Indo–Europeans were controlling much of the steppe area between West Asia and Northern China, which has suggested to some the possibility of stimulation from that direction (Powell 1981). Not only is it the most recent, it is also the most clearly pictorial in its logographic characters. Of these there are some 8,000 in current use, although basic Chinese for popular literature needs a range of only 1000–1500 characters. In these respects it is the most conservative of contemporary writing systems. Although the problem is eased because of the predominantly monosyllabic nature of the language, the complexity of the script clearly limits access to knowledge, and for this reason there have been attempts to introduce alphabetic systems (e.g. pinyin in 1958) in recent years, although as a result all existing works would have to be transcribed. However, the Chinese characters (*hanzi*) make more use of phonetic elements than is commonly supposed. Analyses of logograms show that a large percentage (82–90 per cent of the dictionary) are phonograms consisting of two elements, one semantic (the signific) and one phonetic. The difference between this and an alphabetic script is that the phonetic notation is holistic, not atomistic or segmental (Wang 1981:232).

The nature of the Chinese script meant that 'full literacy', a complete knowledge of the system of characters, could be acquired only by the few. But the corollary is that the many can gain a knowledge of a few characters without having to master a system. The gradation is steeper than with an alphabetic script and it becomes difficult to think of literacy (in the individual sense of the term) in the same way. Nevertheless, Rawski (1979) has produced ample evidence of the wide extent of some knowledge of writing in the Ch'ing period.

Uniquely in early societies, achievement in the written word, tested by the examination system, became the criteria for eligibility to high, but not the highest, office; the top of ladder of success in Imperial China was the mandarinate that governed the country. Restricted (in one sense) largely because of the nature of the script, writing dominated the socio–cultural system in other ways, not only from the standpoint of administration but also of scientific and cultural attainments.

The Chinese *hanzi* ('Han character') script spread eastwards to Korea (*hanja*) and thence to Japan (*kanji*), although these Altaic languages were structured in a very different way; this was also true of its adoption in Vietnam, where a language of the Mon–Khmer family is spoken. Elsewhere speakers of Sino–Tibetan have adopted alphabetic scripts of Indian origin. Moreover, Vietnam abandoned *hanzi* in favour of a western alphabet in the seventeenth century, Korea developed its own Hangul alphabet in 1443 and the Japanese created the *kana* (as distinct from the logographic *kanji*) based on the mora (a sub-syllabic unit) and displaying an Indic influence (Wang 1981:231).

The development of phonetic transcription

In theory, individual word signs can provide a relatively exact equivalence of sign and sound, of image and speech. However, a repertoire that included a different sign for every word would be enormously cumbrous and difficult to work. As we have seen, in the three West Asian scripts, Mesopotamian cuneiform, Egyptian hieroglyphics and Anatolian, there developed a type of semantic indicator that was not pronounced and that was originally used to distinguish between word signs that had more than one meaning. For example, in cuneiform the word sign AŠŠUR stands for both the city and the patron god; an additional 'determinative' may be added to the initial sign to indicate the class to which the intended meaning belongs, that is, adding either the sign for 'city' or the sign for 'deity'. In the course of time these determinatives were used for all members of a particular class, whether or not there was any danger of ambiguity.

The use of such determinatives added to the complexity of writing, though in other ways it limited the number of different signs and aided the interpretation of the existing ones. However the most important development, which opened the way to the modern alphabet by way of the introduction of syllabic writing, was the systematic employment of the phonetic principle. By the use of the 'rebus' device, signs need no longer distinguish separate meanings of a specific sound (e.g. AŠŠUR) but could rather denote the sound itself, irrespective of the meaning. In this way, as we have seen, the Sumerian word TI, 'life', a concept which is in any case not easy to put in pictorial form, can be expressed by means of the sign for arrow, which is also TI. This shift entails over-riding semantic meaning in favour of phonetic equivalence, the latter representing a more abstract method of transcribing language and one that enabled powerful economies to take place.

Phonetic indicators were frequently used with word signs (as were semantic ones) to specify the way the sign should be pronounced. The phonetic principle was particularly important in rendering proper names. Such words could be broken down into their constituent syllables (i.e. various combinations of consonant and vowel, of stop and breath) by using word signs already in the language, as in the use of the word sign for 'man' as a syllabic sign in the transcription of a name such as Manfred. Such syllabic signs might then be used in other words, as in the case of 'mandrake'. In this way the various systems that combined the use of word and syllabic signs gave birth to syllabaries working on the phonetic principle and employing a much reduced set of signs. In general this development took place on the fringes of the major civilizations; the Japanese worked out a syllabary using Chinese signs, which included some phonetic ones; the Elamites and Hurrians did the same with Sumerian; various minor syllabic scripts of Cyprus and the surrounding Aegean area were derived from neighbouring forms; and the Egyptian can possibly be seen as the parent (with Akkadian, see Powell 1981:434) of the West Semitic 'syllabaries' which are the progenitors of the alphabet. Indeed many scholars would count these West Semitic systems as true alphabets, though they transribed only consonants.

Systems of syllabic writing employ a limited set of signs and are relatively easy to learn and to work. For this reason they have also been much used by missionaries developing writing systems for non-literate peoples. In North America one such system was current among the Cree while in the Eastern Arctic the Rev. James Evans of the Canadian Methodist Church invented a writing system based on forty-eight 'syllabic' characters (Flint 1954).

There have also been a number of recent indigenous inventions of syllabaries, again in 'peripheral' areas, by individuals or small groups who have made deliberate efforts to introduce writing to their own peoples. Two well-known instances of this process took place among the Vai of West Africa and the Cherokee of North America in the first quarter of the nineteenth century. In both cases we know the names of the individuals concerned and some of the background to their invention. The Cherokee syllabary was invented by Sequoyah following twelve frustrating years of trial and error. Obsessed with his vision that Indians, like the more educated of the White people, might learn to communicate with 'talking leaves', he neglected his farm, defied his family, and was ultimately tried for witchcraft because of his behaviour. However by 1819 he had perfected the syllabary and had taught his daughter to read. He was asked to demonstrate his discovery before a group of Cherokee elders and so successful was his innovation that within a few years, thousands of Cherokee became literate in their native language. Subsequently a printing press was set up and by 1880 the Cherokee had a higher level of literacy than the neighbouring Whites.

A similar series of events occurred among the Vai of Liberia where Bukele created a syllabary of some 226 signs at about the same time. This invention also arose in the competitive context of European and Arabic writing, and the script, as explained in chapter 9, is still widely used by Vai speakers. As with the Cherokee, individuals often learn to read as adults since the ability is not of much use in childhood; given motivation most adults have relatively little difficulty in learning to write down their maternal language using a syllabary. A number of other syllabic scripts have been invented in West Africa during the present century, many of them clearly stimulated by the achievement of the Vai. In the Mediterranean and Near East, early syllabaries were modified by the further simplifications of phonetic transcription, and the fact that Japanese continues to make use of a supplemented syllabary shows they have many of the advantages of the alphabet.

The alphabet

There are two views about the invention of the alphabet; the first holds that it was invented in Greece around 750 BC, in the period immediately before the great Ionian and Athenian achievements; the second that it was invented by Western Semites, some 750 years earlier.

In certain respects both views are correct, the first claim referring to a full alphabet consisting of consonants and vowels, the second to the consonantal alphabet. However the importance of Greek culture for the subsequent history of Western Europe has led to an over-emphasis, by classicists and others, on the addition of specific vowel signs to the set of consonantal ones that had been developed earlier in Western Asia (Coldstream 1977; Havelock 1973; Goody and Watt 1963). The consonantal system itself, as the order and shape of the signs demonstrate, was the achievement of speakers of Canaanite, a Semitic language. At one time it was thought that this earlier invention had taken place among the workers in the turquoise mines of the Sinai peninsula, whose Proto-Canaanite script was said to have been derived from ownership marks on livestock and pots. Now the proposed location has shifted to Northern Canaan, that is, to contemporary Syria, which formed a bridge between the socio–cultural systems of Egypt and Mesopotamia.

Many scholars like Gelb have insisted that the alphabet was an invention of the Greeks, who created a complete alphabetic system by introducing signs for vowels in addition to those for consonants. This view holds that all previous forms of this system were 'syllabic'. The other camp has argued that, whatever the merits of this nomenclature, this position tends to distract attention from the decisive problems concerning the origin of the alphabet.

The extension of the Canaanite system to a fuller notation by the Aramaeans in the eleventh or tenth century to permit systematic notation of final vowels, and the further elaboration of vocalic notation by the Greeks . . . were, relatively speaking, minor adaptations of the alphabet. To restrict the term alphabet to one of these late systems is also to ignore the historic origin of the term "alphabet" which goes back to the names of letters and the order of these names which were part of the invention of the Proto-Canaanite script. (Cross 1967:11)

An important early step forward in the work on the origin of the alphabet took place with the discovery by the archaeologist Sir William Flinders Petrie of the inscriptions at the turquoise mines of Serābît el-Khâdem in Sinai in the spring of 1905, inscriptions that he dated to the fifteenth century BC, though his contemporary, A. H. Gardiner, placed them two centuries earlier. The signs resembled Egyptian hieroglyphic writing but there were so few characters that an alphabet was indicated. The decipherment of the script was suggested by Gardiner in 1915. He noted a recurrent series of pictorial signs, 'oxgoad' (or shepherd's crook) – house – eye – oxgoad – cross and saw that, if the signs stood for the initials of the names (on the acrophonic principle), their Canaanite value would be "for the lady". This was a favourite epithet of the Canaanite goddess, Asherah (or Ba'alath'), identified with the

Egyptian goddess, Ḥatḥor, whose temple dominated the site of the mines worked by the labourers (or slaves). This Proto-Canaanite script was finally deciphered by Albright in 1948, by which time additional inscriptions relating to the emergence of the alphabet had become available from other areas.

These inscriptions consist of three groups, the most important of which came from Ugarit in the very north of the Canaanite area. There, beginning in 1929, the French archaeologist, Schaeffer, had made a series of very significant discoveries. The main group of materials relating to the development of writing consisted of epic and mythological texts inscribed in a cuneiform consonantal alphabet in an early Canaanite dialect of the fourteenth century BC. This cuneiform alphabet of thirty-two letters, written from left to right, seems to have been developed under the inspiration of the pictorial system of Proto-Canaanite on the one hand, and of Babylonian on the other. The latter was the form of cuneiform used in the Late Bronze Age for diplomatic and commercial communication throughout the Near East. The same alphabet seems to have been used by the Canaanites throughout Syria–Palestine, and other specimens include a commercial tablet from Ta'anach from the late twelfth century. There are indications that this cuneiform alphabet followed upon the invention of a linear script in the area where North Semitic languages were spoken. Scribes who were accustomed to write by impressing a stylus in wet clay may have wished to continue to write in this way even when they had seen the advantages of an alphabetic script: this suggestion would explain the invention of a cuneiform alphabet that derived from a linear one.

The second group of discoveries includes early texts in linear Phoenician characters from Byblos, dating from a later period, the eleventh century. The third group consists of Proto-Canaanite evidence that comes from Palestine. Fragmentary as this is, it includes two important finds, the Gezer sherd (*c.* 1600?) and the Lachish Prism (late fifteenth or seventeenth century) which were roughly contemporary with the corpus from Sinai; moreover they are written in the standard alphabet.

So the order of these early alphabetic texts and their scripts can be summarized as:

1 the Proto-Canaanite texts
   a Old Palestinian (or Early Canaanite), seventeenth–twelfth centuries BC

b Proto-Sinaitic (or Palaeo-Sinaitic), fifteenth or seventeenth century BC

2 Canaanite cuneiform texts

a Ugaritic, fourteenth-thirteenth centuries BC

b Palestinian, thirteenth-twelfth centuries BC.

These scripts were succeeded by Old Phoenician linear texts in the eleventh century BC, also known as the North Semitic script and consisting of twenty-two signs. The Israelites borrowed either a Phoenician or a similar Palestinian script, the type that also formed the basis of the Greek alphabet, sometime after the thirteenth century; but even at the beginning of the eighth century the scripts are still virtually the same. The Aramaic script, so important for the history of writing in Asia, was derived from the Phoenician, which had been borrowed in the eleventh century, and this in turn led to the Arabic and modern Hebrew scripts.

Thus the consonantal alphabet developed in an area situated between the early written civilizations of Egypt and Mesopotamia, among a people known as the Canaanites, the Semitic-speaking inhabitants of Syria and Palestine before the coming of the Israelites from whom they are difficult to distinguish. The land of Canaan, with its rich western slopes covered with cedars of Lebanon, and its dry eastern ones leading down to the desert, was the entrepôt for trade in the metals of Anatolia and copper of Cyprus as well as itself producing wine, olive oil, wood and the purple dye which later gave the coastal lands the name of Phoenicia. This region of small kingdoms and rich merchant princes was the meeting place of invaders and cultural influences not only from Egypt and Mesopotamia, but also from the north where the Hurrians and their Mitanni rulers, probably originating in central Asia, spoke an Indo–European language. It was these latter who "revolutionized society with the introduction of the horse and chariot", and what Gray calls "the feudal order which that involved" (1964:51) later subjugated the whole area. And from the sixteenth century, the region has strong contacts with the Aegean – it has been claimed there was a Mycenaean quarter in the port of Ugarit itself – for the movement was mainly in a westerly direction.

In Mesopotamia, Sumerian had been replaced as a spoken language by its contemporary, Akkadian, though it continued as a written language especially for religious texts; in this way the scribal monopoly was maintained. Akkadian was a Semitic language in which some early texts had been compiled; even scribes of the Fara period had Semitic names. But it later became the medium of international diplomacy throughout Western Asia, even in the Hittite Empire where Indo–European was the language of the rulers. Under this empire, local scribes were trained to employ both language and script for the purposes of administration. Trade with Egypt, and the Egyptian conquests of Canaan, made its inhabitants familiar too with hieroglyphic writing, which may have had some influence on the development of the alphabet. Both Akkadian cuneiform and Egyptian hieroglyphics were elaborate scripts, with logographic and syllabic elements complicated by determinatives which indicated the semantic category and the pronunciation. Thus their use was virtually limited to specialist scribes serving the temples and palaces of Mesopotamia and the priestly and adminis-trative bureaucracy of Egypt. Such scripts were less well-adapted to the business of Mediterranean merchants in Canaan, the region that saw the beginning of the experiments that resulted in the alphabet, the area that had already in the middle of the third millennium used cuneiform for writing down the early Canaanite spoken at Ebla.

Between 2000 and 1500 BC other attempts were made to invent a simpler script based upon hieroglyphics as well as upon geometric signs and proprietary marks. One such example is the pseudo-hieroglyphic script used in texts from Byblos written and dated between 2300 BC and 1750 BC; the script appears to be a syllabic system for writing an archaic dialect of Canaanite in an area which had slightly earlier (2400 BC) used logographic cuneiform for a similar purpose. While the Proto-Canaanite script probably arose under the influence of Egyptian hieroglyphics, this influence may have been mediated by the pseudo-hieroglyphic syllabary.

Helped by the morphological structure of their language, in which consonants, rather than consonants plus vowels, make up the combinations that carry fundamental semantic notions, the Can-aanites were able to develop consonantal alphabets, one based upon cuneiform characters (Fig. 8) and the other linear. This linear script, known as Proto-Canaanite, was found widely spread in the Late Bronze Age from South Sinai to the coastal Canaanite town of

Byblos, and it appears to have been more practical for writing on papyrus, leather and similar materials.

Despite the reference in the Wenamon papyrus (*c.* 1100) to the import of papyrus rolls from Egypt to Byblos, and despite the records of commercial transactions using the same medium, little remains of the Canaanite writings on this material. Contrary to what happened in Egypt, the humid climate of the coastal areas destroyed such documents, so that our knowledge of Canaan is dependent upon the more cumbrous cuneiform texts from Ugarit, in which were preserved literary products such as the Baal myth and the legends of Krt and Aqht. The new script adapted to the new materials seems to have led to a considerable extension of literate activity; cuneiform on clay tablets was not adapted to long texts (Powell 1981:435). Quite apart from the script's appearance in the ledgers of the merchant princes of Canaan, its successor alphabets were widely used throughout the Mediterranean by Phoenician traders, while immediately to the south, it was used for the annals of the kingdoms of Israel and Judah; in this alphabet Baruch, the friend of Jeremiah, wrote down the prophet's oracles (Jeremiah 36); and it later developed into the script used for the scrolls of the renowned community, thought to have been of the Essene sect, living on the shores of the Dead Sea, as well as for all later manuscripts of the Hebrew Old Testament.

The Hebrews apparently adopted the Canaanite alphabet in the twelfth or eleventh century BC. It was certainly being used in Palestine before their arrival, but apart from the recently dis-covered Afeg Tablet (eleventh century), there is only one Hebrew inscription that antedates the eighth century, namely the Gezer Calendar, probably of the late tenth century, the time of Saul and David. The Aramaeans established their small kingdoms and tribal states in Mesopotamia and Syria respectively in the twelfth and eleventh centuries, with the decline of the great powers of Egypt, Assyria, the Hittites, and of Minoan and Mycenaean Crete; they appear to have adopted the script slightly later than the Hebrews and passed it on to the Arabic-speaking Nabataeans living in what is now Northern Arabia, South Jordan, South Israel and Sinai.

The Phoenicians emerged in the Late Bronze Age (about 1400

BC) as the inhabitants of the coastal belt of Canaan from Tartus in the north (situated in the south of present day Syria) to Dor or Jaffa in the south. There they created a special brand of Canaanite culture which they carried, by trade and by conquest, throughout the Mediterranean. In the late thirteenth century they were conquered by, and amalgamated with, the Philistines, one of the many groups of Sea People who were probably of European origin.

The Proto-Canaanite script is the common ancestor of the Phoenician, Hebrew and Aramaic variants. In about 1500 BC it seems to have consisted of twenty-seven pictorial letters which were reduced to twenty-two in the thirteenth century; by this time most of the letters had dropped their earlier form and taken on a linear one, while by the middle of the eleventh century the direction of writing was stabilized from right to left. Indeed these particular changes mark the shift from the Canaanite to the Phoenician script which was used by the Hebrews and Aramaeans before they developed their own versions.

It was this consonantal alphabet that the Greeks in turn adopted, adding their own five characters to represent vowels. The earliest Greek inscriptions date from the eighth century BC and it is generally believed that, following the disappearance of the Mycenaean script in the twelfth century, a Dark Age of some 300 years followed at the end of the Late Helladic period.

For some time scholars of Semitic languages have tried to date the Greek alphabet to the previous century on the grounds that the Phoenician alphabet was by then widely diffused through the Mediterranean. In Cyprus, an inscription on a Phoenician tomb dates from the first half of the ninth century. The earliest Punic text in Carthage, the great Mediterranean base of the Phoenicians founded *c.* 814 BC, dates from about 600 BC, but in Sardinia we find a stele fragment from Nora which is said to date from the eleventh century (Cross 1974). It was from the Phoenicians that the Greeks claimed to have borrowed their script which spread through the Mediterranean; and the Phoenician script, directly or indirectly, gave rise to the alphabet used in Italy for writing Etruscan and the Italic dialects, possibly having been borrowed from the Cumaean or Ischian Greek colonists. More recently Semitic scholars such as Cross, Harvey and Demsky have pointed out that the forms of the archaic Greek script are in many ways more consistent with the idea that an earlier form of Canaanite served as their model, the one current around 1100 BC. So it is suggested that the Greeks adopted their alphabet at about the same time as the Hebrews and Aramaeans, possibly through the occasional visits of Canaanite merchants to the Aegean islands, possibly from the Sea Peoples (or Philistines).

The argument for the earlier invention of the Greek alphabet is not archaeological (as we have seen, the earliest inscriptions are from the eighth century) but epigraphical. The American archaeologist, Narveh, has argued for the earlier date, around 1100 BC, on the basis of the similarity between the writing of the eighth century in Greece and the Proto-Canaanite script from the Late Bronze Age (1973). In both these scripts, writing went first from left to right, then turning in the other direction in a form known as *boustrephodon*, from the movement of the plough over a field. One objection to the idea of early diffusion has been the absence of a particular letter in Proto-Canaanite, namely the long-legged *kaf*, which could have served as a model for the Greeks. Light on this matter is shed by the discovery in 1976 of the 'Izbet Sartah Abecedary (a Canaanite ABC for an alphabet with twenty-two letters) in the Sharan Valley in Palestine, near Afeg, site of battles between Israelites and Philistines around 1050 BC. This new find provides an example of this missing letter, and the form of a number of other letters is closer to Greek than to those of tenth-century Byblos which had previously been held to provide the model for the Greek alphabet; hence it supports the suggestion of earlier borrowing, implying that the so-called Dark Age of Greece was possibly lightened by some element of literacy.

If the Greeks did borrow the alphabet at this period, then the Homeric poems may well have been written down earlier than is commonly supposed. Certainly, as I argue in Chapter 3, the structure and style, despite the so-called 'oral' elements (such as the formulaic phrases), is in many ways unlike those of cultures without writing. From the standpoint of their accepted date of composition, parts are archaic in content. Many have held the present version to represent an earlier oral composition written down at a later date. Is it not more likely to have been a written composition of that same earlier date?

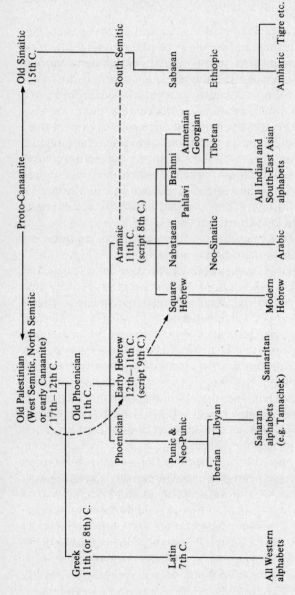

Table 2. The genealogy of the alphabet.

The unity and diversity of alphabets

The consonantal alphabet descended from Proto-Canaanite divided into three main branches, the Phoenician, the Hebrew and the Aramaic. If we accept the hypothesis of the earlier derivation of the Greek alphabet, it split off at roughly the same period, not from Phoenician (as the Greeks themselves claimed), but from Early Canaanite writing itself. In addition, there is a more loosely connected branch, the south Semitic, used down to the present-day in Ethiopia. The spread of the alphabet was extensive and rapid. The Phoenician version, as we have seen, dispersed rapidly throughout the Mediterranean, wherever their merchants and settlers travelled, to Malta, Sardinia, Cyprus and to Carthage, where it gave birth to new scripts among previously non-literate peoples, in Italy, North Africa and Spain.

The Early Hebrew alphabet, which is often seen as acquiring its distinctive character in the eighth century, continued in use until the re-establishment of Assyrian rule in Palestine and the exile of the Jews to Babylon, when the conquered people took over the language and script of the Aramaeans, though the Square Hebrew which resulted was partly influenced by the earlier form. Early Hebrew writing virtually died out, though it was used on some coins in the Hasmonean period of the first century AD; it left as its only descendant today the script used by the Samaritans of Nablus (Shechem) in Palestine, a small band of co-religionists now numbered in hundreds rather than thousands – a remnant of a branch of the Judaic religion that was once as widespread as the southern offshoot, based on Jerusalem, that gave birth both to Christianity and to Islam.

Benefiting from the collapse of the great empires in the twelfth and eleventh centuries BC, the Aramaeans moved into the regions of the Canaanites and Phoenicians and adopted their script, possibly by the eleventh century. Early inscriptions are few though important, but from the seventh century we find a large number of texts throughout the Near East, demonstrating the spread both of the script and of the language. Many Aramaic papyri and *ostraca* (inscribed potsherds) have been found preserved in the drier conditions of Egypt. The earliest evidence from the ancient capital of Memphis may date from the seventh century. The best known example, the Elephantine Papyri, provided details of the religious and economic life of a fifth-century military colony of Jews stationed in Egypt.

The very wide distribution of Aramaic writing shows how, despite the collapse of their kingdoms following the recovery of the Assyrians in the late ninth century, their language (and script) became the *lingua franca* of the Near East through its use as the administrative and diplomatic language in the Assyrian Empire (see 2 Kings 18:26 and Isaiah 36:11) and later in the Achaemenid Empire. It was under those Achaemenid rulers of Persia that Aramaic became the diplomatic language, replacing cuneiform with a more democratic script which was used by traders all the way from Egypt to India. The language became the vernacular of the Jews and was therefore that of the early Christians, only disappearing in the Near East with the advance of Islam after the seventh century AD, though Aramaic continued to be employed by scattered Jewish communities as the language of ritual.

Just as the Phoenician alphabet spread far to the west along the sea lanes, so the Aramaic variant travelled along the land routes to the east. It was adopted by the kingdom of Nabataea, with its capital at Petra in modern Jordan, and from there it travelled into Sinai and the Arabic peninsular to become the progenitor of the script used for writing the Qu'ran. As a result it was widely used throughout Africa and the Old World to transcribe many non-Semitic languages. So, too, was the earlier Aramaic. For it appears to have been carried to India in the seventh century BC by Semitic merchants. There, according to Bühler (1898), it became the prototype of the Brahmi script of India, the writing system that developed after the gap (not longer than in Greece) that followed the disappearance of the undeciphered script of the Indus Basin civilization and the one that gave birth to the numerous alphabetic systems of India and the rest of Asia.[4] The Indo–Aryan migration to Ceylon in the fifth century BC took the script to the south, while at a later date the North Indian version was adopted in Eastern (or Chinese) Turkestan and strongly influenced the invention of the Tibetan script in AD 639.

One of the major factors in the further spread of the alphabet outside India was the rise of Buddhism in the fifth century BC, a religion that was perhaps more easily accepted outside the subcontinent than Hinduism itself, though one would not wish to discount the enormous influence of the latter, as indicated in iconography and literature, on the whole of Indo-China and Indonesia. Buddhist monks travelled widely, converting the masses and helping to develop varieties of the South Indian scripts over a vast area that included Burma, Thailand, Cambodia, Laos, Vietnam, Malaya and Indonesia, and as far as Tagalog in the Philippines, perhaps even influencing the development of the *kana* script in Japan. On the other hand the Korean alphabet, *Han'gul*, dating from the fifteenth century AD and connected with the use of movable type, was possibly the result of stimulus diffusion from the West during the *Pax Tartarica*.

Apart from its influence on Arabic and the Indian scripts, Aramaic writing was also adapted for the Iranian (Persian) form known as Pahlavi, for Armenian and Georgian writing of the fifth century AD as well as for a range of alphabets used by early Turkish and Mongol tribes in Siberia, Mongolia and Turkestan.

The more distant branch of the scripts developing from Early Canaanite (*c.* 1400 BC), and possibly influenced both by the Old Sinaitic script and by the North Semitic, was the South Semitic branch, which was confined to the Arabian peninsular and to the adjacent African shore, including the mountains of Ethiopia. These are the scripts that flourished in the kingdoms of southern Arabia, the best known of which was that of the Sabaeans (the land of the Queen of Sheba). All of these forms of writing were swept away by the rise of Islam and the consequent spread of the Arabic script derived from Aramaic. Today the South Semitic branch survives only in the alphabets of Ethiopia used for transcribing Amharic and the other major languages of that country.

I earlier discussed the derivation of the Greek alphabet from Phoenician, possibly from Early Canaanite. Given that the Greek alphabet was the first systematically to isolate and transcribe both consonants and vowels, and given that it provided the basis for subsequent European writing, we need to look at its development in slightly greater detail.

The first adaptation of the Greek alphabet was to transcribe the languages of non-Hellenic peoples of Asia Minor, in the coastal areas of what is now Turkey. In North Africa, it was used by the Copts of Egypt for a script which included some elements of Egyptian demotic writing. As in the Near East generally, the alphabet quickly replaced earlier systems of logo-syllabic writing in a way that emphasizes its greater efficiency for many tasks.

In Europe the Greek alphabet was adopted at a very early stage by the Etruscans of Central Italy; it is already laid out at the end of the eighth century or the early seventh century BC in the Marsiliana Tablet, which was probably used for teaching the alphabet, and it continued in use until long after Latin became commoner as the result of the dominance of Rome. At a much later date the Greek alphabet was adapted by Bishop Wulfilas for translating the Bible into Gothic. Then, in the ninth century, St Cyril and St Methodius utilized the Greek letters for transcribing Slavonic languages, and a modified version of this alphabet became the script of all those Slavonic peoples whose religion was derived from the Eastern Christian Church of Byzantium. It was subsequently adapted, under Russian influence, for the writing of a number of other languages spoken by peoples who were incorporated into what is now the Soviet Union.

Just as the Greek alphabet was probably early on adapted by the Etruscans, so the Etruscan script was soon borrowed by neighbouring peoples. The Runic writing of northern Europe and the Oghamic characters used by some of the Celts were possibly descendants of Etruscan or Venetic writing (Fig. 9). But by far the most important offshoot was Latin, first written down in the seventh century BC. Certain changes were made in the script, especially after the conquest of Greece by the Romans in the first century BC, but that alphabet has kept substantially the same form down to the present day. Its subsequent history has been, first, one of adaptation to the languages of western Europe following the conquests of the Roman Empire, and then to languages throughout the world following the European conquests of America, Africa and Oceania and the spread of European trade and religion into much of what remained independent. Secondly, the script itself has been continuously transformed by varieties of cursive style required for everyday purposes as well as by the development of

Fig. 9. The Kirk Maughold inscription from the Isle of Man. Below the carver's inscription ("carved by Iuan the Priest") appears the alphabet in both Runic and Ogham letters

printing and the use of movable type. Of the cursive forms the most influential was the Carolingian script introduced throughout the Frankish Empire at the time of Charlemagne. This formed the basis of the national varieties of writing that developed from the twelfth century, out of which emerged the contemporary types of hand-writing that use the Latin alphabet as well as the letters that appear on the printed page.

The implications of graphic systems

I have discussed the origin and history of writing and the alphabet but what of their significance? We may think of this at three related levels, storage (intergenerational communication), communication (intragenerational) and internal, 'cognitive' effects. The general implications of introducing a means of recording speech are revolutionary, in its potentiality if not always in its actuality. In the first place it permits the transmission of cultural (non-genetic) information across the generations. So too does speech itself, but writing enables this transfer to take place without face-to-face contact (indeed, independently of direct human intermediaries), and without the continual transformation of the earlier statement that is the characteristic of the purely oral situation. For example, it meant that it became possible to reconstruct the past in a radically different way, so that (to use an unconvincing dichotomy) 'myth' was supplemented and even replaced by 'history'. The kind of transformation this wrought can be understood when we think of how visual recording on film and audio recording on tape have augmented our contact with and understanding of our predecessors. But such understanding is perhaps the least important of its implications. Preservation leads to accumulation, and accumulation to the increased possibility of incremental knowledge. Writing, being in effect the first stage of this process of preserving the past in the present, had the most far-reaching effects. For not only did it create a possibility, but the realization of that possibility changed the world of man, internally as well as externally, in a remarkable way. The process of course is neither immediate nor yet inevitable. Social organization can, and often does, delay its impact. But the possibility is there.

How did it change the world of man? Let me first touch upon the organizational changes. Writing, in the full sense, appeared with the growth of urban civilizations. Nor was it simply a consequence but also a condition of that development, though the complex mnemonic of knotted cords (*quipu*) took the Inca some way along this path at an administrative level. In Mesopotamia, the first written word appears to be that of the merchant and the accountant, though as part of the ecclesiastical organization of the temple city.

What did writing facilitate? Clearly the identification of merchandise, the recording of types and quantities of goods, the calculation of the input and the output, were much helped by the development of a script. None of these activities are impossible in oral societies. But without the written word the scale and complexity of the operation were limited. Apart from mercantile operations themselves, the organization of the temple city was carried out by means of writing, which permitted the elaboration of bureaucratic arrangements related to tax and tribute, as well as playing an important part in the conduct of external affairs and in the administration of the provinces. Law was organized around the written code rather than the more flexible 'custom' of oral society which could react to changing social situations without having to be deliberately set aside. While early writing was employed in the service of the political economy, the training of scribes was often connected with the temples. Moreover, the comparative complexity of logographic systems and the desire of scribes to control education, meant that while literacy was restricted to a small proportion of the population, the tasks it could perform were further limited by writing on clay. One of the tasks that later cuneiform did perform, however, was the recording of information about the movements of heavenly bodies that formed the basis of subsequent advances in astronomy and mathematics. The possibility of preservation led to accumulation and then to incremental knowledge. Such a process was not seriously inhibited by the nature of the system of linguistic notation, since mathematics remains a logographic rather than an alphabetic system. Many logograms made use of sound values, but holistically, not in terms of the minimal phonological segments of vowels and consonants.

The invention of the alphabet, and to some extent the syllabary, led to a considerable reduction in the number of signs, and to a writing system which was potentially unrestricted both in its capacity to transcribe speech and in its availability to the general population. The descendants of the Canaanite alphabet/syllabary spread rapidly through Europe and Asia, and, later, the remaining continents, making available a script that was easy to learn and easy to use.

The results are seen in the apparent growth of literacy in the Syrian–Palestinian area, where the uses of writing seem to have expanded in the religious and the historical–literary domains relative to the political and economic; of this expansion the Old Testament of the Hebrews may be considered one of the major products. A further extension of literacy, fundamental as far as the range of writing was concerned, took place in Greece, with its fully developed alphabet, possibly a more open political system, and a type of instruction that largely released literacy from the constraints of the temple organization and the religious domain. In this new context, writing managed to place some restrictions on the development of centralized government, which it had elsewhere helped to promote, by providing an instrument of control in the shape of the ballot. The same period saw the development of new fields of knowledge and the encouragement of new ways of knowing. The development of the visual scrutiny of the text had supplemented the aural input of sound over wide areas of human understanding; linguistic information was organized by means of tangible records, which affected the way in which man's practical intelligence, his cognitive processes, could work on the world around. This potential was there with logo-syllabic systems; indeed, in China great advances in the accumulation, transmission and furthering of knowledge were made using this system, although with the advantage of brush and paper. It is a gross ethnocentric error of Europe to attribute too much to the alphabet and too much to the West. Nevertheless, a potentially democratic form of writing, one that could, if allowed, make the easy transcription of language and direct access to learning a possibility for the vast majority of the community, followed the development of the alphabet and syllabary, though it was not until the emergence of mechanical means of reproducing these texts by movable type that the alphabet came fully into its own. Equally it was the limited number of alphabetic signs that enabled Europe to exploit the benefits of movable type, first used in the East. And it is in this same direction that other systems of writing have found themselves pushed, sometimes under political and religious pressures, often by the mere idea that modernization somehow depends upon it. But other languages (Chinese with its monosyllables, Japanese with its homonyms) may be more adapted (or have adapted themselves) to their present scripts. In any case the act of changing the script, like changing one's language, carries much emotive and cultural significance. Additional learning difficulties there may be, but it is the written word itself that has brought most of the gains (and costs), both at the level of social organization and of cognitive capacity.

II

The influence of early forms of writing

2

Literacy and achievement in the Ancient World

It is clear from the historical picture that one cannot regard the impact of writing as a single phenomenon. The so-called 'literacy thesis' covers a range of possible variables, a series of changes in the way human beings communicate with one another, and the effect these have upon the content and style of communication, and upon social life in general. And it includes the cumulative historical consequences of such changes. So that we should not think of a simple binary shift between oral and literate, but a whole sequence of changes that have to be defined in terms of the means of communication (or what I have also called the technology of the intellect) and the mode of communication, if by that sibylline phrase I can indicate elements of social organization and ideology that may inhibit or favour the adoption of a specific technology, the realization of its full potential and the opportunity for its further development.

It has been suggested that in placing so much emphasis on literacy in an attempt to face up to the differences between what have been described as primitive and advanced, traditional and modern societies, we are simply replacing one dichotomy, one set of binarisms, by another. That is not at all the case; we are concerned with a whole set of changes, from clay to papyrus, for example (Powell 1981), as well as with the difference between what in a Popperian way I am, only for the moment, calling closed and open religious or ideological systems.

In any case I would argue that even if I were simply replacing one set of dichotomies by another, at least this particular set attempts to include some sort of general explanation; it implies a statement of a causal (or at least correlative) rather than simply of a descriptive kind. It points to a mechanism by which the difference came about, not only in Greece or Babylonia, but elsewhere as well.

By a phrase 'pointing to a mechanism' I don't mean that I am offering a mechanistic, deterministic, explanation. Those who work in the humanities and social sciences are too apt to talk in terms of single, determining causes, because their mode of discourse (that is, linear exposition by the written word) makes it difficult to present a multifactorial analysis except in a vague and eclectic manner. But essentially we should be involved in weighing one variable against another – it is our techniques and data that inhibit us from going very far in this direction.

The first chapter has shown that there are important developments in the study of the history of writing since the article by Watt and myself, published in 1963, and since the earlier work by Havelock and others, and the suggestions arising from these studies ought to be considered, if not accepted, in considering the implications of literacy. Two of these are the result of the work of Semitic scholars. One should remember that it was the Afro–Asiatic languages (which include Semitic) that were widely used in the early development of writing in the Near East (apart of course from the very early use of Sumerian), so it is not surprising to find important contributions coming from this academic source.

The first point has to do with the date and origin of the Greek alphabet. Received opinion, which we earlier followed, had it that the Greeks adopted the Phoenician alphabet around 750 BC. This date fits with local archaeological evidence, that is, with the material from inscriptions recorded by Jeffrey (1961). It fits with certain historical data, and with the idea of a Dark Age between the loss of Linear B around 1100 BC and the subsequent adoption of the alphabet, a period of some 350 years, equivalent to the gap between the time of Shakespeare and the present day.

But the hypothesis does not fit with certain other data I have noted in the previous chapter. The distribution of Phoenician throughout the Mediterranean is held by some to have occurred at least a century earlier, possibly longer. According to F. M. Cross (1974), a fragmentary stele from Nora in Sardinia (not the Nora Stone of the ninth century BC), "can be no later than the eleventh century BC" (1974:492).

Again the early date does not fit with the supposedly archaic features of the Greek script which look to many Semiticists as though they had been borrowed much earlier. We can put the technical arguments in the following simplified way. Many modern scholars of the ancient Greek script have followed Rhys Carpenter who, on the basis of the similarity of the letters, argued for a Semitic script borrowed during the eighth century (Carpenter 1933; Jeffrey 1961:15). Negative support for this date was provided by the absence of earlier Greek texts, obviously an important consideration. Nevertheless, Semiticists like Albright, Cross, Driver and Gelb, advanced the date by a century because of the wide diffusion of the Phoenician alphabet throughout the Mediterranean in the ninth century (Albright 1949:195–6; Gelb 1963:180–1; Cross 1967:23; McCarter 1975:123ff.). More recently a study by Narveh makes a much more radical claim, dating the Greek borrowing as early as 1100 BC because of the palaeographic similarity between the direction of the Greek script and the Proto-Canaanite letters of the Late Bronze Age, at a time when the direction of the script was not fixed. The major difficulty in this thesis has been the absence of a long-legged *kaf* in Proto-Canaanite which could serve as the archetype for the Greek form (1973:7), for a suitable *kaf* had made its appearance only in the second half of the ninth century. The recent discovery of the twelfth century sherd at 'Izbet Sartah in Palestine has removed this obstacle; the sherd is inscribed with eighty-seven letters, making it a long alphabetic text of the period, and includes an abecedary of twenty-two letters, one of which provides a suitable model for the missing form (Demsky 1977).

We have treated the alphabet here (as Diringer and others have done) as a unique invention. There are good empirical reasons for such an assumption, in terms of its known history and present distribution. But there are also good theoretical ones, since the alphabet is a very abstract device; it consists of (in the case of English) twenty-one stops and five voiced elements. It also represents a terminal point in a scheme of 'logical' development. You get to that point of high abstraction by starting with:

1 logograms ('word signs'),
2 moving to syllables, e.g. signs for BA, BE etc.,
3 then proceeding to the further break-down by using the initial (or

other letter) to stand for the common phonetic element in a group of syllables; the alphabet may only emerge when the whole range of syllables are put together in a matrix, that is, in a graphic form consisting of the combination of x and y co-ordinates.

It is possible for a society to go straight to a syllabary as its first system of writing, and it is a form that has many advantages for the process of learning to read. Even so, all the examples we know of where this has happened appear to have been stimulated by contact with already literate societies outside. To go straight to a new alphabet, on the other hand, means jumping to a level of abstract analysis which only earlier literate operations appear to allow. This step is not a matter of invention *de novo*, nor does it follow automatically from morphologically 'simpler' systems. However, the development is implied in those earlier forms and was not possible without them.

Before we ask what difference these developments make, not simply to our earlier hypothesis but to an assessment of the consequences of changes in human communication, there is a second point that needs to be considered. In arguing for the pre-eminent character of the Greek contributions to the alphabet, Watt and I were following a line of thought that was clearly congenial to the European experience and to the role of a classical education. Following Gelb and others, we accepted the term 'alphabet' as appropriate only to the Greek script, which provided signs for consonants and vowels, but not for the parent script that represented consonants alone. That position needs to be reassessed. Current opinion would certainly modify the radical distinction in modes of writing, suggesting that the breaks between logographic, syllabic, and alphabetic systems are less clear cut than the terminology implies. The nature of a logographic system, in particular because of the number of signs involved, leads at an early stage, to some kind of phonetic representation, signs signifying the sound rather than directly representing the semantic reference of a word. Such was the history of developments in the Near East. Since phonetic signs were additions to, rather than replacements of, other signs, their introduction added to the complexity of the script itself. Nevertheless the phonetic principle was embedded in these scribal systems and the second millennium saw the development of a kind of alphabet consisting of consonantal signs alone. This development was partly a matter of shedding non-phonetic elements, leading to the and evolution of the syllabaries and alphabet as the simplest and most efficient systems for societies that did not desire the access to past records which scribal modes entailed. In this process of shedding non-alphabetic constituents, which makes possible the 'describalization' of culture and lays the basis for an 'unrestricted literacy', social as well as technical factors play an important part.

The first systematic transcription of consonants was used to write down a Semitic language, all of which give great weight to consonantal roots. A greater amount of information is contained in the consonants, which typically outnumber vowels by ratios of 3 or 4:1 (Wang 1981:224). Should this be described as an alphabet? The point is arguable. It was only the later Greek alphabet that systematically provided graphemes for vowels as well as for consonants, and its comprehensive character was surely one element in making it such a versatile instrument for writing, and specially for reading. On the other hand the Greek alphabet is closely linked to the consonantal system that was developed long before, from 1500 BC onwards. First used by scribes, that is to say, by the advocates and practitioners of a restricted literacy, these consonantal systems were adapted for scripts that became in some ways almost as flexible as the Greek; for another great branch used for writing down Aramaic gave birth to written Arabic as well as to the numerous alphabetic scripts of the Indian subcontinent, of Southeast Asia and much else beside. It was possibly the adoption of these scripts that formed the background of that intellectual revolution of the East, of the development of Sanskrit knowledge in the form in which we know it, as well as constituting the prerequisite and tool of Brahmin authority, and at a slightly later stage leading to the rise of the reformist movements of Buddhism, Jainism, and the alternative modes of Hinduism.

The notion that the gap between the Greek and earlier 'alphabets' is less extensive than many have assumed derives partly from the wide diffusion of the consonantal alphabet, the Phoenician version in the West and the Aramaic in the East. These forms of writing exploded rapidly over a large part of the Eurasian continent in a manner very different from the impact of earlier systems of writing. The nature of their impact is indicated by the continuity of their form, for it is a remarkable fact that the purely arbitrary ordering of letters in the Roman alphabet, A, B, C, D, which once memorized, gives us such a formidable power of recall and of control over information, has remained relatively constant from 1500 BC to the present day, that is, over a period of 3,500 years. This ordering has no 'rational' justification, except that once established, continuity pays off. Change the order to a more logical one, vowels first, then consonants, and you upset the organization of every dictionary and telephone directory that has been pro- duced. The arbitrary order ABC is basic to our understanding of the universe we have created.

But there is yet another point. Not only may the Greek alphabet be earlier than we suspected, not only may it be closer in form to consonantal alphabets, but even the earlier types of writing may have had some of the liberating effects that certain authors (includ- ing Watt and myself) attributed to alphabetic literacy. The point is obvious in the Chinese case. The logographic script inhibited the development of a democratic literate culture; it did not prevent the use of writing for achieving remarkable ends in the spheres of science, learning and literature. The same point holds true for the Ancient Near East. In other words, we may need to modify our ideas not only about the uniqueness of the techniques available to the Greeks (i.e. their alphabet) but also about the uniqueness of their achievements in other respects.

The question of the relationship between the achievement of the Greeks and the development of writing systems has recently been raised in G. E. R. Lloyd's distinguished work, *Magic, Reason and Experience: studies in the origins and development of Greek science* (1979). To put a sensitively phrased thesis in simplistic terms, Lloyd argues that what happened in Greece constituted a defeat for magic and the victory of reason. Greek society developed a general scep- ticism which was related to the growth of specific methods of proof; and he suggests that since the consonantal alphabet was invented earlier, we should not look at the advent of a new technique of literacy for the cause of this development but rather at the uses of argument that characterized the judicial and political process.

We need to consider again what is involved. In the first place there is the question of how unique was Greek science, specifically in its procedures and its assumptions. Secondly, there are clearly some links between the general growth of science and the growth in the development of more abstract writing systems; and, thirdly, we need to relate the growth of Greek science to the freedom given by an easy form of writing not only in a technical sense (through its possession of the first consonant–vowel alphabet, a fact that is probably of less importance than we had earlier supposed) but also in a wider sociological sense (that is, in the relative freedom from ecclesiastical or scribal control, permitting more freedom of expression and communication). But I have no wish to imply that everything is due to a unique causal factor; it is a matter, as I have said, of weighing one element against another. While accepting much of Lloyd's argument, including the importance of argument itself, I would want to emphasize the longer term effects of communication by writing.

The general questions that face us are indicated by the title of the book itself. Lloyd writes of the origins of Greek science. Yet he is also dealing with the origin of Western science and its dissociation from magic. From the standpoint of explanation and fact, two different situations need to be distinguished. Are we trying to account for the origins of a form of systematized knowledge or for the adoption of one such form in a particular place at a particular time, as, for example, in explaining the recent transfer and adaptation of western science to West Africa.

Lloyd is clearly concerned with the more general problem, and this he relates to the development of criticism directed at magic and to the growth of a general scepticism. At the same time he is aware of the fact that to speak of "the emergence of philosophy and science" in Greece is to use a shorthand phrase which requires some qualification. First, because 'magic' still persisted, even among the scientists and philosophers (indeed the very concept was perhaps a shifting one, depending on one's point of departure). And secondly because science, even in the restricted sense, had already made its beginning in Babylonia and Egypt. In this context, Lloyd discusses the continuities, and even the comparability of achievement, in the fields of medicine and astronomy; "in both cases, the production of *written* records transforms the situation as regards the preservation, diffusion and utilisation of the knowledge in question" (p. 232). What earlier societies lacked however was "the notion of proof" (p. 230); they failed to acquire "a concept of rigourous mathematical demonstration" or "self-conscious methodologies" (pp. 232–3). The Greeks

were certainly not the first to develop a complex mathematics – only the first to use, and then also to give a formal analysis of, a concept of rigorous mathematical demonstration. They were not the first to carry out careful observations in astronomy and medicine, only the first – eventually – to develop an explicit notion of empirical research and to debate its role in natural science. They were not the first to diagnose and treat some medical cases without reference to the postulated divine or daemonic agencies, only the first to express a category of the "magical" and to attempt to exclude it from medicine. (p. 232)

One of the problems lies in the use of the term "magical" as an analytic tool. The title of Lloyd's book, *Magic, Reason and Experience*, provides a kind of counterpoint to Evans-Pritchard's well-known empirical study of the Azande, *Magic, Witchcraft and Oracles* (1937). The terms 'magic' and 'magical thinking' are the common coin of discourse in the social sciences, in philosophy and in history, but they are concepts that require some elucidation. In the language of the LoDagaa of northern Ghana, whom I use as a sounding board, there appears to be no equivalent word that one can reasonably translate as 'magic'. Indeed the notion does harm to their own categories or forms of knowledge, for it cross-cuts their way of understanding the world. It is sometimes the case that a person will remark of another *o tera tĩi*, 'he has medicine', referring to powers which we would describe as 'magical', for example, the ability to appear and disappear at will. On the other hand, the same term is used for curative medicines, whether in the local or in the European repertoire (Goody 1961), as well as for efficacious materials like gunpowder. Indeed the same phrase can be used, sometimes with a nod or a smile, of a good hunter, to indicate that he has some external, non-human, help, perhaps as an acknowledgement of his prowess and powers.

Where and how did the term and usage arise? For Herodotus, as Lloyd explains, the *magoi* were a distinct tribe.

But already in the fifth century magos and its derivatives came to be used perjoratively – often in association with ... other words for vagabonds, tricksters and charlatans ... for deception, imposture and fraudulent claims for special knowledge ... Thus these texts already exhibit what was to remain a prominent feature of the words from the mag-root (and of their Latin equivalents ...). They were never clearly defined in terms of particular beliefs and practices, but were commonly used of such activities or claims to special knowledge as any particular author or speaker suspected of trickery or fraudulence. Pliny, for instance, attacks the "magical art" at length ... But that does not prevent him from including in his work a mass of homeopathic and sympathetic remedies, amulets and the like, which he is half inclined himself to believe to be efficacious; he often mentions, for example, the special ritualistic procedures to be used in their collection and preparation ... (1979:13)

Even at this stage, the term 'magic' was used of the beliefs and predictions of other people, and hence of ideas and procedures that were foreign to one's own. The coming of the Magi was the visit, obviously, of non-Christian, but also of non-Jewish 'wise men', to pay homage to the infant Christ. Already the concept had a slighting implication of beliefs that were not altogether worthy to be held and of practices not altogether worthy to be undertaken; later on it designated beliefs and practices that lay outside the Church and were condemned by it. I would argue, therefore, that the LoDagaa have no concept of magic not because they lack the necessary scepticism but because they lack the bounded system of beliefs that excludes 'magic', or defines it as being 'other'. This lack is not so much a matter of 'tribe' (since in West Africa beliefs and practices cross the often shaded boundaries of groups in the same way as kola nuts, cloth or salt) but of the definition of a boundary between systems of belief that literacy encourages, even if this feature is not tied in any absolute way to Religions of the Book (Goody 1975).

The problem of magic is linked to that of scepticism. Examining the pre-Socratic texts, Lloyd traces the growth of general scepticism and hence of rationality. He also points out that Keith Thomas remarked upon the sceptical approach to astrologers in sixteenth- and seventeenth-century England, where the recognition that some were charlatans and quacks "only served to buttress the status of the system as a whole" (Thomas 1971:401), an argument that Evans-Pritchard had already used of scepticism about the work of the Azande diviner. He recognizes too that this attitude was not confined to 'rationalizing' Europe in the throes of developing capitalism. For Joseph Needham (1956) presents an account of the sceptical tradition in Chinese thought, on which Lloyd comments, "there are some admittedly rather limited signs of critical and rationalistic attitudes towards divination in two third-century writers ... In fragment 210 of Huan T'an ... we read: 'Today all the artful and foxy, magicians of small talent, as well as the soothsayers, disseminate and reproduce diagrams and documents, falsely praising the records of prognostication. By deception and misinformation, by greed and dishonesty, they lead the ruler astray. How can we fail to suppress and banish such things?'" The criticisms of another Chinese writer are "strikingly similar" to that of Lucretius, while a third claims that "As a matter of fact, diviners do not ask Heaven and Earth, nor have weeds or tortoise shells spiritual qualities"; at the same time this last writer rejects the idea that dead men become ghosts (1979:19); although in a different form, that notion is still part of many world religions, and held by many who are scientists or sceptics in other contexts.

Nevertheless, Lloyd claims that while scepticism existed before the Greeks, as well as among other peoples, there is a significant difference between general and specific scepticism. He quotes the well-known passage from Evans-Pritchard's study of the Azande, to which I have referred, where the author points out that while individual witchdoctors might be frauds, there was no scepticism about witchdoctoring in general. "I particularly do not wish to give the impression that there is any one who disbelieves in witchdoctor-hood. Most of my acquaintances believed that there are a few entirely reliable practitioners, but that the majority are quacks" (1937:185). Evans-Pritchard went on to remark that "faith and scepticism are alike traditional. Scepticism explains failures of witchdoctors, and being directed towards particular witchdoctors even tends to support faith in others" (p. 193).

The difference between general and specific scepticism, Lloyd suggests, can be seen in the work of the Greek author of *On the Sacred Disease* who is against all purifiers, and against the idea that ritual purification can influence natural phenomena. The difference, moreover, constitutes "a paradigm switch ... the Hippocratic writer rejects the notion of supernatural intervention in natural phenomena as a whole, as what might even be called a category mistake. Even when we have to deal with the divine, the divine is in no sense *supernatural* ..." (1979: 26–27).

The last point can be most easily cleared away. The designation 'supernatural' is clearly one that derives from the observer's point of view. Despite the insistence of Lévi-Strauss on the existence of a general divide between nature and culture, or of other writers on that between the natural and the supernatural, it is difficult to grant that these concepts have any universal or even widespread roots in the notions of the actors themselves; like 'sacred' and 'profane', they are basically to be regarded as analytic tools or as specific folk concepts (Goody 1961).

Returning to the difference between specific and general scepticism, on which great importance is placed, we should note that Greek society as a whole did not reject the intervention of supernatural agencies. Moreover any scepticism must be related to a particular universe, so that generality and particularity become matters of definition. The common anthropological argument, expressed by Evans-Pritchard, that you can reject diviners without rejecting divination, has something to be said for it, but only a limited amount. It is difficult to see how worries about the morality of a particular Pope do not raise doubts about the papacy in general, do not lead to the asking of other questions about the institution. What is critical here is the way these doubts are recorded, the way they accumulate over time for the individual and for his successors, as well as the way of accounting for the failures that occur in, say, divination, since the question of the handling of the evidence directly impinges on the question of scepticism. The certain knowledge that a notebook I have kept shows that my dreams have come true in only five out of a hundred cases must tend to modify my initial attitude towards dreams as indices of future events. In oral memory the many misses tend to get forgotten in favour of the occasional hits; this is the memory of the gambler who recalls his wins more frequently than his losses. It is the systematic recording (or even the possibility of so doing) rather than an initial attitude of mind that allows us to be 'generally sceptical'. In other words there is perhaps not the radical division between particular and general scepticism that the theory demands. Those differences that do exist need to be related to literacy (that is, to recording), as well as to other specific factors in the culture which Lloyd discusses.

The specific factor to which he links the general scepticism of the Greeks is the nature of argument, especially as it appears in legal dispute. He concludes his book with the following remark. "The sterility of much ancient scientific work is . . . often a result of the enquiry being conducted as a dispute with each contender single-mindedly advocating his own point of view. This is easy to say with hindsight: but an examination of the Greek evidence suggests that this very paradigm of the competitive debate may have provided the essential framework for the growth of natural science" (p. 267). That growth is related to "the experience of radical political debate and confrontation in small-scale, face-to-face societies" (p. 266).

This interesting argument is in some ways similar to that pro-pounded by Horton when he replaces the open–closed dichotomy which he had used in an earlier discussion of the difference between western science and African thought (1967), with the idea that under certain circumstances the opposition of theories, the clash of cosmologies, produces the kind of ferment to which Lloyd refers. He attempts to specify some of those circumstances.

The political situation in Greece was undoubtedly an important element in the intellectual developments that occured there. Even more important perhaps was the relatively free religious life to which Lloyd refers in his opening chapter. "These texts", he writes,

show that in the sixth and early fifth centuries it was, within broad limits, perfectly possible both to criticise existing religious ideas and practices and to introduce new ones. To put it negatively, there was no dogmatic or systematic religious orthodoxy. Although there were certain widespread and deeply held beliefs, there was no common sacred book, no one true religion, represented by universally recognised spokesmen–priests or prophets backed by an organised religious authority such as a church. The expression of new and quite individualistic views on god and the divine was, as our examples show, not only possible but quite common, and by the end of the fifth century we have evidence of a series of rationalistic accounts of the origin of religion. (1979:13–14)

The argument is convincing. Greece was on the periphery of the Ancient World, both politically and religiously. Just as the alphabet developed on the periphery of the great civilizations – if not in Sinai, then at least in Syria, so too the freedom from the constraints of the great empires and their accompanying cults gave speculation a freer rein. We do perhaps find greater freedom in the Eastern religious traditions of Hinduism and Buddhism in both India and China. And we have that interesting example which Baines (1983) compares with Greece, of Akhenaten. Indeed Baines provides some support for Lloyd's argument. Discussing what he considers to be a roughly parallel "cognitive revolution" (that of Akhenaten), he notes that "what is ... missing in Egypt is the abstract form of textual argument that arose in Greece", where "plurality may have helped to formulate a mode of discourse that allowed different areas to be discussed in the same terms without necessary recourse to ultimate values" (1983:592). But the development of science is not simply a matter of speculation, of which there is often a good deal about. As Lloyd repeatedly insists, it is also a matter of proof, evidence, of *recorded* scepticism that builds upon the thoughts of more than one man, of more than one doubter, and creates a body of new knowledge based on a tradition of cumulative scepticism.

Clearly ideas of evidence and proof are already present in oral societies, not to mention the Ancient Near East. In his account of Barotse jurisprudence (1955), Gluckman provides us with an excellent analysis of the use of evidence in an oral society. This use is different from that of European courts, with their restricted ideas of 'factual' relevance. Concepts of relevance are differently phrased in multiplex situations where people interact with one another in a variety of contexts, any one of which may be relevant to any other. I would suggest that the differences in the nature of evidence in these societies is related in a fairly direct way to the absence of written codes. And furthermore that the forms of refutation linked by Lloyd to this politico–legal activity are again closely associated with the development of writing, including that used before the Greeks.

In his account of the early work *On the Sacred Disease*, the one which undertakes a general rather than a specific attack on puri-fiers, Lloyd points out how the author, who makes only a rare use of empirical evidence, supports his thesis by deploying "critical and destructive arguments to defeat his opponents" (p. 24). The first of these weapons is an implicit form of the argument later known as Modus Tollens; "if A, then B; but not B, therefore not A". This "powerful technique of refutation" was being utilized long before it is stated in general terms by Aristotle and formally analyzed by the Stoics in the early Hellenistic period.

I would suggest that these forms of refutation are in many respects not so very diffferent from the forms of argument found in oral societies. Proof, evidence, witnesses, forms of argument, all these are present. But they do not take the same shape; there is not the same degree of formalization, largely because the Greek versions were developed in a written tradition, which, operating in a single communicative channel, necessarily introduced a tighter formulation. One clue lies in the use of the letter A, an alphabetic sign, in the procedures themselves. Such signs are of great generality, high abstraction, but of considerable power. Try under oral conditions to formalize a general proposition using concrete cases instead of, as in the present instance, appealing to arbitrary data, to non-sense.

Try, too, expressing ideas in the form of the syllogism. Try comparing versions of the same story and perceiving the diversity and contradictions. Try formulating opposition and analogy, in which both opposition (across) and analogy (down) exist in the same time-frame, let alone exist in the 'decontextualized' way that is characteristic of the work of Pythagoreans and of anthropologists. Try all this *without* writing, without the use of graphemes.

In one sense this type of formalization is implicit in writing itself, although its explicit formulation is a specific historical event. Certainly it seems to have appeared in an implicit form before the Greeks, with earlier systems of writing than the alphabet. One example is given in a study by J. Bottéro, entitled "Les noms de Marduk, l'écriture et la 'logique' en Mésopotamie ancienne" (1977). The author analyzes two tablets found in the Library of Assurbanipal, which consist of a 'commentary' on the fifty names of Marduk, listed in parallel form, the Sumerian and Akkadian terms side by side in columns. Here the process of offering equivalents, of adopting a translation procedure, has interesting consequences:

Dans cette culture, comme qui dirait diplopique, essentiellement, enracinée dans le monde sumérien et épanouie dans l'univers accadien, de telles listes ne formaient pas seulement l'armature de la lexicographie, mais, pour les lettres au moins, la propre assise de la pensée. (p. 15)

The procedure was essentially a literary one, if only because Sumerian was a 'dead language' and could hardly be anything else.

... dans le but d'obtenir, en partant du Nom, autant de sumérogrammes qu'il leur était necéssaire pour retrouver l'intégralité du texte de l'*En.el.*, les auteurs de notre pièce ont traité ledit Nom en procédant suivant les règles de leur propre *écriture*. (p. 16)

They proceeded by decomposing words, using of course determinatives which were written but not pronounced.

These lists produce a series of equations, of polarities and analogies, which the commentator tries to explain:

So we suggest that all the rare equivalences, unused (*inusuelles*), unknown, between the sumerograms in the first column and the Akkadian words in the second, have been in a way demonstrated and "acquises", even "conquises", either by our authors, or else before them by their lexigraphic authorities, by means of real modes of reasoning which employed, in essence, the procedure of analogy and successive equations of one term and another, ending up by placing in a relation of equivalence the first and last of the series: if A=B and if B=C, then A=C.

These are the procedures by which our 'commentators' came to draw from the different names of Marduk "l'integralité du texte consacré par l'*En.el.* à leur paraphrase", showing the way that just as the universal encloses the particular, each of these names contains "la totalité des attributs, des qualités, des mérites et des hautes-faits de ce dieu: bref, de sa nature telle que le poème la détaille" (p. 24).

The argument is very similar to the one Lloyd is making about proof in connection with another syllogistic form, that known as Modus Tollens, except that the latter is formulated in an abstract, explicit way. It is an argument that is correct but requires supplementation. I would suggest that:

1 this particular formalization is a product of a written tradition at whatever specific moment of historical time it may appear
2 it constituted a relatively small step from oral reasoning but one of considerable significance

3 such types of formalized inference appeared before the Greeks,
   though less explicitly than later
4 they were critical to science and to all systematic knowledge.

The earlier existence of such procedures would support Neugebauer's contention that we can already speak of the development of
science in the Ancient Near East. But what sort of science? He
himself argues for the creation of "ancient science" in the Hellenistic period, "where a form of science was developed which later
spread over an area reaching from India to Western Europe", and
remained dominant until the creation of "modern science in the
time of Newton" (1969:1). But there was a yet older science, if by
that expression we mean systematized knowledge, stemming from
earlier oriental civilization. Of course knowledge that is systematized to a certain degree existed and exists in oral cultures. I refer
here to the kind of systematization, developed before the Hellenistic period, whose nature is indicated by the titles to the chapters of
Neugebauer's book on the exact sciences in antiquity: Babylonian
Mathematics, Egyptian Mathematics and Astronomy, Babylonian
Astronomy. In addition we find developments in the fields of
medicine and the natural sciences, in the study of drugs, plants and
stones. The first advances are critically dependent upon recording
natural phenomenon, while the formal classification of the constituent elements of the world seems implicit in the whole use of lists
that dominates Sumerian and Akkadian literary work to such an
extent that it gave birth to a contemporary branch of Assyriological
knowledge known as *Listenwissenschaft*. But it is astronomy that
Neugebauer regards as "the most important force in the development of science since its origin sometime around 500 BC to the days
of Laplace . . ." (1969:2). Significantly astronomy, which had been
closely connected with divination (1969:101–2), was developed on
the basis of a series of mathematical operations (the early texts
dating from 1800 BC) and observational records (from 700 BC),
producing a consistent mathematical theory around 500 BC. These
developments gained little from the invention of the alphabet;
indeed mathematics rests on what are now universal logographic
symbols rather than restricted phonetic ones.

The invention of writing around 3000 BC provides not only an
admirable instrument of storage, of precision and of conceptual

analysis, bringing revolutionary changes in culture, but to the emergence of a class of 'lettrés', specialists in the difficult art and technique of writing and in the ways of looking at things, an intellectual approach to reality. "These mandarins, grouped together in schools and academies around palaces and temples, began very early to interest themselves in a certain range of phenomena, to study them and to compose works that one can hardly call anything except 'scientific'. And these were copied, studied endlessly, adapted, enriched and republished until shortly before the beginning of our own era" (Bottéro 1982:426). So we are left with fragments or entire works dating from the first third of the second millennium, works that deal with matters interesting the learned men of the country: lexicography and grammar, encyclo-paedias, divination, mathematics, medicine, as well as juris-prudence.

In looking at this literature we need to examine the elements and the order in which those elements are placed. As with Hammura-bi's Code, the elements consist of a series of conditional propo-sitions, if so and so, then this and that, which may represent the fundamental logical procedure of their rational thought rather like our syllogism (Bottéro 1982:427). *We* put forward premises in order to draw a conclusion from them: *they* begin with a hypothesis, then draw a conclusion from it by means of a judgement based on this hypothesis. Again 'science' involves selectivity and here the Mesopotamians laid bare its essential attribute, "namely that it relates not the individual, the casual, to all and sundry, but to the universal, the necessary" (p. 429). This process is achieved through "repeated observation, no doubt discussed and criticized". Through the notion of "necessity" we have "le sens de la causalité" but not the law of causality which was never formulated by the Mesopotamians (p. 430).

The move in the direction of 'science' had much to do with the uses of writing itself, as well as to the rise of specialists, of 'savants', that it encouraged. For example, the stripping away of the individual and the casual, as well as the process of selection this involves, is part of the process of recording a court case or any other set of events. Moreover the very fact of writing them down means that one can make, record, and hence *compare* repeated observations in a precise way. The Mesopotamians failed to predict the appearance of Halley's comet largely because they did not have a sufficient run, not of observations, but of *recorded* observations. It is the record that makes the difference and enables the 'necessary' relations, the universal, the general, as distinct from the individual and the particular, to be revealed.

The record is capable of revealing regularities because it provides a measuring instrument. Regularities may suggest a sense of causality but these only become a law of causality when they are explicitly formulated. It was the Greeks, according to Bottéro (and many others) who pushed this process a stage further, who took us further "towards the concept of the universal, the hard and fast formulation which allowed the clear perception and definite statement of principles and Laws in all their abstraction" (1982:437). Nevertheless the Babylonians had already taken us along the road to 'science' and this journey, I argue, was intrinsically linked to their ability to communicate in the written channel.

I have used the opportunity to comment upon part of the discussion in Lloyd's important book in order to rectify some aspects of the argument put forward by Watt and myself respecting the Greek achievement. From the technical standpoint the invention of the Greek alphabet, while clearly marking an important advance, was a less dramatic event than we claimed. But then some other aspects of the Greek achievement also need to be seen against a wider background as researches into earlier literatures can only make increasingly clear.

Of course, other important factors in the Greek situation led to the development and use of this type of proof or demonstration at this particular time. Here the periphery argument seems to me strong. So does the related argument concerning the fluid nature of political, legal, and religious institutions. But without wishing to fall into the jargon of necessary and sufficient causes, these developments are linked, in the long run, to communication in the written mode. Moreover, the changes did not all occur at once; the struggle against 'magic' did not only take place in Greece; it occurred in China, among the Romans (Christian and pagan), as well as at the time of the European Renaissance (Thomas 1971). It was a continuous struggle, for reasons to do with the God who failed ('magic' at times representing an alternative as well as a rejected belief) and the gradual adoption of more complex modes of discrimination among 'theories'.

The struggle continued long after the decline of Greece; the battle wasn't won there and then, nor perhaps even now. Indeed was there ever a general change of the kind that many theorists want to explain? Was there really a sudden, single change in modes of thought, just like that, as distinct from changes in ways of thinking that have been influenced by a variety of factors, but especially by systems of communication and the knowledge they permit us to develop and accumulate?

The Greek achievement has to be seen in the context of other achievements, other attempts to systematize knowledge. In respect of certain of these achievements writing was the *sine qua non*. It made possible a special kind of debate, not I think based exclusively on a particular political system, nor upon the clash of cultures in a general sense, but upon the framed opposition of theories set down on paper which permitted a different form of scrutiny, the analysis of the text. Writing also renders forms of contradiction and proof explicit – though the processes themselves are certainly present in oral societies. And it not only makes possible a particular type of formalized proof (e.g. Modus Tollens), it also accumulates and records these proofs (and what they prove) for future generations and for further operations.

3

Africa, Greece and oral poetry

Writing, indeed any form of visual transcription of oral linguistic elements, had important consequences for the accumulation, development and nature of human knowledge. Here I want to turn to its influence upon those standardized verbal forms we literates discuss under the name of literature. The term is misleading in one way though it has its defenders (Finnegan 1970, 1977) since it specifically designates letters and may tend to introduce a certain bias into the analysis of oral forms. But poetry, tales, recitations of various kinds existed long before writing was introduced and these oral forms continued in modified 'oral' forms, even after the establishment of a written literature. The co-existence of an 'oral' and 'literate' tradition, the situation of the interface, has led to a vigorous discussion about the nature of early poetry (our knowledge of which is necessarily mediated by writing) and its relation to yet earlier oral forms, a discussion that, as with so many other topics, centred on the great achievements of early Greece where the alphabet came into its own.

The notion that Homer's poems were essentially oral compositions received support from the fieldwork of Milman Parry and A. B. Lord in Yugoslavia and from the seminal analyses they made of that material, leading to the formulation of the so-called "oral theory". However neither Yugoslavia nor the Heroic Societies with which Greece is often compared were in fact oral cultures in the sense that literacy was completely absent. To find a truly oral culture, to be sure that the form and content of poetry and prose are uninfluenced by writing, one has to look elsewhere. My own experience of recording oral compositions and my more general conclusions about the role of writing (the so-called 'literacy theory') suggest that we should look again at early Greece in the context of contemporary, or near-contemporary, Africa with a view to re-assessing our ideas about these important contributions to the European tradition.

The Africa I want to discuss is mainly West Africa; it is there, among the LoDagaa of northern Ghana, that I have recorded the long myth of the Bagre (1972 and 1981) and it is this part of the continent, too, that has produced a number of published versions of epic poems, especially the cycles relating to Sunjata in Mali and to Silâmaka among the Fulani and Bambara peoples. There too we find the Soninke legend of the dispersion of the Kusa, edited by Meillassoux and others (1967) and in Nigeria, the Ozidi Saga of the Ijo (J. P. Clark 1977); further south, in the Cameroons, we encounter the *mvet* 'epics' of the Fang (Pepper and De Wolf 1972; Boyer 1983), and in the Congo the Lianja cycle of the Mongo-Nkundo peoples published by Boelaert (1949, 1957), de Rop (1964) and others, as well as the Mwindo epic of the Nyanga recorded by Biebuyck and Mateene (1971).[1]

Of Ancient Greece I know little and have no knowledge of the language. My comments about oral and literary influences on the form or content of Homeric poems have to be read in this light, though the same *caveat* is just as necessary in the case of those numerous scholars dealing with translated material, whether anthropologist, historian, or literary critic. But the appreciation of poetry derives partly from widely-shared human experiences and partly from the specific personal and cultural situations surrounding the act of communication; while the outsider can recognize the general, he is at a loss when it comes to the particular. A sound judgement must clearly take both into account. For instance, it may be very clear to those brought up in a European educational system which has its direct links with the 'classical' past that the Homeric poems are 'unique', 'monumental' products which have no equal in any other tradition. But this judgement is not immediately obvious to members of other cultures, nor (and this is where my lack of linguistic ability makes itself apparent) is it wholly so to me.

The oral traditions (one can hardly call them oral cultures) with which early Greek verse has been compared comprise, above all, the Southern Slavic poetry, especially that recorded by M. Parry

(1971) and A. B. Lord (1974), and secondly, the western European
epics and sagas of England, Ireland, Scandinavia, France and
Germany, and, thirdly, in the works of Chadwick, the so-called
Heroic poetry found in more distant parts of Eurasia. I want to look
at some aspects of these comparisons and then widen the discussion
to include Africa, not simply to bring in data that I myself have
collected but because there are specific reasons for considering that
these other traditions raise questions about the nature of 'orality'
which Africa does not, and because there is an obvious value,
brought out in the stimulating work of Parry and Lord, in looking at
the past against the background of the present. In Africa we still
find long recitations carried out, not frozen in the pages of a
manuscript nor relegated to the café but performed in central
contexts of cultural life.

  Before commenting upon this discussion, we need to make
certain points about the terminology in which it is phrased. There is
no great difficulty in assigning poetry to *cultures* with or without
writing, although there is obviously a question of the extent of
literate influence on the form itself. The problem of assigning a
work to an oral or literate *tradition* is that we are not dealing with a
clear-cut division. In the first place there is the important distinction between composition and performance, with the further
possibility of having to differentiate between performance and
transmission. Secondly, there is a meaningful sense in which all
'literate' forms are composed orally, if we include the use of the
silent voice, the inner ear. And there is also a meaningful sense in
which all earlier oral works are known only because they have been
written down, usually by a literate member of that very society,
possibly by the poet himself, an action that in itself may transform
that composition to a greater or lesser extent. This, at least, was
largely true before the studies of ethnographers; indeed only with
the coming of the recording machines so successfully used by Parry
and of the now standard tape-recorder utilized by every fieldworker, has it been possible to transcribe long oral recitations with any
great exactitude. Earlier the only method was dictation, involving a
much more deliberate delivery than recitation itself, and one that
was necessarily decontextualized. How far the differences between
the earlier (1972, dictated) and the later (1981, taped) versions of

the Bagre are due to the different modes I used when recording is difficult to say, but in the first case the speaker was obviously not reciting in the situation of performance and his delivery was much more carefully considered as he often had to pause while I hastened to write down his words. Historical factors and technological processes are of the utmost importance in the analysis of oral discourse. Until the advent of recording devices we possessed oral material only in written form; it is therefore difficult if not impossible to know how far the 'utterances', the oral compositions, have been transformed into literary 'texts' in the course of being written down.

While it is right to emphasise the 'creative' aspects of much oral performance, which is often a combination of composition and commemoration, of creation and memory, one must also recognize the variability of this activity from performer to performer, from occasion to occasion and from 'genre' to 'genre'. Among the LoDagaa, an individual will sometimes sit down at the xylophone and deliberately compose a short song; at other times, the same individual will sing a song he knows 'by heart', yet the music will often consist of free variations on the common theme in the manner of many jazz musicians. The words and melody of the new song may have been 'deliberately' worked out beforehand. Or they may be 'improvised' in the heat of a funeral or a dance. This distinction is less obvious in longer recitations of the Bagre type, but it is clear that some individuals are more 'creative' – that is, their versions show greater distinctiveness from the rest of the sample. However, in analyzing the recitations of one speaker over time, which we have done in the case of one man, Sielo, the versions of a single individual (or a least this single individual) are closer to each other than to the versions of any other performer, whether performed on the same ceremonial occasion or not. This is what we would expect. Once a speaker has delivered his first recital, which has been 'learnt' in an informal manner, he stores what he has given (or 'improvised') and then tends to reproduce his original version. He does not memorize someone else's recitation (certainly not in a verbatim manner), but he does memorize (after a certain fashion) his own.

Finally there is a further distinction to make that is very relevant

in considering 'epic' and similar poetry. We sometimes speak of
an oral and literary tradition as present in the same society,
identifying the former with popular culture and the latter with 'art'
forms. There are certain marginal situations in which an orally
composed and performed 'literature' could remain quite independent of the written tradition. On the other hand literacy may
profoundly influence the 'oral' product. In an extreme case this
may be orally performed (recited) and orally transmitted (i.e.
memorized, even without using the book) and yet it may have been
composed with the help of writing. Such appears to be the case with
the Ṛgvedas, which I discuss in chapter 4. But take another
example. Egyptian mathematics carried out multiplication and
division by a cumbrous process of doubling and then adding or
subtracting, except for cases in which numbers had to be doubled or
multiplied by ten (James 1979:123). Even so, writing was certainly
necessary for any complicated calculation. We, on the other hand,
are able to carry out quite complicated multipliction tasks 'in the
head' by means of 'oral arithmetic'. In order to do this we have
first to learn 'by heart' a set of tables, usually from a printed copy,
although possibly from the speech of another person. But we
cannot doubt that the arithmetic *tables* were the product of writing,
that they are part of or are influenced by a literate tradition. The
problem raised here is the degree of influence that the presence of
another register, another channel of communication, has on any
specific 'oral' composition, genre or author, when both exist
within the same, or possibly neighbouring, societies. I would argue
that almost no 'oral' form can be unaffected by the presence of
written communication, especially as the latter is so often associated with high status of one kind or another.

With these points in mind, we can look at some aspects of the
recent debate about the composition of the Homeric corpus. I want
to intervene in this venerable discussion among classicists with
Adam Parry's comments (1966) on Kirk's earlier thesis (1962) and
with Kirk's reply in his subsequent book (1976). Two points made
by Lord began this exchange. He maintained (1) that an orally
composed poem cannot be handed on by the tradition of oral song
without fundamental changes taking place – Dow elsewhere comments that: "*Verbatim* oral transmission of a poem composed orally

and not written down is unknown"; and (2) that the oral poet's powers are destroyed if he learns to read and write. Kirk rejects the first point and accepts the second; Adam Parry thinks he has made the wrong choice. Kirk's own argument about the composition of the Homeric poems runs as follows: The *Iliad* was created in the eighth century by the monumental poet Homer, an *aoidos* with a lyre, living in an oral culture. He produced a work that was unique in many ways, in length for one thing, for Kirk rightly observes that oral cultures have provided little evidence of long poems, as well as in other, poetic, qualities. The poem was then transmitted more or less exactly, at first by "reproductive singers" of the type found by M. Parry and Lord in the Yugoslav town of Novi Pazar. Subsequently, during the period 625 to 575 BC, the poem was handed down by "semi-literate" *rhapsodes* (whose badge was the staff rather than the lyre) until finally written down in the sixth century, in the form known as the Peisistratean recension. In this last phase the poem was associated with the Panathenaean festivals of which the recitation became an intrinsic part. It became embodied in a ritual and mainly aristocratic context, whereas it had been largely popular in origin, like the Yugoslav epic, having its roots in the café songs of an antiquity that was giving birth to the city-state, the *polis*.

While accepting the notion of Homer as an 'oral' poet, Kirk is also anxious to emphasize the possibility of the transmission of his work, in substantially the same form, from the post-Mycenaean period which he regards as the proper setting for the Trojan story – the 'heroic age' with 'epic' as its typical art-form. But to be able to identify the present written version of the *Iliad* as the work of the monumental poet of the earlier period, we have to accept the capacity of oral cultures to transmit long poems in a relatively exact manner from generation to generation. It is this assumption that seems open to question.

As we have seen, comparisons of the Homeric works with modern oral poetry are generally based upon the important collection gathered by Parry and Lord in Yugoslavia in the 1930s. Most of these compositions are shorter than the Homeric ones; only one recitation, by Avdo Međedović, attains a comparable length, possibly as a result of the circumstances of the recording. But

irrespective of length, Yugoslav oral poetry provides little support
for the thesis of exact or verbatim repetition, a mode of recitation
that is in apparent contradiction with some of the singers' statements about their intentions. So Kirk places his future hopes on
finding some "remote and inbred region" (1976:122) where we
might come across a singer of local pre-eminence who hands on his
version to his pupils in a form a good deal more exact than the poets
of Novi Pazar, that is, in the same manner that he suggests obtained
in Ancient Greece. In any case, accuracy, he argues, was more
likely in Homeric than in modern times because of three factors:
1 the greater reliance on formulas
2 "the much greater metrical rigidity of the Homeric hexameter"
   (1976:123)
3 the fact that the poems came "at the end of the true oral
   traditions", so that their transmission depended for much of this
   period not on singers but on reciters or rhapsodes (1976:124).
  This argument encourages him to reject the statement made by
Bowra that it is not poems that are transmitted but their substance
and technique; and it enables him to bridge the gap between the
supposed composition of the poems in the eighth century and their
first appearance in written form in sixth-century Athens.
  Although generally shorter than the Homeric works, the epics
recorded by Parry are often of considerable length, especially those
sung by Avdo Međedović; those recorded on discs in 1935 consisted
of the following number of lines (though words would obviously
make a better basis of comparison): 2,436; 6,290; 6,042; 2,624;
13,331; 5,919; 645; 1,302; 6,313. "The Wedding of Smailagić
Meho", a translation of which was published by Lord in 1974, was
dictated and contained a total of 12,323 lines. However, even epics
on the same theme were very variable in length. Lord returned to
visit Avdo in 1950 and recorded another version of the Wedding,
which consisted of only 8,488 lines, being shorter by one-third. A
particular epic would also vary in content over time. We know this
because earlier versions of this epic already existed as texts, notably
that dictated by Šemić and printed in 1886 which formed the basis
of two more popular published versions. In addition another
version, dictated by Malkoč in 1916, existed in manuscript form.
Lord comments that, although the Šemić tradition is somewhere in

the background, the later versions have been influenced by it "only slightly or very generally. Moreover, other story elements, some akin to those in the Malkoč tradition, have joined with the Šemić tradition, or been joined by it" (1974:282). In other words the written texts influenced but did not dominate; composition still took place. In a special chapter of his book, Lord stresses "Avdo's originality" (pp. 13–34), just as Kirk insists upon Homer as "the monumental composer"; and it is an interesting fact that many recorders of oral poetry attribute similar powers to the poet with whom they have worked. Faced with several versions, some will undoubtedly appear more pedestrian than others. But given the accident of 'recording' we do seem to encounter a lot of tellers of tales judged to be outstanding by those with whom they come into contact. Which suggests that originality was not in such short supply as some have suggested. Indeed the oral tradition was characterized by continual creation; it was the written that encouraged repetition, at least of established texts.

In Avdo's case, this originality persisted despite the fact that he was working within a literate culture which certainly affected the content or style of his work. While he claims to be illiterate, he belonged to a world religion, Islam, a religion of the Book, which had its own tradition of chroniclers and chronicling. Although he had not himself been to school, he had been in the army, could recognize characters from the Latin and Cyrillic alphabets and had learnt some of his songs from song books. What is the significance of the latter? The existence of the song book would tend to promote the notion of a fixed text. Moreover it would actually help to fix one in practice. For example, a schoolboy could read to Avdo the same version over and over again until he learnt it 'by heart'; although a singer can repeat his song to himself in a purely oral situation, he is unlikely to do so in exactly the same manner if it is a song of any length, even if he held the idea that precise repetition was a valuable exercise.

Despite these written prompts, Avdo maintained his originality. It is difficult from this evidence to accept the idea of a 'fixed utterance' for long songs of this kind. The weight of testimony would seem to support Bowra rather than Kirk, though the former's argument about the transmission of 'substance' presents its own problems. When Parry made a trial of Avdo's ability to learn a new song in 1935, he arranged for him to be present while another singer, Mumin, performed a song that was unknown to him. When it was over, Avdo sang the song, but his version was nearly three times as long, being embroidered with verbal ornaments, some created, some introduced, reshaped, from other songs.

Transmission between singers is clearly a different matter from repetition by the same singer. At the same time exactness was certainly more difficult to obtain in the informal atmosphere of a café than in the highly structured situation in which, say, the Vedic 'texts' were passed on. In the present case, Avdo does not appear to have committed his version to memory in any precise way, let alone made any attempt to transmit it, at least according to the interesting comment on the dependence of the poet upon his immediate audience. When Lord revisited the singer in 1950, Avdo said he had not sung the song since Parry's visit, "because there was no one with a deep enough interest (*meraklija*) to listen" (1974:298). The long gap in time would obviously have made it more difficult for the singer to repeat his earlier performance; he would have been forced to be 'original'.

The question of 'originality' raises three other aspects of this discussion that require further clarification; first, the relation of verbatim memory to oral cultures, a problem I discuss in greater detail in chapter 8 when I examine the Bagre but which here I consider with the question of the formula; secondly, the nature of 'orality', to which attention has been drawn in the general remarks; and, thirdly, the relation between the epic (and other long 'standard oral forms'), oral society and the Heroic age, a subject central to the Chadwicks' comments on the Homeric corpus which have been a continuing point of reference in attempts to specify the connection between the presence of such poetry and the wider society in which it was found.

Memory and verbatim memory

On the question of verbatim accuracy, the argument of Adam Parry seems to carry more conviction than that of Kirk. There is little evidence either for verbatim transmission or even for verbatim repetition of long oral utterances, as distinct from short poems, though the two processes are not always distinguished in discussion. Let us take the more difficult case of repetition. Finnegan quotes the example of the Bamba Suso's two versions of the Sunjata epic of West Africa. She concludes: "The most striking point to emerge from a comparison of the two is their close similarity, in places amounting to word-for-word repetition" (1977:76, discussing Innes 1973). But looked at from another standpoint, what is surprising is the fact that the words are clearly not learned by heart; an individual does not simply reproduce verbatim his own performance. When we examined the different versions of the White Bagre recited by Sielo in 1975, the remarks of my collaborator, K. Gandah, were very revealing in this respect; he was surprised at Sielo's inconsistency, whereas I was struck by the similarity. In any case, we were a long way from verbatim reproduction.

Here we were dealing with the question of consistency between the versions of a single singer recited in the same ritual context within a short space of time. Adam Parry has pointed out that, despite Kirk's dismissal of the percent changes in the two versions of Zogić's "Alija Rescues Alibey's Children", these would add up to a 4.4 per cent change over seventeen years. In the case of transmission between different singers, these changes would be cumulative at a much higher rate. The question of innovation cannot be set aside.

One problem is that both for the 'oral singers' and for their commentators, the notion of sameness or identity is a subjective matter, quite different from that facing an editor of two written versions of a text which he can compare side by side. However oral singers are often pushed towards variation, by their own ingenuity, by their particular audiences or by the wider social situation. In this aspect there are interesting differences in accounts of the Silâmaka wars from the neighbouring Bambara and Fulani peoples of West Africa, as one sees by comparing Silâmaka and Poullôri (C. Seydou 1972) for the Fulani side, and *La Prise de Dionkoloni* (eds. Dumestre and Kesteloot, 1975) for the Bambara. Here wandering minstrels or *griots*, belonging to the same patronymic group, had to 'change their tune' as they moved from camp to camp; in the same way a Trojan version of the *Iliad* would be a very different one from the Greek.

The question of whether or not the speakers think of themselves as reproducing or producing the Bagre, i.e. reciting the same or different versions, appears to be a simple problem but is in fact complex. In making a distinction between reproductive and creative (my 'productive') bards, Kirk argues that Parry's recordings with the singers of Novi Pazar showed that they aimed at '*verbatim* precision' (1976:276), even though Lord and Parry insisted that songs were composed by the singers. For example, Derro Zogić asserted that he sung "the same song, word for word, and line for line. I didn't add a single line, and I didn't make a single mistake ..." But in answer to a further question, he admits that "two singers won't sing the same song alike ... They add, or they make mistakes, and they forget" (Lord 1960:27). Commenting on this passage Adam Parry notes how far the bard is "from any understanding of verbal accuracy in our sense", and "is psychologically incapable of grasping the abstract concepts" (1966:188).

It is not a failure of understanding nor a lack of psychological capacity that is at stake; without a written text it is difficult for anyone to know whether two versions of a long recitation are the 'same' or not. Even the deliberate intention of the author to produce an identical version of a song is thwarted by the impossibility of juxtaposition, of visual checking – only sequential comparison, often with long time intervals, is possible. Then there are the limitations of 'normal' memory, the recall of the heard recitation. While recall can obviously be improved by rehearsal, that requires particular techniques, a teacher (as distinct from the Speaker in the performance) and a non-ceremonial context, the need for which may not be apparent if the absence of identity is not realized or not required. For in this situation the concept of sameness may be much looser; it may refer not to verbal identity but to some kind of unspecified structural similarity, for example the fact that all the versions of the White Bagre present an account of the ceremonies. Ceremonies, seasonal events, spatial positions, and especially narrative can provide a continuing framework which is sometimes the core of the recitation, sometimes no more than a peg on which to hang a different sort of discourse.

In working on the Bagre we have also encountered sets of statements about intentions that appear to contradict one another, as was the case with Derro Zogić. The oneness of the Bagre, whether we are referring to recitations or to ritual, is often insisted upon in answer to a direct question. But what is oneness (*a in boyen*) here, except an assertion of the absence of duality? The Bagre is a ceremony as well as a recitation, and every performance is Bagre. The conditions of recital are such that not only are differences inevitable but, as in Yugoslavia, a good version is considered to be an elaborated one, that is, one in which the Speaker elaborates certain incidents. In the White Bagre, it is often the account of the ceremony that is developed. Since the ritual schedule presses heavily on the organizers, and participants and the senior members have their own ideas of how long a recitation should continue, limits are placed upon such elaboration, and the consequence may well be the curtailment, even the elimination of other incidents.

The Black Bagre does not have the ceremonial framework of the White. Here one major theme is "the coming of culture", which constitutes a necessary part of any myth of origins, of dawn beings, of the Creation; it is the Genesis theme of "In the beginning". In this case the greater variation both in presentation and in the elements chosen to be included in the recitation seems to arise out of this process of elaboration, which is at the same time inevitably a process of exclusion, elimination and forgetting. For in this part there is no framework of ceremonies to provide a way of recalling something that has been, or might be, included. As a consequence change is more radical, differences more extensive. As the singer of Novi Pazar remarked: "They add, or make mistakes, and they forget" (Lord 1960:27).

On a more microscopic level the question of variants bears on that enduring problem of the formula as a characteristic of oral poetry. Milman Parry defined a formula as "a group of words which is regularly employed under the same metrical conditions to express a given essential idea" (1930:80). In an ingenious article entitled "Towards a generative view of the oral formula", Nagler has attempted to focus "on the real nature of the formula as a mental template in the mind of the oral poet, rather than on statistical aspects of 'repetition' found among phrases in the text" (1967:269). Taking up some aspects of the ideas of what Rosenmeyer calls the "soft Parryists" (1965:297), who consist of Hainsworth, Russo (with his notion of "the structural formula") and others, he attempts to offer a more flexible and extensive definition that the one provided by Parry.

How can we treat resemblances other than exact, *verbatim* repetition, and hence examine the problem of the creative ('original') use of 'traditional' materials? For Nagler the question is how can Homer be so creative and at the same time so clearly an oral poet in his use of formulas, for "it is obvious on statistical grounds alone that Homeric poetry was fundamentally oral poetry" (1967:274). We do not have to accept the assumption behind the remark nor agree with the conclusion in order to recognize that the problem is a real one, similar to that posed by the variant 'versions' of the Bagre (chapter 8).

Nagler in fact avoids the term formula and thinks of the recurrent phrases as constituting an open-ended family (rather than a closed system or class), each phrase in the group being "an allomorph, *not of any other existing phrase*, but of some central Gestalt which . . . is the real mental template underlying the production of all such phrases" (p. 281) The idea, he claims, derives from Wittgenstein's linguistic philosophy ("family resemblances"), Chomsky's linguistics ("deep structure") and particularly from structuralist studies of myth and folklore which have analyzed "the fluidity of the living mythopoeic process as repeated fresh realizations of a basic structural idea along similar but ever-varying lines, rather than as repeated presentations of finished products which are copies of earlier finished products accidentally or otherwise altered by their successive inheritors" (1967:283). This simple notion hardly requires such an authoritative genealogy to give it legitimacy. Moreover, while the structural model of a myth or folktale can theoretically be deduced from "a given array of allomorphs by simply eliminating as ornament those features which are not invariably present in each allomorph, and then deducing the basic similarities underlying the variations of what remains", no clearly discernable pattern emerges in dealing with phrases, which others have also claimed for folklore. So Nagler adopts a very flexible concept of the deep structure of these phrases, which is "not yet differentiated enough to be verbally definable" (p. 289); in other words, we cannot specify the deep structure that generates the 'formulas', nor can we set boundaries to the possible transformations at the surface level.

It may be possible to analyze the verbal formulas in this way, though it is doubtful whether this process necessarily requires the idea of a permanent core, nucleus or focus at a deep structural level. Indeed the idea of the transformation of unchanging, unspecified, entities raises profound theoretical problems, including the danger of falling into the fallacy of 'misplaced concreteness'. At the macrostructural level of the recitation the process has even greater dangers. To sketch out an outline of the White Bagre is not problematical; at one level the structure can be seen as the order of ceremonies. That sequence is performative, in that it transfers *dakyume* into *bag*; that is, the non-member passes through the status of neophyte (*bagbil*, 'little Bagre') and becomes an initiate. However the Black Bagre presents quite another problem since the result of such a summarizing process would be, in my view, to divest the recitation of the most important aspects of meaning. The benefits would be few; the general claim that the decomposition into elements leads to some inclusive understanding by establishing homologies through the parallel process of stripping down other social institutions has yet to be established, certainly as a general procedure for socio–cultural analysis.

Oral composition and oral transmission

Some Homeric scholars regard the question of literacy as a matter of binary distinction; a poem is either written or it is not. Others have argued the case for a transitional status. This discussion requires a clarification of what we mean by an oral poem and by an oral composition. Because Milton, like Homer, was blind when he composed *Paradise Lost*, Kirk comments that he used a "semi-oral mode of composition" (1976:98), which is evident in his 'cumulative' style. He also refers to the question of the oral transmission of the Sanskritic Ṛgveda (p. 118), as well as the mixed

oral and literary origin of the Epic of Gilgamesh. He had earlier
treated this Mesopotamian epic, which was composed in Akkadian, using Sumerian components, in the second millennium BC
(p. 93), as a true 'myth' but its status is now questioned. There is
clearly an element – variable of course – of oral composition in all
written works, if one includes the silent speech events that precede
or accompany much reflective creation. The line is never easy to
draw if we are talking about societies in which writing is a common
means of communication.

While the question of the mode of composition is important, it is
not the only way in which writing influences the poem or other
literary product. Obviously Milton used verse forms and styles that
were developed through writing; the theme itself was based on a
written text of another age; *Paradise Lost* is the creation of high
literate culture, the product of a developing tradition. "Oral
composition" in such a context is quite a different process from
composition in a purely oral culture.

Some of the same considerations apply to *Gilgamesh*, for there
seems little doubt that the form of the written epic that has come
down to us is the result of aggregating (and so transforming) earlier
products, possibly of an oral tradition. But we need to appreciate a
further point if we are to understand the position of this epic in
relation to literacy. For even before the version we know was
brought together in writing, the constituent parts existed not simply
as "oral poems" but as part of a culture in which writing had played
an increasingly important part since the fourth millennium. For
Mesopotamia had not experienced a truly oral culture, a purely oral
tradition, since that time. It is true that writing appears to have
been relatively little used for 'literary' activity in the usual sense.
However its poetry was subject to influences both in form and in
content, in composition and in reproduction (memorization), that
emanated from the other changes that writing had wrought, promoted or accompanied.

Most examples of the epic or the prose saga that have been
looked at in the context of the Homeric discussions also come from
societies where writing existed in some form or other. At one level,
the point is obvious, for how otherwise would we have any record
of them? Anglo-Saxon England, Norse culture, the Germanic

society that produced the *Niebelungenlied* – we could run through the list mentioned by Chadwick – all had writing. The original poems or sagas may have been oral. But the text we possess was written down by insiders, i.e. either by dictation to a countryman or by the singer himself, if he was able to put pen to paper. And the text itself may have been influenced by the advent of writing in stronger ways than simply being subjected to the process of transcription, although that itself is capable of effecting a radical transformation.

Just as the epic has been found in societies with writing, so have many other so-called 'oral' products. It is only recently, in general, that outsiders (as distinct from insiders) came and recorded oral forms, as Parry and Lord did in Yugoslavia. But these could, indeed were, set down by insiders, for Yugoslavia, like the Heroic societies, was far from being an oral culture, that is, one without writing. Indeed the very emphasis placed upon these performances by the singers of tales may have arisen partly from the fact that writing was largely confined to the Arabic, Greek or Church Slavic languages, being little used for the local tongue; the singing of epics was a 'low' vernacular activity contrasting with the 'high' activities of church and state. Politics and religion were the subject of dominant literate influences, leaving 'popular' culture in the quasi-oral sphere of activity until it caught the attention of nineteenth-century nationalists.[2]

In this context let me return to the problem of dictation. Because of his idea that the bard could not write, Lord suggested 'dictation' as the only way the *Iliad* could have been put down on paper. The suggestion is founded on the assumption made by Lord and Parry that these poems were oral compositions, an assumption resting largely on the presence of formulas and similar features that were seen as the product of the improvising style of the bard, the *aoidos*. When we look at poetry in oral cultures, we find some grounds for modifying this view but the point I want to make here has to do with the process of dictation itself. Before the 1960s virtually all the oral literature from simple societies was dictated, since recording machines required the use of mains electricity or heavy batteries. With the appearance of the transistorized tape-recorder, these problems vanished within a few years; dictation gave way to transcription.

What were the consequences of the earlier restriction? Although the invention of recording machines goes back to the previous century, before the 1960s most oral communication, whether it took the form of discourse or of standardized oral forms such as poetry, could be recorded only by the laborious process of dictation. Thus very little could be set down in the natural context, during a ceremony itself. An observer would make a few notes at the time but in order to get a 'text' he had to entice an 'informant' to withdraw from the scene of activity and 'repeat' the words or the music, that is, to dictate or rehearse the utterance. Needless to say, the matter was yet more problematic with music and with dance before the advent of the tape recorder and the camera, since the notation used for setting down these standardized communicative acts was non-linguistic, less well known and hence more difficult to employ.

In other words, the context in which earlier recitations were recorded was inevitably different. In the first place the recorded version had been redirected in various ways towards the interest of the writer; he it was who became the new audience, rather than the congregation, the chief's court or the domestic group. The ways in which this new context affected what we have presented to us as 'oral' productions are many. For example, a young lad is called to the terrace of some missionaries in the South American jungle and asked for a 'story'. His understanding of what his interrogator wants may lead him to extract the narrative element from a more complex work as the one most likely to amuse his audience, the one they may find easier to understand, the one he finds easiest to recall in the new context. Narrative has its own internal 'logic' which is not always present in other forms of discourse. Consequently the whole content and form may be radically transformed and what we are left with as 'the myth of the X' may turn out to be a much impoverished version of the 'real' thing. At the same time we get to know little about the context of recitation, as in the case of Gê material from Brazil (Wilbert 1978).

On the other hand, the process of dictation may work in another direction. I have analyzed some eight recordings (more now) of the White Bagre. The first was dictated to me by Benima in 1950, necessarily outside the formal ritual situation in which it should have been recited. The other seven versions were recorded by tape-recorder either in the course of the ceremonies or at a special recital. What are the differences between the dictated and the transcribed versions?

With only one dictated version, comparison has its obvious dangers. But there are some broad points that can be made. Benima's version is substantially longer than the others, and it is also both more elaborate and more deliberate. Nevertheless he makes a mistake in the order of the ceremonies around which the White Bagre is constructed. This error presumably arose because he did not have the rituals, as it were, in front of him, in play; for the mnemonic framework is not provided by narrative but by the sequence of ceremonies. However we also find similar errors in the transcribed versions since the Speakers are looking back at the ceremonies that have been performed up to that session.

Benima's recitation was not only longer, it was 'tighter'. Let me explain what I mean here. In virtually all the other versions, the commonest phrase (one cannot call it formula) was *fu nye* – 'you see?' or *fu nyaa*, 'don't you see?'. Benima had less need of such devices since he paused after every two or three lines to allow me to catch up with writing. In the second place, the Speaker in the ceremony is addressing, almost instructing, the new initiates. Hence the phrase "do you see?" (or, "you see" – it is difficult to tell the inflection in a dictated version) has a specific purpose, drawing the attention of the neophytes to a particular point. To address me in the same fashion would have been to disregard the context of our communication

I claimed that Benima's version was more elaborate. The complexity is much clearer in the case of the second part, the Black Bagre, which always has a greater narrative and 'philosophical' element than the first, the White Bagre, where the ceremony provides the framework. Benima was certainly a verbal and imaginative character, and some of his ability comes through in his choice of words (that is, in the use of unique words, related to number of lines.) Partly because of the nature of the measure I used, he does not tower above the others. It would be difficult to make any adequate comparisons of the various Speakers based on their handling of words in ordinary discourse, although I have known all of them over many years. Benima did seem to have a greater agility with words in other contexts. But the situation itself, that of dictation, gave him the opportunity to elaborate what might otherwise have been left unsaid. Or rather, let me say, 'uncreated', because for reasons I will give later I need to avoid the supposition (critical for many analytic approaches) that in considering each of these versions we are dealing with 'the same myth', which in some unspecified form exists at a deep structural level; once again analysis is not advanced by positing such hypothetical entities, which assume an underlying unity, whereas that implied by the actor's use of the term Bagre seems rather to be a surface identification. But first I conclude this section by remarking that my own material appears to show that even when the context is closely controlled, a dictated version can differ considerably from one that is recorded electronically. This is important to remember when virtually all earlier oral material was dictated while contemporary versions are transcribed.

Heroic societies and the epic

The third problem concerns the relation between forms of society and 'literary' forms, in particular, the relation between the Heroic Age and the presence of the epic, a tale telling of the great deeds of a warrior society. The concept of the Heroic Age was elaborated by H. M. Chadwick in a series of books of remarkable range and depth that included a three-volume work attempting to analyze the epic and other forms of literature throughout the world, entitled *The Growth of Literature* (with N. K. Chadwick, 1932–40). Here the Chadwicks discuss the literary correlates of the Heroic Age, a concept which had been formulated twenty years before (H. M. Chadwick 1912). The reference in the title of that earlier work was of course to the age Hesiod interpolated between that of Bronze and that of Iron, when the world was inhabited by "a godlike race of Hero men" who, it is claimed, formed the subject of the oldest literature (1932–40: i, 13). The characteristic form of heroic poetry was the epic, that is, a narrative of adventure, designed for entertainment and dealing with the activities of the Heroic Age itself. The Chadwicks went on to compare the Homeric poems, which they took to be the archetypes of the epic, with the earliest known poetry in Britain, Germany, Norway and Ireland.

In evaluating this central notion of the Chadwicks, which has influenced much subsequent scholarship, I want to consider briefly the general relationship of 'literature' to society in Africa. To begin with, were these societies Heroic in any sense? Certainly there were complex state organizations. In West Africa, Asante, Dahomey, the Mossi kingdoms, all had warlike rulers of the kind found in the Middle Eastern and Central Asian societies where the epic is found. Their rulers were warriors, or descended from warriors, some of them horsemen. From this standpoint they were certainly Heroic. They differed substantially from the states of Eurasia. As I have argued in another context, neither feudalism nor the "Asiatic mode of production" were to be found in Africa, if only because the means of production were less developed than in Europe and Asia (Goody 1971a). The critical events that led to the intensive cultivation of food crops, to the use of the plough and to the production of a large transportable and transformable surplus did not occur in Africa, despite the presence of centralized, warlike and often complex societies. As a result, the economic base and the system of stratification were substantially different. And it is important to note that, together with these economic disadvantages, went the absence of writing, for although the invention of logographic scripts occurred during the Bronze Age of the Near East, they never spread south of the Sahara. Only at a much later date did alphabetic writing spread with Islam, Judaism and Christianity. It was an age that Africa effectively missed out, going more or less straight from the use of stone to the use of iron. So in this matter of communication, too, African states were different from the model of Heroic societies, whose literature we know largely from their own writings.

In discussing written and oral 'literature', Chadwick distinguishes three conditions:

1 where writing is unknown, e.g. in Polynesia and Africa
2 where writing was used for restricted purposes but not for literature, e.g. among the Tuareg, the Teutonic peoples at the time of the Runic script, in Ireland in the time of Ogham, and probably among early Gauls, Italians and Greeks

3 where written literature is current. Here, he argues, the written
tends to replace the oral, except where writing is restricted by
class or by its use of a non-current language. This latter situation
existed in Orthodox Slavonic countries, in Abyssinia and in
India, where an otherwise obsolete language (or form of a
language) was used for religious purposes. It was the same with
Latin in Europe, and with Arabic in many parts of Africa and
Asia today (though here the language was foreign rather than
obsolete). "A vernacular oral literature may flourish by the side
of these, as in Yugoslavia, where Ecclesiastical Slavonic, Latin
and Arabic have been known as literary languages for centuries"
(Chadwick, H. M. and N. K. 1932–40:iii, 698). When writing
used the vernacular, then oral literature tended to decline, as was
the case in nineteenth-century Russia.

It is in those early literate societies, which had been influenced by
the profound changes of the Bronze Age, that Chadwick locates his
Heroic Age. It is here that he finds the epic, not in truly oral
societies, those without writing, but in ones that had been influenced in some measure by the advent of literacy and of 'civilization'. Is not this where Homer belongs? Not in a truly oral
culture, even though the poem we know may possibly have been
based upon an earlier product, originating in the gap in access to
writing that most scholars consider to have existed between the end
of Minoan B in the twelfth century BC and the appearance of the
alphabet in the eighth century. In any case, composed in a region
which saw the emergence of great libraries and archives such as
those of Boğazköy, Ebla, Ugarit, composed by the compatriots of
the Greek merchants who had established their quarters in the
trading ports of Phoenicia with their long-standing written traditions, and composed *about* an area of Anatolia, Ionia, that lay near
to the lands of the Hittites, it can hardly be considered as a typical
product of cultures without writing. Discussion of the oral character of the Homeric poems has concentrated upon the analysis of
the formulas, but we need also to look at other features, at lists, at
metrical forms, at narrative structure, that seem to have more in
common with the literate culture that was coming into being than
with purely oral forms of communication.

I have already mentioned Nagler's view, which is also held by

M. Parry and Lord implicitly, if not explicitly, that the more formulas, the closer to the oral. In this connection Adam Parry observes "The Homeric line is evidently more formulary than the Yugoslav" (1966:202). But it is also more "formulary" I would maintain, than that of the Bagre, an unambiguously oral poem. The domination or *tyrannie de la formule* may resemble the tyranny of rhyme in later poetry, or of alliteration in early English verse. Might it be suggested that all these three, in their elaborated forms, were written developments of features found in oral works but not in the extent and consistency with which they are later used. The suggestion receives some support from Kirk's observation that the 'oral' tradition of the Greeks, was "more highly organized" than any modern equivalent – he had the Yugoslav material in mind. And in Hainsworth's discussion of the poems, which generally follows a Parryist line, he is forced to conclude that "the greater architecture of the poems appears to be unlike typical oral poetry" (1970:98). Like Kirk, he regards Homer as "a very special case". It might however be possible to explain all these features in terms of the early influence of writing in formalizing and elaborating poetic utterance, making the particular case of Greece perhaps less unique, and at the same time more understandable.

Another feature that is characteristic of early literacy is the making of lists, of catalogues. I do not mean that lists are not found in oral poetry. In the Bagre itself we run round neighbouring settlements (though in a 'contextual', journey-like, 'clockwise' fashion), greeting them in order, just as we run through the ceremonies. But lists of a largely decontextualized kind are a dominant feature of much earlier writing. Hesiod's *Theogony*, presumably a written poem, was roughly contemporary with the Homeric poems but composed in Boetia on the Greek mainland. It has been described by Adam Parry as "the great catalogue poem of all time" (1966:208), although the catalogues are largely of gods. Homer contains less, though there are the lists of Trojan rivers and of ships.[3]

A further pointer to the nature of this composition, which it is very difficult to study in an intensive way without the aid of writing, is that "minor slips are very infrequent in Homer" (Hainsworth 1970:92); equally significant are "the perfect recall of a repeated passage, the copious catalogues, the unbroken linear narrative, the maintenance of . . . the 'epic illusion' ". The firmness of the metrical as well as the narrative line seem to set the poem apart from the looser constructions of the oral poet. That is why, like Adam Parry, I would see "in the use of writing both the means and the occasion for the composition, in the improvising style, of poems which must have transcended their own tradition in profundity as well as length", although I would be less happy with the claim that "that tradition itself surpassed all subsequent traditions of heroic song" (1966:216). It is writing, he claims, that enables the poet "to compose a long but coherent work without immediate dependence on the vagaries of his audience" (p. 215).[4] I would go further and suggest that writing effectively led to a new 'tradition', involving a new mode of transmission and possibly of creation, modifying and developing both form and content.

The argument can be supported by looking at cultures where writing is totally absent. The main areas of the world where such a situation existed in recent times were parts of Africa and South America (together with Australasia and the Pacific). Much of South America was transformed by the Spanish and Portuguese in the sixteenth century, though a few remoter areas escaped their overwhelming influence. Africa offers the most straightforward case, even though influenced by the written civilizations of Europe on the West, of the Mediterranean on the North and of the Arabs on the East. It is also a continent whose oral literature has been systematically examined. The main work of synthesis has been carried out by Ruth Finnegan. On one point about the epic she is very definite: "Epic is often assumed to be the typical poetic form of non-literate peoples ... Surprisingly, however, this does not seem to be borne out by the African evidence. At least in the more obvious sense of a 'relatively long narrative poem', epic hardly seems to occur in sub-Saharan Africa apart from forms like the [written] Swahili *utenzi* which are directly attributable to Arabic literary influence" (1970:108). What is called epic in Africa is often prose rather than poetry, though some of the lengthy praise poems of South Africa have something of an epic quality about them. Most frequently mentioned are the Mongo–Nkundo tales from the Congo; these too are mainly prose and resemble other African tales in their general features. The most famous is the Lianja epic running to 120 pages of print for text and translation. It covers the birth and tribulations of the hero, his travels, the leadership of his people, and finally his death. Finnegan suggests that the original form might have been "a very loosely related bundle of separate episodes, told on separate occasions and not necessarily thought of as one single work of art (though recent and sophisticated narrators say that ideally it should be told at one sitting)" (p. 109). In other words a similar type of amalgamation may have taken place as apparently occurred with the Gilgamesh epic.

We do find some poetry of a legendary kind in the *mvet* literature of the Fang peoples of Gabon and the Cameroons, as well as in the recitations of the *griot* among the Mande peoples south of the Sahara. She concludes: "In general terms and apart from Islamic influences, epic seems to be of remarkably little significance in African oral literature, and the *a priori* assumption that epic is the natural form for many non-literate peoples turns out here to have little support" (p. 110).

Since Finnegan's earlier book, the picture with regard to longer compositions has somewhat changed, both in respect of 'mythical' and of 'legendary' (including epic) material. As far as longer 'myths' are concerned, we now have two published versions of the Bagre of the LoDagaa (Goody 1972, Goody and Gandah 1981), the first consisting of some 12,000 short lines in length, and taking some eight hours to recite. This is a work concerned with the creation of the world, with the position of man in relation to his God and his gods, with problems of philosophy and of life.

It contrasts sharply with the recitations of the *griots* of Bambara and Mali. The *griots* (the word is in general use) are a type of minstrel belonging to an endogamous caste-like group. They mainly perform at the courts of chiefs but also on other secular, public occasions, for the societies in which they are found have state systems, unlike the acephalous LoDagaa where praise singing is little developed and legends are no more than migration histories of the clan or lineage (Goody 1977a).

Listen to the account of his profession given by the *griot* Tinguidji, who was recorded by Seydou.

Nous, le mâbos, nous ne quémandons qu'auprès des nobles: là où il y a un noble, j'y suis aussi. Un mâbo ne se préoccupe pas de ce qui n'a pas de valeur: s'il voit un pauvre et qu'il quémande auprès de lui, s'il le voit dénué de tout et qu'il le loue, s'il en voit un qui en a l'air et qu'il le loue, un mâbo qui agit de la sorte, ne vaut rien. Moi, celui qui ne m'est pas superieur, je ne le loue pas. Celui qui n'est pas plus que moi, je ne le loue pas; je lui donne. Voilà comment je suis, moi, Tinguidji. (Seydou 1972:13–4)

It would be wrong to assume that all the activities of the *griots* were directed towards pleasing or praising the aristocracy in return for favours. There were those who adopted an aggressive attitude, "griots vulgaires et sans scrupules dont le seul dessein est d'extorquer cadeaux et faveurs et qui, pour cela, manient avec autant de desinvolture et d'audace la louange et l'insulte le panégyrique dithyrambique et la diatribe vindicative, la langue noble et l'argot le plus grossier" (p. 15). But among the "gens castés", the *nyee-nybe*, which included smiths, wood-carvers, leather-workers, weavers (who are also singers, the *mâbo*), there were minstrels, "artisans du verbe et de l'art musical", who include

1 the *intellectuels-griots* who have studied the Qu'ran
2 the *awlube* or drummers, who are attached to a particular family whose history, genealogy and praises they sing (i.e. drummers)
3 the *jeeli* of Mandingo origin, who play many instruments, are unattached and make their living by their profession, and
4 *nyemakala*, wandering singers and guitarists who organize evening entertainments (pp. 17–20).

The *griot*-intellectuals were those who had studied the Qu'ran, giving support to Finnegan's point about Islamic influences. Certainly the bulk of these epics are found on the fringes of the Sahara where such influences are strong and of long duration. The Fulani epic of Silâmaka and Poullôri recounts the story of a chief's son and his slave plus companion, who attempt to relieve their country of its debt of tribute. It is an epic of chiefship recited within a society that was linked to the written tradition of Islam; A.-H. Bâ has described the society of that time as village-based, with each village headed by a man who was literate in Arabic (Seydou 1972:81) but in any case the language and its writings were known in the towns of the region, influencing the nature of local historiography (Hiskett 1957; Wilks 1963; Hodgkin 1966).

Note that the content of this epic was "fixed" in certain broad narrative features but varied enormously in its telling. Seydou describes how the legend crossed frontiers, was spread by the mouths of *griots* who, "chacun à sa guise et selon son art propre, l'ont enrichi, transformé, remanié à partir d'élements divers empruntés à d'autres récits". So that the epic ended up as "une véritable geste dont il serait fort instructif de reconstituer le cycle complet, tant dans la littérature bambare que dans la peuple", that is, in Fulani (1972:9–10). As a result we find a great number and variety of versions (e.g. Vieillard 1931; Bâ and Kesteloot 1969), which develop one particular episode and exalt this or that hero, because it is recited for both the contending parties in the struggle, the Fulani and the Bambara. Each time the *griots* are playing to a specific but varying audience. They live by the responses of that audience; they travel, play the lute, and change their song to fit the community in which they are working. In other words, while the Fulani epic, like the epic in general, seems to occur in a society influenced by writing, the form it takes varies considerably depending upon the bard, the time, the situation. Such variants should not to my mind be regarded as part of a definitive cycle, for that exists only when inventiveness has stopped and the epic has been circumscribed in text, but rather as part of an expanding universe around a narrative theme.

In making a contrast to the work of the minstrel, who is concerned with the legendary, with the epic, I turn to the Bagre of the LoDagaa in which the narrative element is small and variability considerable even over the short term, at least in the section of the recitation that does not constitute the equivalent of a "ritual text". One of the consequences of an initial point of departure from written genres (from 'literature') in which the processes of composition and reproduction are rather similar, is that we tend to ignore the diversity of contexts in which oral compositions are produced and the variety of the forms they take. The diversity exists even if we confine ourselves to considering the longer forms on which we are concentrating. The Bagre is recited in a formal, ceremonial situation, during the course of a long series of initiatory rites. The form is rhythmic recitativo, unaccompanied in a musical sense except by the terminal beat of a stick. Each phrase is repeated by the audience and the whole recitation is performed three times on every occasion. The Speakers are senior men, one of whom generally recites the whole poem (Black or White), though a change of Speaker is possible. Younger men are sometimes brought in towards the end, and by this means they pick up the style of delivery and composition, though in fact such changes were only common in the session that was specially arranged for us to record. The general content is learnt by listening but it is not learnt verbatim. Indeed a premium is placed upon elaboration, and elaboration inevitably involves some contraction unless the recitation is to proliferate continuously. The result is continual change, as in the case of the Yugoslav singers of Novi Pazar (Lord 1960; Kirk 1976).

Let us summarize the conclusions on the relationship between society and this form of recitation in West Africa.

(1) We find some long poems, such as the Bagre of the LoDagaa of Ghana (Goody 1972, Goody and Gandah 1981). If I describe this as myth rather than epic, I simply mean that its content is "sacred"; it is not performed by wandering minstrels, praise-singers or entertainers, but is recited in a ceremonial context, during the entry rites to an 'association'. Other examples are the Ozidi 'saga' of the Ibo and the *mvet* of the Fang. We have other long poems associated with initiations, such as those of the Fulani presented by A. H. Bâ, namely *Koumen* (with G. Dieterlen 1961), *Kaïdara* (with L. Kesteloot 1969) and *L'Éclat de la grande étoile, suivi du Bain rituel*, A. H. Bâ *et al.* (1974), but these probably constitute an intermediary category.

(2) We find types of epic, that is, legendary stories, sung by the *griots* of the Mali, Bambara and Fulani areas, about Sunjata (a thirteenth-century Mandingo King) and Silâmaka (a nineteenth-century Fulani ruler). The Soninke legend of the Kusa falls in the same category.

The first type, epitomized here by the Bagre, seems to have a loose link with acephalous societies (which were also the purely oral ones), since they are part of the ceremonial performance of associations that are more commonly found in the absence of central government, though 'secret societies' of a different complexion sometimes arise in opposition to the state. Under the impact of centralized government, oral forms tend to become more specialized, even in the absence of writing; or to put it another way, the 'holistic universe' of the 'savage mind' is partially fragmented under the pressures of differentiation and inequality. It would be easy to exaggerate the point. I have elsewhere argued that in Africa behavioural differences between estates, strata, do not lead to the development of distinct sub-cultures, for marriages take place extensively between groups (Goody 1970, 1971a, 1982). That remains the case. But clearly there is differentiation and one form it takes is in standardized oral forms. Among the Gonja it is not so much that each group has its own genres of music, poetry, legend, for the audience is largely (but not always) the community as a whole and the performers, as so often, are of lower status than the recipients, that is, the section of the audience to whom the performance is specifically directed, usually a senior chief and his entourage.

The second type of recitation is found mainly in centralized societies influenced by a written religion, that of Islam, which had its own chroniclers and its own extensive literature. Here, as in Eurasia, the epic seems to be characteristic not so much of purely oral cultures, whether they have warrior rulers or not (though the former certainly celebrate their deeds and genealogies in standardized ways), but of those more complex situations in West Africa where writing was employed in restricted ways and yet had some influence both on the content and the form of such compositions.

With this point in mind, let us return to early Greece. The stress we gave in earlier publications to the contribution of widespread literacy to the Greek achievement has been interpreted as a Great Divide theory (Finnegan 1973) separating cultures with and without writing. On the contrary, we were attempting to avoid the binary divisions current in much scholarship and in all folk perceptions and to use changes in the methods and content of communication to try and explain in a more satisfactory way some of the differences that the divisive divisions implied by books on 'Oral Poetry', 'Primitive Classification' or the 'Savage Mind' tend to assume. In the first place, even in terms of the stress on changes in the means of communication, these shifts are multiple

rather than single in kind. It is not a question of a simple division
between oral and literate; the introduction of logographic scripts
had different implications for human intercourse than the introduction of the alphabet. But secondly, factors other than immediately 'technological' ones are critical in defining the mode (as
distinct from the means) of communication; it is these factors
(religious, political, economic and so forth) that restrict or enlarge
the potentiality of different channels or registers. Thirdly, writing
provides a new way of accumulating as well as presenting communicative acts, one that inevitably changes the character of the cultural
tradition over time; the cumulative historical factor becomes of
major importance in the cultural repertoire. Fourthly, and this is
the important point for our present purpose, the division between
'literacy' and 'orality' is never a question of crossing a single
frontier, a simple binary shift. If it were only a matter of the way
poetry is presented, in writing or in recitation, there would perhaps
be some reason to entertain a sharp division of this kind, though as I
have insisted even the composition of literary (written) verse
obviously involves oral (or sub-oral) processes. But there is more to
the point than this. The very existence of writing leads to the
creation of verse forms which would be as inconceivable in a purely
oral culture as, say, the kind of mathematical table that decorates
the back cover of an exercise book, a copy book. Yet once learnt,
such a table or such a verse form (the hexameter, perhaps) may
appear as a part of the 'oral tradition', or at least of oral
manipulation, in a literate culture; people may internalize the
stanza formation of a sonnet just as they do the table. The one
becomes a tool of 'oral arithmetic' just as the other sets the frame
of an 'oral composition'.

No one, I think, would take the sonnet form to be typical of or
even conceivable in a purely oral situation. But there are other
aspects of oral discourse that may be influenced, even transformed
by writing, and that are less easy to specify. The strong statement of
the dramatic unities by Aristotle in the *Poetics* could be regarded as
essentially a literate formalization of the more fluid structure of oral
practice, imposed by the nature of the theatrical production as
well as by the written page, but one that can as it were be 'read back'
into the processes of oral composition to produce a more formal

oneness by considering in a more explicit fashion the widespread demand for a beginning, a middle and an end. Explicitness is at the same time formalization; set in writing, a tendency becomes a 'rule' (unqualified because 'decontextualized', generalized). Once again feedback effects on composition in the oral register are possible. Indeed such effects may manifest themselves not only in the oral products of the culture in which this literate channel is found, but even in the compositions of neighbouring societies where it is not.[5]

To whatever period in the first or second millennium we allocate the creation of Homeric verse, we cannot regard the Greece of that time as being an archetypal oral culture. Even the so-called Dark Ages had knowledge of a past displaying the restricted literacy of the Mycenaean period (and hence a culture marked however minimally by this fact) while the immediate future was to see a sudden flowering of a literacy of the most advanced kind. In addition we have to consider the influences even on oral culture of the extensive literate activities that marked the neighbouring societies of the Near East, societies with which the Greeks were in frequent and continuous contact.

It is true that the use of writing for literature was not one of the major features of these societies, whereas in Greece the newly introduced alphabet, whose use was unrestricted by centralized religious, political or scribal interests, penetrated into most areas of culture. Indeed, right at the beginning we find a wide range of non-oral uses which incorporate literacy and are not simply straightforward adaptations of the new channel to the oral mode, suggesting at the very least a readiness to welcome this development. These uses include the following:

1 lists of names are written up in a public place from the sixth century (Jeffrey 1961:50), the lists of Olympic victors, Spartan ephors and Parian archons being traced back in literary sources to the eighth or seventh centuries (776, 756, 683 BC)

2 legal texts are found in the seventh-century temple of Dreros in Crete and in sixth-century Gortyn in the same island;[6] a number of other secular and sacral laws are known. This listing of laws in an 'organized' way pulls them out of their particular contexts of pronouncement (probably in judgements) and collects the rules

together in a sequential order like that of the Ten Command-
ments, or, as we shall see, of the constitution of the Misila
association of the Vai, so that they can be rearranged, reordered,
in more 'logical' and consistent ways

3 while there is no evidence of early treaties between states, we do
find records of public works connected with temple affairs.
"Records by temple treasurers of valuables collected for the
temple in about the middle of the sixth century have been found
at Ephesos and Athens, the latter in the form of a dedication"
(Jeffrey 1961:61)

4 monuments are inscribed with the names of the dead, providing
a degree of personalization that marks the inherited products
which written cultures often leave to posterity ("I am Ozyman-
dias . . .")

5 personal property is marked linguistically, not simply graphi-
cally, sometimes in hexameters. Graffiti took the form of "I am
X"s, i.e. the object speaks, a use parallel to that of "X wrote me"

6 lists of the alphabet are found in the form of that widespread
learning device, the abecedary. Writing was never an esoteric
craft, being open to a large segment of the population, and this
constituted one of the most significant contributions to the Greek
achievement.

The arguments I have pursued in this chapter are two-pronged.
Reviewing the general literature on the comparison of the Homeric
composition with other 'epic' forms, I concluded the genre was
less typical of oral cultures than of early literate ones, a suggestion
that is supported by other features of the style and content of the
poems; the structure is not inconsistent with literary influence. In
making this point I do not mean to suggest that the author of the
Iliad was necessarily literate. But the poem as we know it appears
to have been considerably affected in form and content by the
existence of writing, if only by being inevitably transformed when it
became transcribed, by the author or by another, as a written text.
On more general grounds it is difficult to imagine a Greek culture in
750 BC whose major verbal achievements did not experience some
effects of writing. A partially-literate background was certainly
typical of other epics of the so-called Heroic Age. African examples
of long recitations that come from purely oral cultures differ

significantly from the Homeric poems. And while the idea of 'communal composition' has obviously to be rejected, the whole notion of a unique, monumental composition – or composer – runs contrary to what we know of the reproduction of such standardized forms in societies that rely on the oral channel alone for linguistic communiction. As we shall see from our studies on the Bagre, such oral forms are both more variable and less 'authored' than the Homeric poems.

4

Oral composition and oral transmission: the case of the Vedas

La mémoire la plus forte est plus faible que l'encre la plus pâle.
Chinese Proverb (L. Lavelle, *La Parole et l'écriture*, Paris, 1947)

The other major verbal achievement that is often regarded as a product, if not of an oral culture, at least of an oral tradition are the Vedic recitations, the sacred texts of orthodox Hindus. Certainly these pose a problem for scholars interested in the cultural consequences of writing. Emphasis is always placed on the way in which Brahmins are taught to recite these works in a verbatim fashion, the written text being little valued, while at the same time great stress is placed upon the truth (*satyam*) of exact repetition (Staal 1961:1). The explicit contrast to the role of the book in other world religions extends to claiming that the Vedic hymns were composed before the advent of writing.

In Sanskrit the term 'vedic' is used to refer to the older forms of literature, namely the four Vedas: Ṛgveda, Sāmaveda, Yajurveda, and Arthavaveda, and it is derived from the root *vid*, know. Each of the Vedas comprises a metrical section, known as *mantra*, and a prose section, composed of explanatory material, called *brāhmaṇa*. The latter consists of a later commentary on an earlier text.

Yet in apparent contradiction to these claims, the recitation of the Vedas – and at times in Indian history, the learning of Sanskrit itself – was confined to segments of the Brahmin caste (Staal 1961:18). Thus *oral* tradition was vested in a caste of *literate* specialists. The question immediately arises, why did literates insist upon the oral transmission of these sacred works and claim that the 'texts' themselves were orally composed? The word 'text' is deliberate, for it is placed in opposition to 'utterance' (following Olson 1976) because what is striking here is the claim made by scholars that an orally composed work has been transmitted with exactitude over the centuries by purely oral means.[1] As I argue in chapter 8, the claim runs against the conclusions that have emerged from studies of the transmission of even narrative works, much less those of a more 'philosophical' bent, that have been carried out in cultures of a purely oral kind. It is a claim about which in the previous chapter I have expressed doubt in the case of the Homeric poems, not only because of the evidence from oral cultures, including my own work on long recitations in West Africa, but also because the proposition itself seems incapable of proof, or even support, before the advent of writing itself. Only then can we tell if we have a similar or identical work being transmitted over time. The Bagre of the LoDagaa has been composed and transmitted orally and we have records of some versions over time (Goody 1972; Goody and Gandah 1981). But we certainly cannot claim identity, exactitude, even though the actors may insist that it is the same work. Are the versions of the Ṛgveda identical? If so, are they dependent upon exclusively oral modes of transmission, uninfluenced by the literate dimension? And why should literate specialists insist upon oral transmission?

In looking at these questions from the standpoint of an interested outsider, I present my remarks in the form of comments on an article by Oliver who relates his discussion of Ancient India to the 'literacy thesis' (1979); it is obvious that I am heavily dependent on his analysis, even in reaching partially different conclusions. Oliver puts forward three propositions. First, the Vedic corpus has many of the characteristics posited by Havelock (1963) and others (for example, Goody and Watt 1963) for the parallel products of literate societies (1979:60). Secondly, it "was composed and most of it arranged . . . before writing became available" (p. 60). Thirdly, even when writing became available, Vedic literature was "meant for memory and voice" (p. 60) and more specifically was "learned orally".

With the first proposition one can readily agree. As he remarks with regard to classical literature more generally, the composition of these works appears to be virtually "inconceivable without writing" because of their particular characteristics; indeed, India may have "preserved written compositions by oral transmission"

(p. 58). If that were the case, we would have no need to go any further. For many early literate cultures, especially in the religious sphere, insist that the holy word should be internalized by the pupil, who may even be required to transmit it by the same means as proof of true knowledge. The question of how exact repetition is achieved without direct recourse to a book is a matter to which we will return, but in fact the claims of many Sanskritic scholars are more far-reaching. However, the second proposition (which the author prefaces with the words "it is clear") is far from self-evident, no clearer for the Vedic than for other classical literature. Oliver himself remarks that whilst the "vedic mantras almost certainly were oral compositions, it seems at least possible that their redaction involved the use of writing. But the brāhmaṇas must have been for the most part oral compositions, though they presuppose the existence of the saṃhitās" (1979:61), that is, the constituted text. It is suggested that oral composition continued until the first century AD when "literature eliminates most of the basic features of oral composition", with the appearance of elegantly elaborate verse, but it is at least five centuries more before a "sophisticated prose style becomes common". Indeed, he states that "no one disputes the claim that all this literature was composed orally and transmitted orally for many generations ... " and that "extraordinary efforts were made to ensure the preservation of this sacred knowledge by oral transmission" (p. 59). At the same time, all these works were composed in a society with alphabetic writing and display features acknowledged to have much in common with the products of a written culture. The problem is that India "produced a great deal of variety of highly developed, specialized knowledge, and at the same time maintained that the only sanctioned method of transmitting this knowledge is oral" (p. 58).

Let us look at the historical argument concerning the advent of writing in the sub-continent. Oliver rejects the conclusion of many writers (see Gough 1968) that the Vedas were not written down until the fourteenth century AD, pointing out that, on the basis of a critical study of the lists of teachers contained in the brāhmaṇas, one scholar has suggested the period around 150 BC (R. Smith 1966); it is even possible to interpret a remark of Yāska as indicating a date as early as 500 BC. While the texts appear to have been written, or written down, over two thousand years ago, there was an expressed taboo in writing out the Vedas, which is formulated in the *Mahabharata*. A fourteenth-century commentator adds that recitation must be perfect "because reading manuscripts is prohibited", despite the author's evident reliance on one. Oliver draws from this discussion the second proposition, that the Vedic literature was composed and most of it arranged before writing became available. But is that conclusion so evident? As we have seen, writing of a kind was present in the Indian subcontinent as early as the third millennium BC (*c.* 2200 BC), long before the dates we are now considering. There appears to have been a gap, from perhaps 1000 BC, between the use of this so-far undeciphered logographic script, and the adoption of a form of the Semitic alphabet, from Aramaic merchants travelling to India from the Middle East.[2] The diffusion of this new form of writing, which was certainly much less cumbersome than the earlier one, took place in the seventh century BC, at the very period when, according to Oliver, there was a general trend towards the formalization and organization of all known fields of knowledge. Given these dates, the role of writing in the composition (or possibly transcription) of the Vedas must remain a serious possibility.

Oliver's third point, like the first, seems essentially correct. But the statement about the Vedas being meant for memory and voice conceals an important ambiguity that is crucial to the whole discussion of the role of literacy, the nature of oral transmission and related questions. He argues that, as far as India is concerned, Havelock was wrong to assume that the "material for memorization" was narrative verse. For, in fact, "every kind of 'inexpressible and also unthinkable' analytic statement – the sheer catalogue, technical information, moral judgement, universal definition, Kantian imperative, mathematical relationship, epistemology, logic – mentioned by Havelock (1963, esp. chapter 10) is found in abundance in Indian literature, and while some may be the product of writing they were none the less meant for memory and voice" (p. 60). The implications are significant. Firstly, that writing is not necessary for the developments described by Havelock. Secondly, that even if writing were a prerequisite, oral processes continue to be of primary importance in the reproduction of these works.

To pursue this argument we first need to be clear about one distinction. If the material with which we are dealing is the product of writing (even indirectly), or has been transformed by being transcribed, then the question of how it is subsequently delivered is of less significance as far as theories to do with changes in 'modes of thought', cognitive style, are concerned. Referring to the kinds of analytic statement listed above, if in mathematics we include the use of multiplication and division, then it would seem that these operations are virtually impossible, beyond a limited point, without the existence of writing or some similar notational (that is, graphic, visual) system. Our mathematics does not of course require the alphabet, or even a complete writing system; if that were so, mathematics would not have the potency it does as an instrument of international communication, nor would elaborate calculations have been possible in pre-Columbian America (assuming for the moment the absence of a full writing system). While such mathematical computation may require a graphic system as a prerequisite, it can be operated 'orally'. An illiterate can be taught to memorize the mathematical tables without recourse to written sources. Such learning becomes more difficult since there is no doubt that verbatim memorization is facilitated by the existence of a written 'crib'. It is also more restrictive. For there is one obvious way in which literate transmission is easier than oral: the learner does not need the physical presence of a teacher to impart the knowledge nor to make the corrections necessary for exact reproduction; that he can do himself. Writing creates the possibility of the autodidact and makes the acquisition of information potentially less personal, less 'intensive'.

Writing may affect the procedures (that is, the cognitive operations) and content of the knowledge of individuals in a society, even though they are unable to read, let alone to write. Scribal cultures were of this kind, so too were many colonial ones. Even non-literate peoples or cultures may acquire, be influenced by, even be dominated by, forms of knowledge developed through literacy.

It is possible, therefore, for literates to communicate the products of writing to non-literates by oral means. It is also possible that those who were able to read may have to reproduce orally, even among themselves, the knowledge they have acquired, either by reading or by having someone read to them. While reading and writing were major aspects of the role of the custodians of the Vedas, the Brahmins appear to have continued over a long period to reproduce orally knowledge that derived from literate sources and to have developed special techniques for this purpose. We should not be surprised that material of this kind, even if disseminated by word of mouth, tends to display some of the characteristic features of early, and indeed of many later, systems of writing.

These features, which include the development of lists and other formalizing processes, are rightly seen by Oliver to be characteristic of early Indian achievements. He takes as his example of these processes the use of the sūtras, or 'threads', brief formulaic statements that were used to analyze ritual so that "simple, self-contained actions could be organized into complex wholes, elaborate sacrificial ceremonies lasting days or longer" (p. 60). The actual form used was that most thoroughly developed by the grammarians, and especially by Pāṇini (*c.* 450 BC) whose major work consisted of nearly 4,000 sūtras. The technical devices employed included two special uses of the alphabet. First 'a table or array' was organized on phonetic principles, to form a complete and symmetrical system for the consonantal stops and the nasals. As Oliver points out, "the use of this table led to its being filled out in all places, since the palatal nasal is a predictable allophone in Sanskrit and need not be accorded the status of a phoneme". This is the phenomenon of the 'empty box' (Goody 1977b). The use of graphic devices for organizing linguistic information, in particular the matrix, pushes the user to fill all the boxes he creates whether or not completion is demanded by the material itself; it pushes towards a certain type of binarism or quadripartism, characteristic of much recent anthropology and sociology. Indeed 'rational' procedures often demanded such complete, 'logical' systems which have a certain affinity with the syllogism. Filling the empty box provides emotional and intellectual satisfaction, but sometimes at the expense of an understanding of the material being analyzed.

The second use of the alphabet involved the employment of a list of fourteen groups of letters to construct abbreviated statements, each group being "terminated by a letter which was by definition not part of the list"; the groups were then employed to form abbreviations, taking one letter plus an end-letter, which were in turn used to express grammatical propositions of a very compact kind. Again the notion of a letter that appears in a list and yet is not part of it, indeed the notion of a letter *tout court*, requires the representation of elements of language by a visual notation which then becomes partially independent of speech. It is a highly abstract achievement, the end of a long line of experiments with writing, and it has (apparently) only been invented once.

The same process is illustrated by another example. Oliver points out that the sūtras are "supplemented by lists of words read with indicatory terminators in prescribed order. Some lists, such as the verbal roots, are meant to be exhaustive, and in fact this list contains more roots than are found in the literature" (p. 61). The question of exhaustive lists is another feature that I have earlier seen as encouraged by early writing systems (1977b). In an oral society the contexts in which an exhaustive list would be called for are few and far between. By putting them in writing they acquire a generalized, decontextualized, authority. The process that Oliver is describing seems to imply the use of writing, as does the method of sorting out and rearranging information by way of re-ordering the lists once they have been spelled out.

In all these features, the materials from early India resemble other early written traditions. There is no difficulty in conceiving a written tradition being passed on largely by oral means, and this, I suggest, is the most parsimonious hypothesis of what was happening in the present case. There can be little doubt that Pāṇini used writing to enable him to formulate the 'rules' of grammar. Nevertheless the instruction of a pupil began by memorizing the sūtras which were only later explained to him; the procedure is not uncommon in forms of Islamic literacy, and in less obvious ways in our own. According to Oliver, a good grammarian learned and still learns the basic classical works "by heart, directly from a teacher without use of a manuscript or book" (p. 61). Nevertheless a book did exist and could be referred to if necessary.

While we cannot doubt the remarkable performances of Sanskritic scholars in memorizing the grammars of Pāṇini or the Vedic hymns, we do not find any features in this literature that would radically modify our earlier comments on the implications of literacy (Goody and Watt 1963). In that paper, as well as in subsequent work, we concentrated upon the accumulated cultural repertoire rather than upon individual performance. Whether arithmetic or grammar is learnt by oral or by literate procedures, is a question independent of the origin of those tables or rules in literate composition. This statement is obviously true of the mathematical tables but is equally so for Pāṇini's grammar. In any case, by origin I mean more than oral or literate composition in the strict sense. For, as I have remarked earlier, I may compose a sonnet in my head, if I have that particular ability; but no-one doubts that the sonnet form is an invention of literate culture, a fact of our cultural environment, a 'representation'. At one level, it is precisely this cultural input into cognitive processes that define the implications of literacy, irrespective of the mode of transmission in any particular case.

It is in this very general context of the influence of literacy that we should judge whether the Vedic songs, as we know them, are the product of an oral or a literate culture. For Staal, in his work on Nambuduri recitation of the Vedas, the situation is clear cut: "it seems certain that only many centuries after the beginning of the Vedic literature writing was used in India" (1961:14–15). It is difficult to see how any claim of this kind can be substantiated historically, since presumably the first records must date from the time when writing was introduced. Scholars may be misled by the actors themselves. But the attribution of the Vedic texts by Brahminical authors to the beginning of the world cannot be taken as anything other than an attempt to legitimate Holy Writ.[3] How can these claims for oral composition be reconciled with the internal evidence which surely suggests, as Oliver implies, the existence of a text? This same evidence led the great Sanskritic scholar, Renou, to remark that "the organisation of the Vedic canon is hardly conceivable without the help of writing" (1954:70). From which he concludes that "we cannot deny the possibility that from the period of the brāhmaṇas the recitation of religious texts was accompanied by the use of manuscripts as an accessory". It is this possibility that constitutes our preferred solution.

However one question we should be asking is of a different order. Whatever the original mode of composition, we know that these texts were taught orally even when written texts existed. Why should the oral transmission of texts continue when reading is available to the learner, the teacher, or to both? Why do we find the oral transmission of texts vested in the literate caste? Probably every lecturer has asked himself this question when making an oral presentation of a written speech, when he is in fact giving a 'reading', that is to say, a lecture. Sometimes he will have taken a further step and memorized the written text, so that he no longer reads but recites, that is, delivers a speech. In this way it appears more 'natural' to the face-to-face situation. Few such speeches are orally composed in their entirety, and even the style, structure and content of those that are will have been heavily influenced by the written learning of the speaker and of his instructors. There are clearly occasions when the oral presentation of literate material is appropriate. These situations include the academic one, when it is important for the author of a paper to receive the verbal comments and questions of his audience, to have the immediate feedback of which he is largely deprived when his word appears in print or in manuscript.

Another advantage of the oral communication of a written text is that the author retains control over the material, whether his own or someone elses, since he remains indispensable to its communication. It is like a poetry-reading of unpublished verse. I knew a distinguished anthropologist who refused to publish a particular paper he had written on the ground that if he did so, he would no longer have something to deliver to university audiences when he was asked to give a talk. The publication of the written word, especially when deposited in a library or printed in a journal, obviates the need for the personal mediation of the author, or indeed of any other literate intermediary.

There are three constraints upon direct access to written materials in early literate cultures. The first is technological; in a manuscript culture, copies of books are rare and expensive. They can be produced only by the long and arduous labour of the copyist. Consequently access is often more simply gained by listening rather than by reading, until printing makes mass access a possibility.

Secondly the process of reading aloud means that the pupil can ask questions and hence improve his opportunities for learning. Thirdly, and most importantly, by retaining control over the process of transmission, we render our jobs more secure. When the book is freely available, the priest may no longer be necessary; so the Protestant sects discovered when the Bible was translated into the newly-acceptable vernacular and printed by the newly-invented printing press, making knowledge accessible through the language of the people and the multiplication of the text. The Catholic Church on the other hand insisted on the essential role of the priest in mediating the written word of God. So too with the Brahmins of India. At certain periods of Indian history, only Brahmins were taught to read at all. Later, and this is true today, only Brahmins were allowed to read the Vedas. They learn them by rote, and thus internalize their content, making these works part of themselves in a very special way, capable of being recalled without the presence of the text.[4] The written word is no longer dependent upon the book, at least for transmission. The fact that reading and learning the Vedas is restricted to the Brahmins, who internalize them, places the members of that caste in a very central position in relation to the theory and practice of Hindu religion.

Some years ago we visited the house of an engineer who ran the highly complex station distributing electricity to a district of Gujerat, on the occasion of a *pūjā*, an offering to the gods. His wife, a school-teacher, had prepared a special meal. Other distinguished guests gathered around the house at the appointed hour. But all stood waiting there for some two hours because the Brahmin who had been called to carry out the performances and to read the Vedic texts had not arrived. It is impossible to carry out such rites for oneself or even to call upon another Brahmin to help; neither the patron nor the priestly group would break the specific *jajmani* arrangement.

The priest of course received food, honour and money for his appearance. For it was only he who could bring the sacred book, finger its pages and recite the ritual. Thus he not only had considerable power over the ritual proceedings in the household, a power that he may have intended to stress by his late arrival, but he also sustained himself in a temporal way by virtue of his indispensable mediation with the book as well as with the gods. Access to both was through the priest. It is understandable that lower castes of the area tended to stress more inspirational forms of teaching that placed less emphasis on the reading and reciting of texts, and more on direct communication with the supernatural, by song, by prayer or by motion. They stressed, in other words, 'visionary' rather than 'tutorial' religion.

One movement of this kind was the Swami Narain worship practised by the followers of Vishnu, who are generally more inclined to the inspirational Bhakti, to popular Krishna cults and to communal signing, than the more Brahminical followers of Shiva, with their orientation towards philosophy (*toro*) and towards contemplation. But for all Hindus, Brahmins remain at the top of the religious hierarchy, a hierarchy that they themselves had defined in writing, so it was *their* practices, *their* ideology and *their* interest, that constituted the framework of 'proper' action as constituted by the text. Control of the Vedas by oral reproduction helped to keep the world this way.

The stress on oral transmission has important consequences for spiritual instruction. As well as emphasizing the necessary role of the guru as intermediary, it acknowledges the validity of Platonic fears about the inadequacies of written communication. Perfect knowledge of the written word (especially of the fixed corpus of religious doctrine or ritual texts) consists of that which the learner is able to reproduce out of his own mouth, verbatim, parrot-fashion, knowledge which he has internalized, made part of himself, not simply left as a resource on the library shelf. Indeed at one level this is what we mean by 'learning' a poem, for example, rather than just reading it. Then there is the more general aspects of the communicative problem raised by Wittgenstein in his oft-repeated phrase, "what we cannot speak about we must pass over in silence". These considerations are of particular relevance when one is brought face to face with the ineffable truth, with the ultimate reality (Staal 1961:14), an understanding of which is perhaps easier to indicate in the flow of speech rather than in the more precise statements of writing – and perhaps even more satisfactorily brought out in a 'dead' or 'deep' language which the gods comprehend more clearly than mankind.

Given the possibility of the 'oral transmission' of a 'text', that is, of a work that may have been written, or written down, as early as 500 BC, we should ask what procedures were available to assist the verbatim memorizing of such a long text and to overcome the limits on exact oral transmission. The priestly schools developed a number of ancillary disciplines known as the six vedāṅgas or 'limbs of the veda'. Of these six vedāṅgas, four concerned linguistic matters, that is, phonetics, metrics, grammar (morphology and syntax) and etymology. The other two dealt with sacrifice and astronomy, which had also been important areas of written authority in Mesopotamia (Neugebauer 1969) where the recording of the movements of heavenly bodies led to the development of a mathematical astronomy that subsequently spread to India and the East. The aim of all these six fields of study, notes Oliver, was "to preserve the knowledge of the correct performance and meaning of the mantras' (1979:59). As Brough has pointed out, "the study of words and of the meanings of words was undertaken in the first place primarily to meet the needs of Vedic ritual and the text material required by it" (1953:161). For if you preserve a text over a long period of time, words and their meanings tend to become obscure as language changes, making it necessary to offer some apparatus of interpretation, whether scholarly or allegorical, unless the text is to become complete mumbo-jumbo, mouthed for its own sake, uncomprehendingly.

Serving the same purpose as the vedangas were five metrical indexes giving lists of ṛṣis (seers), metres, deities, sections of the Ṛgveda and the number of stanzas in hymns. Another class of work contained rules for the formation of each word of the Veda, which were important in constructing a special version of the 'text', and involved "a recognition of the individual word abstracted from the flow of speech" (Oliver 1979:59), reflecting a thorough knowledge of phonology and forming the basis of further exegesis.

From a special form of the 'text' are created three different renditions in which the words are repeated in various orders: the *krama* text arranges the words in the sequence ab, bc, cd, etc.; the *iaṭā* text reads ab, ba, ab, bc, cb, bd, cd, etc.; and the *ghana* text reads ab, ba, abc, cba, abc, bc, cb, bcd, dcb, bcd (Staal 1961:24).

These accounts make it possible to understand how most male

Brahmins could be taught to memorize, over a twelve year period, the mantras of at least one Veda. For the 'oral transmission' of the Vedas can take place without reference to the book when use is made of techniques which are themselves clearly derived from literate activity, both in the wider sense of the study of phonology and in the more particular one of breaking down speech into words and using complex mnemonic devices (as in the *ghana* text) which depend upon the visual perception of linguistic phenomena and constitute the equivalent of the mathematical table in 'oral' arithmetic. Indeed, as I later discuss with regard to Frances Yates' interesting study on memory (1966), the development of certain important memorizing techniques for speech seems almost to require the prior reduction of language to a visual form, providing speech with a spatial dimension (chapter 8).

In conclusion, most Sanskritic scholars claim that the Vedas were composed and transmitted by oral means, that they constituted 'utterance' rather than 'text'. But we cannot know whether the Vedas emerged when India was purely an oral culture and are therefore to be taken as examples of 'standardized oral forms' in this important sense. Much of the early literature, as Oliver suggests, displays features that we would associate with the advent of writing, that is, with 'literature', books and 'texts'. Even if they were not written down at the moment of composition (and this we can hardly know), these works, including the Vedas, bear the hallmarks of a literate culture. Moreover these texts have existed side by side with oral transmission for at least 600, possibily 1,800, or even 2,500 years. There is no reason to doubt that the hallmarks represent the process of 'writing down' which is itself transforming. Whatever the date of written composition or transcription, the question of oral transmission is quite different from that of composition. It seems clear that not only is the organization of the Vedas influenced by writing, but also the mnemonic devices used by those who teach and learn them. Is it not time to recognise the Vedas as 'texts' rather than 'utterances'?

III

Written and oral cultures in West Africa

5

The impact of Islamic writing on oral cultures

In chapter 2 I considered some aspects of the long-term impact of forms of writing on human cultures in the context of the Greek achievement, following which I examined the status of the Homeric poems as products of an oral or literature culture. I suggested that like most 'epics' of the Heroic Age they too were products of the interface within such cultures. So too, I argued were the Vedic recitations, although the interface here seemed to be between a written tradition of composition and an oral tradition of transmission. In this section two chapters deal with other aspects of interface, connected with the coming, first of Islamic literacy, then of European literacy, to West Africa and with their impact on local societies. The following two chapters treat of differences between written and oral societies in West Africa, especially as these concern the form, content and reproduction of verbal art forms.

The first system of writing to make its impact on West Africa south of the Sahara was Arabic, a form of script that, as we have seen, stemmed from the same source as the Phoenician that via Greece conquered the Western world and the Aramaic form that spread throughout the East. Of course writing had developed in North Africa, in the Nile valley, as early as the third millennium BC. And subsequently alphabetic scripts were spread by the Phoenicians, the Jews and later the Christians, especially to North Africa and to Ethiopia. But before the coming of Islam the impact upon Africa south of the Sahara was negligible. It was the advent of Islam to the Niger bend around 1000 AD that brought a form of restricted literacy to parts of West Africa. I stress its restricted nature because, in discussing its influence on these societies, we need to try and distinguish the role of Islam from that of the writing

125

that accompanied the advance of that religion. While a complete separation is barely possible, at least we should have the question in mind.

One of the main problems was that writing was firmly linked to a Religion of the Book which was written in the Arabic language as well as the Arabic script. On the one hand, that language was foreign to West Africa, so that learning to read was generally a parrot-like activity, unless accompanied by the learning of the new language. On the other hand, the adaptation of the Arabic script to local languages was not encouraged although this became an important feature of Hausa life in northern Nigeria from the eighteenth century. While the advent of the Roman script also entailed learning one of the European languages, its use for writing down the vernaculars was promoted, especially by Protestant missionaries anxious that people should be able to read the bible in their own tongue.

The general range and content of Islamic writing in West Africa has already been discussed by a number of scholars (Hiskett 1957, Wilks 1963, Hodgkin 1966, Goody 1968b, etc.). The ability to read and write and understand Arabic was very limited. Even in Hausaland the uses of writing were restricted. Nevertheless the halo effects of Islamic-derived literacy were experienced over a much wider range of activities than might appear.

The title of the chapter refers to the impact of Islamic literacy on oral cultures. The use of written material for magical purposes in such cultures is a question I have touched upon before (1968b). But there are two other questions, first, the overall historical one, and secondly, the nature of its influence on cultures which are largely non-literate, such as the Soninke of Mali or the Gonja of Ghana, but which contain a Muslim component. For those West African societies that know writing are characterized by a literacy that is restricted in its use and limited in its extent. Their populations are consequently divided into literate and non-literate elements. But the non-literates had a status quite different from the illiterates in a contemporary Western society. In the kingdoms of northern Ghana, for example, chiefs rarely possessed the skills of reading and writing which were associated with the Muslim estate whose members sometimes acted as secretaries to the rulers. While writing had its own prestige as a technical device apart from religion, there was nothing shaming about being unable to read or write. The 'community' consisted of literates and non-literates; neither was automatically deemed to be more prestigious than the other.

I want to illustrate and assess the impact of Islamic writing by looking at two contexts, first at the oral tradition of savannah societies, to which I referred in chapter 3, secondly, at the concepts of time and space in the different Gonja estates, Muslim, ruling and commoner. Elsewhere I have looked at the role of writing in the revolts of slaves and freed slaves of Hausa and Yoruba origin in Bahia in the first half of the nineteenth century (Goody 1986). Disparate contexts, but they will help to define different aspects of this complex interaction.

Oral recitations

As we have seen, the *griots* or minstrels of the Niger bend work within the framework of a 'mixed' society of this kind and their recitals give some idea of the role played by Islam, and by Islamic literacy, in the non-literate sectors. The Soninke legend of the dispersal of the Kusa (Meillassoux *et al*. 1967) offers a number of examples.

In this text, the appeals to Allah (p. 50) and the reckoning of time by the hours of prayer (p. 61) provide strong evidence of literate Muslim influence.[1] But above all, in the legend of "le héros magicien", stress is placed upon the magical knowledge of Islam. At one point, the representative of the oppressed Kusa challenges the tyrannical king by accusing him of geomancy, contrary to the practice of Islam.

Il dit: 'Bien que Koussa,
N'est-ce pas toi qui a interrogé la terre
Chez nous dans le Koussata?'
Il dit: 'Le règne de notre grand Allah,
Sa dignité et sa science infuse,
Surgira de ta géomancie.' (p. 69–1)

When the hero, Jagu Maré, wants to revenge himself upon the tyrant for the death of his father, he goes off to acquire knowledge about the manipulation of things supernatural from elders well-versed in Islamic lore:

Il alla chez un premier sage.
Il dit; 'Sage, ami d'Allah,
Sage, interlocuteur d'Allah,
Sage, confident d'Allah, je suit venu me faire traiter par toi,
Afin de venger mon père à Kelampo.' (p. 93)

The second example I take is from Koumen, by the distinguished authors, A. Hampaté Bâ and G. Dieterlen (1961), a work that is described in its sub-title as *Texte initiatique des pasteurs peul* (of Macina). Although gathered in the contemporary period, the authors see this text as referring to, if not composed in, much earlier pagan times. The text tells the story of the initiation of the first *silatigi* (ritual leader and diviner), who was called "Silé Sadio ou Soulé, diminutif de Souleyman, c'est-à-dire de Salomon" (p. 29). The actual text runs; "Koumen lui dit: 'Silé Sadio! je suis Koumen l'Enchanteur. J'initie les hommes par degrés à l'exemple des génies de Salomon qui trempent l'acier" (p. 35). On this passage the editors offer the following comment: "Les Peul font constamment allusion aux événements de l'époque de Salomon, qui apparaît dans les légendes et les traditions historiques comme un maître et la source de certaines initiations" (p. 34).

A little later in their commentary they suggest that a knowledge of this text permits one to attribute the Tassili frescoes of the bovid period to the Fulani (p. 94) and they go on to propose that a further analysis of the text will throw light on the relations of these nomadic peoples with the Mediterranean and the Near East, "ou de préciser les influences subies au contact des peuples de l'antiquité classique, et dont témoignent, par exemple, les allusions à Salomon" (p. 95). One might remark, however, that such allusions bear witness not to any direct contact with classical antiquity but to more recent communication with written Islamic sources. In much of the cabalistic literature of Christian, Jewish or of Muslim provenance, especially in the books of magic that circulated widely in the Western Sudan, Solomon is regarded as the fount of magical power. The tradition lives on in the Masonic myths of contemporary Europe as well as in the works of magic that have spread wherever writing is found (and in some parts where it is not). The reference certainly demonstrates a link with the Mediterranean world, but a link not through migration in the unrecorded past but through the movement of books and scholars since the coming of Islam.

The same neglect of the probable effects of literacy appears in M. Griaule's (1965) discussion of the zodiac among the Dogon of the Bandiagara scarp. In the course of his explicit effort to establish the equality of humankind and to show that Dogon philosophers lose nothing by comparison with their counterparts in the Near East, Griaule points to the existence of the zodiac among the Dogon, apparently thinking of this as an independent invention (p. 212). So of course it may be. But a much more likely suggestion (which he does not consider) is that, like the Fulani who surrounded them, who lived in amongst their lowland settlements, and who sometimes defeated them in war, the Dogon were also influenced by the 'books' of Solomon. By this I mean the works of Al Buni and other North African scholars who were instrumental in transmitting these off-shoots of Chaldean learning to the diviners, magicians and other religious practitioners located across the Sahara. Here we have an example of the influence of Islamic writing on a prototypical oral culture. Indeed there are other aspects of Dogon culture, such as the domestic architecture (1965: Plate IIIa) and the clothing (Plate IV), which remind us of its proximity to the Niger bend as well as to those long-established Islamic centres of Mopti and Timbuctu.[2]

Writing and magico–religious activity

I draw attention to the content of these oral recitations for two reasons. First, in dealing with any society in the Western Sudan, we have to think of the total context of social interaction; no tribe, state, or village can be treated as a cultural isolate, especially in magico–religious affairs. And an important part of this context of interaction, though clearly more important in Kano than in Konkombaland, has been the circulation of books, largely of Mediterranean origin, but also of local authorship. Here one needs to introduce a caveat.

It does not follow that every mention of a High God, every

manifestation of 'civilized' society, should be attributed to Islam and its works. Much of Islam, as Frankfort has insisted for ancient Egypt, emerges from a wider base, a common source, which can be suggested only by assiduous comparison. But in every case we need to be aware of the possibility.

This first point leads to the second. The area in which the influence of Islam on non-Islamic, non-literate cultures is most immediately apparent is that of magico–religious activity. One example comes from Braimah's (1967) account of the Salaga civil war of 1892, written from the standpoint of that segment of the ruling group of the Gonja division of Kpembe most directly involved in the rebellion. Muslims come into the picture on two main occasions.[3] On one of these the Kabache chief, Isifa, goes to Salaga to consult the Imam and overhears his liege lord who has come there for a similar purpose, that is, to provide himself with destructive medicine (p. 17). The other time is when Isifa flies from Kpembe, the neighbouring 'king's town', and is about to raise the rebellion; through a Nanumba chief he is put in touch with Mallam Imoru of Miong in Dagomba, and it is the help of his magical powers that enables him to conquer the enemy (pp. 24 ff.). The only specific mention of books or writing is in connection with the use of the Qu'ran for swearing oaths.

One does not need to elaborate the point that, even for pagan cultures and for non-Muslim groups,[4] Islam has a considerable magico–religious appeal and its practices are often incorporated in ritual activities of various kinds. Nadel noted the influence of Islam on various aspects of Nupe religion, including divination. Nupe is a Muslim state and we might well expect this fact to be reflected in its divinatory practices. But, even further south among the 'pagan' Yoruba, it is now generally thought that the famous Ifa divination was profoundly influenced by these Mediterranean methods.[5] And from 'pagan' Asante, ninety per cent of the early nineteenth-century collection of Arabic manuscripts that found its way to the Royal Library of Copenhagen was concerned with 'magic' (Levtzion 1966).

Why did such magic have such an appeal to Islamic and non-Islamic cultures alike? The orally transmitted religions of Africa are essentially eclectic in their approach to the supernatural; no written code tells them that this deity must be worshipped and not the other, that "thou shalt have no other God but me". While they have a framework of religious concepts and beliefs, there is much scope for change, for new ideas, for new gods, for new cults. Indeed, as I have argued elsewhere, the process of religious creation is rendered almost essential by the inability of existing shrines or medicines to live up to their promises about curing the sick, banishing witches and outlawing sin. The built-in obsolescence of such cults paves the way for a mobility in religious practices.[6] Given this predisposition, the willingness to accept Islam rested on the following factors: first, the many points of contact between the religious frameworks, which have been well discussed by Lewis (1966:66); secondly, the prestige of a 'superior' culture, whose representatives, being traders, had the goods one coveted; thirdly, the added value accorded to esoteric magic. In addition, the patent effectiveness of writing as a means of human communication made it an obvious candidate for use in intercourse between man and god; and the attainment of effective communication with supernatural powers lies at the centre of religious activity.

The problem for the non-literate cultures lay in the fact that Islam differed from other new cults in one significant particular; being a written and an excluding religion (the two epithets are, I suggest, almost synonymous), its practitioners were required to reject other approaches. First brought in as a supplement, it later emerged as a replacement. Such a situation clearly opened the way to total conversion, but it also put a premium on co-existence and even apostasy since those who were prepared to accept Allah were not necessarily ready to reject existing deities. Hence the process of conversion to Islam is not a matter simply of increasing the numbers and the communities of the faithful but of replacing those who have been drawn back to pagan practice.

The fact that writing had a pragmatic value in enabling Muslims to communicate at a distance, to record the passage of the years, to acquire the learning of past centuries and far-off places, was obvious to anyone; consequently magico–religious activity that made use of the same technique was thought to have similar advantages; divination by the book, literacy magic, magical squares, phylacteries, and the whole paraphernalia of Mediterranean practice has a wide appeal which spreads far outside the boundaries of Islam. Even among the faithful, it is often one of its main attractions.

Time and space

Recourse to the 'magic of the book' was not the only benefit writing brought, even if it is what most impressed the pagan world. The change in the media of communication also altered the basic categories of time and space. Take time, for example. Here Islamic literacy introduced a fixed calendar which set aside the solar system and placed its ceremonies on a lunar cycle. Typically non-literate societies adjust the two by a process of fudging; the harvest moon appears when the harvest is ripe. Only literate societies have to wrest the month away from the moon, or the year from the sun. The week provides another example. While Islam did not introduce this unit, which is an old-established West African institution, the seven-day week was based upon the planetary cycle that derives from Chaldean astronomy and provides the basis for many divinatory interpretations and symbolic constructs. Thirdly, writing introduces the concept of the era, essentially a function of developments in astronomy and mathematics which were themselves dependent upon developments in the graphic arts and first introduced in Babylonia in 747 BC (Goody 1968a, vol.16:31). Writing thus allows the development not only of history in the technical sense (Goody and Watt 1963:321) but also its tool, chronology. Finally, graphic time-measurement divides the day into periods no longer determined by diurnal activities but by formal criteria; in oral societies, the time words cluster around the points where there is a shift from one mode of activity to another, as in the plethora of terms describing the coming of day, first-light, day-break, dawn, etc., words that are largely redundant in an industrialized and electrified society. But under Islamic literacy it is the religious act of prayer that now marks out the day into defined periods, to form divisions of a more abstract character.

The same is true of space. Not necessarily writing itself, but the accompanying developments in graphic techniques encouraged a different attitude; by extending the possibilities of measuring, numbering, recording and repeating observations, spatial relation-ships could be subjected to different kinds of treatment. In the Arabic world, the new treatment of space had led to extensive developments in geography. However, works of the Arab geogra-phers appear to have had little influence in the Western Sudan. It was the same with most of the more empirical branches of Islamic knowledge, for reasons to which I shall later return. But at least Islamic literacy permitted the recording of itineraries such as those published by Dupuis in his account of the mission to Kumasi (1824), which were so valuable to the European scholars of the eighteenth and nineteenth centuries engaged in building up a two-dimensional picture of the interior of Africa. These lists were mainly itineraries of trading voyages. But others existed that included the pilgrimage routes to Mecca; for, even among the mud-huts of the Gonja town of Salaga, the traveller Binger met men who had voyaged through the whole of the Middle East (1892:ii,86).

Two points need stressing. The first concerns the role of writing in Islam. It is, I suggest, mainly because Islam is a written religion that it can exercise the kind of pull upon the lives of individuals made manifest in the great pilgrimage; to make this journey, a man would give up seven years of a life that was considerably shorter than that of today. It is (and I hardly need to qualify such obviously speculative remarks by the phrase 'in my opinion') the fact that Islam is a written religion that makes and preserves its status as a universalistic creed and prevents it from disintegrating, not just into breakaway sects but into numberless 'local cults'. For the Book persists, in whatever land or period Islam is found, as a permanent reference point – communication preserved as a material object and hence relatively immune to the transmuting power of the oral tradition, held only in memory, transmitted only in face-to-face situations. The Qu'ran immortalizes Muhammad, or the myth of Muhammad, as the New Testament immortalizes Christ, or the myth of Christ, so that the sufferings and victories of the Prophet (and consequently the places where these events occurred) remain of continuing significance for their followers over time and over space.

The second point is that the influence writing had, directly or indirectly, upon the cultures of West Africa varied greatly within as well as between societies. It is this fact that enables us to observe some of the consequences of this form of literacy. In the kingdom of Gonja, north of Asante, there were three main estates of the land: the rulers, the Muslims, and the commoners, although formerly slaves and strangers were present as additional groups. The activities and interests of the three main participating groups coincided at various points but at others they markedly diverged.

In recent times members of the three major estates are not greatly differentiated in terms of occupation, anyhow at the village level: most men are farmers, whatever else they do. Before 1900 the differentiation was greater, since chiefs were more involved in ruling and raiding, while Muslims were more involved in trade and magic. The commoners, too, include warriors (*mbong*) and magicians (e.g. *bilijipo*), but their main activities were connected with the Earth and the bush, with farming, hunting and with local cults.

This internal differentiation is mirrored in their myths of origin as well as in their religious practices. But here I want to discuss differences in the space–time perspectives of the three groups, especially in the ways that these reflect the influence of the written word.

The commoners are mainly named groups ('tribes') of autochthones attached to a particular locality where they claimed to have lived before the Gonja state was established. They tend to speak local languages or dialects, to worship at local shrines and to practise local 'customs'. Though they marry across estate boundaries, they marry within divisional ones. Social space is for them largely bounded by their 'tribal' and local ties.

For the chiefs, social space is the state as a whole. Although the primary sphere of political action lies within their own division, they were nevertheless called upon by other such units to assist in war or to give advice.[7] While Gonja can hardly be said to have operated as a unified state in the immediately pre-colonial period, its divisions were part of an interlocking network of political relations which depended upon acceptance of a common myth and upon communication through a common culture and a common language. The orientation of its chiefs was nationwide, from the standpoint of language, marriage and other communicative acts. Their frame of action included the neighbouring divisions competing for royal office and the neighbouring states competing in armed conflict. In their concepts of space, Gonja was visualized as surrounded by a network of states, friendly as well as hostile, between which lay interstitial areas of acephalous peoples who were raided for human booty.[8]

For the Muslims, spatial relationships were yet more extended, partly for religious reasons connected with the pilgrimage, partly because their sphere was trade not war, and partly because of their access to "preserved communication" with its constant references to distant places. Unlike the stranger Muslims, the local Muslim estate had become largely identified with the state. Nevertheless it tended to think more in terms of lines of communication than of opposition between local units. This was (and still is) especially true of some of the Dyula groups who held such an important role in the transmission of learning in the Western Sudan (Wilks 1968). Inevitably these men looked not only to the individual states within which they lived but to the West African community of Islam as a whole, a fact that made them more aware of events in other parts of the region and in the Mediterranean world than their non-literate neighbours. They tended to see the states in relation to the Islamic communities within them and to judge their rulers according to their allegiance to the faith (and the security they afforded to long-distance trade).

The differences in the conception and measurement of time are equally marked. As agriculturalists, the commoners are largely tied to the farming year; their festivals are mainly determined by the passage of seasons; their rural markets (such as they are) by six-day (and sometimes five-day) cycles. They are of course aware of the royal ceremonies, which are religious in origin and political in character, and are firmly set within the Islamic calendar; but their main mode of time-keeping is by 'natural' cycles. Genealogically their reckoning is short; they do not have the extensive lineages of many acephalous societies in the area, for many of the main functions of these groups are taken over by chiefly government. Their history is local legend and their chronology a matter of counting summers.

The chiefly estate operates two calendrical systems, at least as far
as its major festivals are concerned. The great public ceremonies of
the political year are the traditional Islamic occasions that celebrate
turning points in the life of the Prophet; these are based upon the
lunar cycle of twelve moons. But there is another series of ceremonies connected with New Yams and with homicide medicine
(*gbanda'u*) which are set within the solar or seasonal cycle; the
same is true of rites connected with many of the Earth and other
local shrines. The observation of a double set of festivals, each with
their different calculus, corresponds to the ideological position of
the chiefly estate, ruling over both Muslims and 'pagans' alike, and
responsible for practising the rites of both.

History for the chiefs is essentially dynastic history, manipulated
to serve present ends. Genealogies themselves, as reference
systems for social interaction, are relatively shallow, though more
extensive than those of the commoners, especially in their lateral
extension. Owing partly to the rotational system of succession,
whereby office jumps from dynastic segment to dynastic segment,
the memory of past rulers is limited and appeal has often to be
made to the written lists of rulers (of Imams too) kept by some
divisional Muslims; there are no oral remembrancers, though
certain divisional drummers do record enigmatic, proverbial songs
which can indicate the relative seniority of chiefs, some Spokesmen
are more informed than others; in the East praise-singers incorporate information about the past ancestors and elsewhere the
gravestones of chiefs provide their own more solid mnemonic,
though in the absence of inscriptions, the time-depth of the record
is again limited. The chronology that is kept takes the form of the
lengths of reign, but these recollections are rarely acurate beyond
living memory. Unlike the neighbouring kingdom of Asante,
where the formal recitation of lineage legend plays an important
part, the Gonja rulers give little attention to the oral conservation
of the more concrete aspects of their past glories; all distant
achievements tend to cluster around the name of the conquering
hero, Ndewura Jakpa, about whom legends exist in bewildering
multiplicity.

If the commoners conceptualize agricultural time, the rulers
dynastic time, then the Muslims operate the system of religious

time I have already described, tied to the life-cycle of the Prophet. Because their religion is literate, their conceptualization can be more 'abstract', more divorced from other aspects of 'reality' than the alternative systems found within the same society.

As for their history, literate scribes occasionally make precise records (as they did in the eighteenth-century Gonja chronicle, see Goody 1954), using an objective system of annual dating that starts with the Hejira. The content of such history includes not only local events but other significant occurrences in the neighbouring kingdoms, particularly as they affect the Islamic world. The seven-day week is brought in from outside and merges with a local six-day week, though this conjunction does not produce the complex forty-two-day cycle of their southern neighbours, the Asante.

The effects of literacy are important in differentiating the major estates of Gonja. But even the non-literate groups are influenced by the existence of literates in their midst. It should also be remembered that the Muslim estate is itself highly differentiated in terms of literate accomplishments. Indeed so steep is the pyramid of learning and so narrow the base that I have characterized the situation as one of 'restricted literacy'. While the reasons for this situation, and the results in terms of a restriction of the possibilities latent within this innovation in human communication, are important, they are somewhat tangential to my present theme. Here I have tried to map out some of the effects that the existence of Islamic literacy had on oral cultures and groups in West Africa, first by examining examples of their recorded literature, and secondly by looking at the differences between Muslim and non-Muslim groups within the framework of a single state.

I would conclude by suggesting that the initial appeal of Islam to outsiders was frequently magical (or magico–religious), and that writing was at first valued more for its role in superhuman than in human communication. This appeal inevitably influenced the development of Islam in West Africa, since its practitioners had to meet the demands of non-Muslims as well as Muslims. This role in relation to the pagan community paved the way for the conversion of non-Islamic elements; but it also affected, in a contrary direction, the content of Islamic practice and belief, and hence contributed to its losses as well as to its gains.

This situation seems partly responsible for restricted uses of writing in the Western Sudan, since it aggravated the limiting effects which were already inherent in religious literacy, whether of the Islamic, Christian or Hindu variety.

6

Literacy and the non-literate: the impact of European schooling

As we have seen, it is a mistake to think of pre-colonial Africa as the dark continent unenlightened by the lamp of literacy. We do not, it is true, know of any early systems of writing which developed there, though some, such as the famous Vai, and lesser known scripts, such as Nsibidi, were invented after the colonial period had begun. But alphabetic writing of Middle Eastern origin made its mark outside Egypt as Judaism, then Christianity, and finally Islam penetrated into the northern sectors of the continent. Christianity and its literature continued to be important in Ethiopia, and Islam spread in the savannah country of the West and along the coastal regions of East Africa, bringing its teachers, its brotherhoods, its books.

The nature of religious literacy inevitably placed certain limitations on its employment; it was a restricted literacy both in terms of the proportion who could read and the uses to which writing was put. Moreover, its religious basis meant that a major function was communication to or about God. While courts utilized writing for a number of purposes – historical, treaty-making, epistolary, it was the magical–religious aspect which most impressed the majority of the population. They were concerned with writing as a means of communicating with God and other supernatural agencies, rather than as a means of social and personal advancement. Certainly there was nothing to be ashamed of in being non-literate.

But the position is now changing. The new literacy, associated with predominantly secular teaching at European-type schools, lies at the basis of a dual economy, a dual economy of the spirit as well as of labour. What does the advent of modern literacy do to societies that were previously non-literate? The extent to which new commercial and political activities depend upon literacy hardly needs stressing. The growth of towns, the growth of the economy, the growth of the political system involving mass participation, the growth of the media, all these depend to a greater or lesser extent upon changes in the mode of communication. But eighty per cent of Africa, as of other parts of the developing world, remains rural. What effect does the growth of literacy in their midst have on this segment of the population?

It gives rise at once to an extending ladder of mobility. It forces the gaze towards considerations of achievement rather than birth. This criterion may not be universally applied, but it is always relevant. In Africa the result has been a drastic modification of existing elites. Some of the slaves sent to school, when their owners wished to avoid the District Commissioner's pressure to recruit their own sons, have achieved more than members of the ruling lineage. Frailty paid off. The first literate became the first Member of Parliament for his district. This new system of achievement carries a new system of rewards leading to a new system of stratification. It takes the successful individual out of the local setting and enables him to operate on a national level; it permits him to command a national or even international salary. The new elite, seeking to maintain its own position, encourages its children to pursue the same goals, and the system of education, earlier an open channel to social mobility, now becomes the instrument of status preservation.

But even in the early phase it is not simply a matter of individual achievement; there is also a yawning gap between those who have been to school and those who have not, between haves and have nots. For the non-literate, social change is associated with 'knowing book'. In David Rubadiri's novel, *No Bride Price*, the hero Lombe goes to his natal village and is visited by his uncle.

He was an old man who had seen life. In his village he had prepared himself to live a full life. But the change came. It was not a sudden change. A white man with a book in his hand. Every evening this white man with the book had sat at the edge of the village and played with the children.

Under these conditions there is inevitably a sense of inferiority which forces the pace of educational development, thus leading to an over-development of schools. For there are soon too many educated for the available jobs. While people have been educated out of subsistence agriculture (as they see it), there is no alternative occupation. We find the classic dichotomy, typical of Ceylon, of Egypt and becoming more typical of Africa; the educated unemployed, the school leaver who refuses to go back on the land, who regards himself as destined for a white-collar job.

Thus, in many parts of the continent the effect of introducing literacy is, temporarily at least, to split the population into two halves, one of which is largely rural, the other mainly urban. The split may not always take the form of a physical separation. But many of the literates working in the country will be doing so reluctantly, with their eyes on the town and on its life. For literacy achieved through formal education is the main method of self-advancement, of reaching beyond the level of subsistence farming. Indeed it is not only at the subsistence level that agriculture is considered to provide an inadequate life; the stress of school-learnt values falls elsewhere, in favour of white-collar jobs (or 'white-colour' jobs, as they were sometimes called in West Africa), preferably in an urban setting.

Let us look at the situation in northern Ghana in greater depth. Writing was not unknown in this region before the colonial conquest. Indeed that conquest was recorded by a Muslim author, Al-Hajj 'Umar of Salaga, who wrote a widely distributed poem on the coming of the Christians, "A sun of disaster has risen in the West" (Goody 1977b:32).

Literacy was used by Muslims for a variety of purposes, principally religious ones. But the rulers were rarely if ever literate. They used some literates as scribes and secretaries but, unlike the later Fulani conquerors of northern Nigeria, they did not themselves know how to read and write; and indeed knowledge of these skills was seen as inimical to the practice of war and government. In this respect the situation was similar to certain kingdoms in the Ancient Near East, where rulers were not necessarily literate and where those who could write might have a status inferior to some of those who could not. Indeed, to us the very word scribe has something of a pejorative implication: a menial intellectual, at hand for the purposes of administering to the ruling class.

With the advent of colonial rule, the situation changed; the value of literacy as a means of social and personal advancement was immediately clear. The new conquerors used writing at every stage in their administration of the country; once they had locked away the Maxim guns in their armoury, it was the pen and telegraph that took over. The increasing dependence on written communication manifested itself not only internally, but also in communications with the subject peoples. These had to be trained to man the burgeoning bureaucracy and to extend this communication to the people themselves. In northern Ghana the first schools were established by the army and by an intrusive mission, the White Fathers from Upper Volta (now Burkina Faso). More informal instruction was arranged in the remote areas. The District Commissioner of Lawra established a 'Hausa' school for the sons of headmen, who were to act as messengers between district head-quarters and their father's villages. With the introduction of the system of Native Authorities in 1932, chiefs had their own clerks, with their own bureaucracies. And later still, pressure was exerted for chiefs themselves to be literate, so that they could participate in the full gamut of council activities, agenda, minutes, memoranda and returns.

Though it was an advantage for chiefs to be literate, for members of parliament, first elected in 1951, there was no alternative. Consequently it was the school teachers and the clerks who were the obvious candidates for these offices, which turned out to be of such high status in the community. Not only did they command a salary which was initially made comparable to that of a British MP (and hence vastly in excess of their previous earnings, or indeed of what they were likely to get if they were not re-elected), but there were abundant opportunities for doing favours and receiving rewards. By local standards, MPs did immensely well and by 1966 theirs was often the most substantial house in the locality, though some officials such as the District Commissioner and the Clerk to the Council were beginning to catch up.

All this mobility had been made possible by literacy, by edu-cation. Indeed the effects are so dominating that a two-sector economy, trained partly in school, partly in the home, however desirable from the economic standpoint in phasing in the new developments, in maintaining a balance in educational investment, in keeping going the production of food, becomes virtually impossible to accept as part of a deliberate national plan. As citizens, the non-literate population would be excluded from so much, at least on the political level. They cannot read, much less understand, the law; appearing in front of a magistrate or judge, they are offered a book or a 'fetish' on which to swear; acceptance of the latter identifies them as inferior, as illiterate, as 'pagan'. When they receive a letter from a son working elsewhere as a labourer they have to find, and probably reward, a literate to read it. If they want to reply, they may have to approach one of the letter-writers sitting outside the local post-office. When the newspapers arrive, they are again left out. Though in recent years the transistor radio has done something to lessen the divide, it can never bridge it altogether. When the tax-man comes, he can cheat them with the receipt. Even the new religions are written, the priests literate, propagating the knowledge of the Book which contains the secrets of life and death. They are at the mercy of a hostile world, geared to the man who can read and write. That is what development, modernization, independence, is all about.

Yet the world of the non-literate is not dead. His culture continues in a modified form and even finds some favour among the new elite. And there is evidence too of some counteraction. In northern Ghana there have been signs if not of a parents' strike, at least of increasing reluctance to send children to school. Despite the avenues that have been opened up for the successfully literate, the standards of education required for new posts are constantly rising as the output of secondary school, technical college and university increases. With a limited number of jobs available for those who do not go to secondary school, the less successful schoolboy finds himself having to scrape a living loading lorries or running messages. Meanwhile he himself is unwilling to return to the farm. Seeing this happen more and more, and seeing too the lack of help given by educated sons to their old or infirm parents, people in some areas are becoming increasingly reluctant to send their children to school; not only do schoolboys fail to contribute to their own livelihood, they fail to help later on, especially if they are unemployed. The consequence has been the closure of a number of rural schools.

How does the advent of literacy affect the quality of life at the village level? One general feature of writing dominates the process of its introduction into non-literate societies; its ability to preserve speech so that communication can take place over space and over time. It is a process of distancing, which affects the personal as well as the national level.

The way it does so can be seen from a community in northern Ghana. The village of Birifu had had a primary school for some twenty years when I returned there in 1971. Not one of its scholars has remained in the village; all left to get employment elsewhere. How did writing affect those that stayed? Clearly it introduced a radical division between those who 'knew book' and those who did not. The literate returned to the village occasionally, for funerals or for other celebrations, but he was not concerned with its day-to-day functioning. At Christmas there was a great exodus from the towns, and over the official holiday many literates returned to their natal villages, took part in settling some disputes and provoking others, and held meetings of 'The Young Men's Society' which only they were allowed to join. For this purpose, they elected a chairman, treasurer and secretary whose first duty was to keep a written record. In this way, decisions are formalized, made permanent and thus less easy to change.

Because the literates came and went like flocks of migrating birds, they made little direct impact on village life. Yet the presence of schoolboys was nevertheless making a mark. At each funeral, food, drink and money pass between the bereaved and their relatives in a complicated series of transactions. Each is reciprocal, in that it has to be acknowledged immediately and repaid eventually – at a corresponding occasion. The concern of people to keep track of these transfers of property shows itself in the fact that today one often sees schoolboys keeping a record of what has been handed over. Among labour migrants in a town in southern Ghana, one investigator often found himself called upon to write down the income and the outgoings at similar ceremonies. For the absence of writing places a restriction on the number of such items the average man can recall as well as the length of time he can retain the information. Many women who provide drinks or cooked food for salaried workers allow credit by the month. When payday comes at

Thanks For Sympathy

....19...........

We acknowledge with thanks, the receipt of your kind donation

of... New Cedis

....New Pesewas

From ....

To...

In the event of our failure to meet you tomorrow or the day after, we
beg you to accept our sincere thanks for your kind Donation & attendance.

N₵...................

                                    RECEIVER

Fig. 10. Thanks for sympathy. Forms sold in Kumasi, Ghana, to
acknowledge funeral gifts and visits.

the end of that period, they can be seen gathering round the workshop gates waiting for settlement. But the number of customers and hence their rate of profit is limited by their memory (Goody 1986a). Liberation from these restrictions on the efficiency of the memory store comes with pencil and paper. Even a very limited knowledge of writing can be of help to a cook making out a shopping list or a market mammy keeping a record of the credit offered. It is just this need for elementary accounting that marks the first use of writing in Babylonia, Egypt and early Greece (Linear B). This simple computation was a precursor of the flowering of book-keeping in the Italian Renaissance, and its development by the burghers of Western Europe, where painters like Rembrandt pictured the literate merchants poring over their account books.

In southern Ghana, the recording of funeral contributions has been even further formalized by an enterprising printer who has produced books of receipts in triplicate for just such an occasion. One fills in the form, tears out a sheet and dispatches the coloured piece of paper to the home of the donor by the hand of a small boy (Fig. 10).

The format requires a word of explanation. It is an acknowledgement by the bereaved of a monetary contribution to the expenses of a funeral. Thanks are not normally given at the time of the ceremony itself but on a subsequent visit to the giver which is known as 'greeting'. The sentence at the foot of the form (above the legitimating signature) is a prepackaged apology for the absence of a face-to-face encounter. It is a written substitute for oral contact, like the visitors' book of the former colonial commissioner which still stood, at least in the mid-seventies, in a sentry box outside the residency of the Chief Regional Officer in Tamale, the capital of the Northern Region of Ghana, or like the visiting card formerly left at the house of a newly-arrived neighbour.

We are witnessing here a process of distancing, of depersonalizing, social contacts. Indeed, in the spatially mobile situation in which they live, with not only the educated but also labourers travelling from less to more developed areas to sell their services, social relationships inevitably get dispersed widely over the ground and writing becomes the main means by which people can keep in touch. Nevertheless, when communication can be reduced to a few marks on a piece of paper rather than take place in the more concrete ambience of the face-to-face situation, the quality of interpersonal relationships is inevitably thinned; the multiplex relations of the village give way to single-stranded contacts that are more functionally specific, more manipulable, more 'impersonal' (Scribner and Cole 1981: chapter 12).

The change in the quality of life is inevitable; the rural community is no longer the centre of the world even for the majority of those who were born there, though it still retains an important place in the lives of all. The advent of literacy is perhaps the single most important factor in the changing situation, though in Birifu its visible influence on the village is limited, since virtually all literates migrate. Perhaps its most radical effect on those who remain behind is that they begin to see themselves as inferior to those who have learnt book and gone away. Whereas formerly it was the migrant who lost contact with the centre of his world, now he gains by going. Exile is a desirable end. And while literacy was valued in the past even among the non-literate peoples, writing was always an auxiliary mode of communication. More important was the visit, the audience, the discussion, the palaver, where one went into the presence of one's chief or one's peers. Even in the Muslim areas, writing was but one specialization among many. Now literacy dominates the wider social system; the non-literate of yesterday has become the illiterate of today.

Postscript

I wrote this comment on the influence of literacy and schooling in northern Ghana in the mid-70s. It is now the mid-80s. The situation has changed radically in a short space of time, partly because of a rapidly increasing population under conditions where decisive resources remain relatively fixed, indeed diminish because the terms of trade (especially the price of oil) have worsened. Human management must also be held responsible, for the attempt to control an exchange rate that cannot be controlled and therefore produces a black market completely dominating the white, eating at the basis of communal morality and national calculation. Because fixed salaries are unable to keep up with black market prices, many of the educated personnel have left the country for better conditions elsewhere. Those who remain have had to turn to farming, somewhat contrary to my earlier prediction. However in most cases they are the providers of capital and the source of decisions and supervision, leaving the unschooled or the partly schooled to do the agricultural work itself.

Under these conditions education has suffered badly. During the school year of 1983–4 Tamale Secondary School, the premier boarding establishment, could only keep open for about half the normal time as the money allocated for food was too little. Books and materials are in very short supply. Discipline is poor because of the government's earlier encouragement of Workers' Defence Committees in each school. The salaries of catetakers and university graduates are virtually the same. Many teachers have gone abroad and those who remain are often so concerned, at least in the towns, with getting their daily bread that they have little time for their job. Under these conditions it is the villagers who benefit. With few external demands, they can live off their land and sell their surplus at a price they regard as just. The rural life comes to be invested with greater value than before; paper will not fill the belly.

7

Alternative paths to knowledge in oral and literate cultures

We have seen that Islamic literacy had an important if restricted impact on West Africa. However the new literacy that came from Europe was more open in that Christian missionaries were no longer tied to the language of the Holy Book, neither the original Hebrew or Greek nor yet the later Latin. It has to be said that the study of the European classics lived on in the prestigious secondary schools established by the missions and later by the government, so that many bright students were encouraged to do advanced work in the field by their classically trained masters; it was not accidental that the first Department at the University of Ghana, Legon, to be africanized in its personnel was that very non-African Department of Classics. But missionaries worked in English or in the local vernacular, while the nature of European administration and commerce (which was also bureaucratically organized through large trading companies) entailed the use of written English in a way that had radical effects on the country. Local personnel had to be trained, communications established, a bureaucracy created; for this schools were encouraged – though with some reservations.

The implications of the introduction of the written register were great for society but so too for the members themselves. I have seen, I might almost say lived through, the experience of individuals in a small society in northern Ghana, that of the LoDagaa, who have acquired writing over the last forty years and I have watched the internal differentiation that emerged with the establishment of schools. What I want to consider in this chapter is the different paths to knowledge that this has created in contrast to those in oral cultures. While I shall touch briefly on its other forms, my main emphasis will be on knowledge acquired through the use

148

of language. This approach is adopted not only for simplicity's sake but because the LoDagaa themselves make this connection.

Traditional knowledge among the LoDagaa

For the LoDagaa, traditional knowledge (*tenkouri yil*) is speech (*yili*), because all knowledge in this sense is acquired not necessarily by means of speech (much ritual, much dance, is acquired by action, imitative action), but with the accompaniment or intervention of speech. So that the term *yil* has a much wider semantic field than simply the flow of words; it can mean practically any 'matter', almost a human action (a 'social act').

On the other hand it is unlikely that certain forms of knowledge would be classified by the LoDagaa as *tenkouri yil*. Though it is the basic medium for acquiring knowledge, language would not be so described, though the meanings of particular words, 'deep' ones, 'secret' ones, might be, for example, some special words that are used in the Bagre, an 'association' that has restricted entry as well as an elaborate myth. In the version of this myth I call the First Bagre, language is the one cultural instrument the beings of the wild, those intermediaries between men and gods, the 'fairies' or 'dwarfs' of West African English, did not teach mankind; it is assumed to be part of his natural make-up (Goody 1972). Again, farming would not usually be so described, yet the myth tells us this was taught to man by beings of the wild, and it is more clearly an activity in which an element of instruction is explicit; there is an obvious handing down, whereas with speech, as with motor development, there appears to be simply an unfolding. *Tenkouri yil* is then an explicitly mediated knowledge, although not a category in which the LoDagaa (if I may be so bold as to speak on their behalf on such a topic) would normally include the practice of farming or that of cooking.

Tenkouri yil may be literally translated as 'the speech (or matter) of the old country', 'the matter of old times', more idiomatically 'traditional knowledge'. Continuity is emphasized, for such knowledge is acquired from one's elders, and in general the older a man is, the more knowledge he is assumed to have – indeed the more knowledge he *does* have, since he remembers incidents, practices and people of earlier times. In an oral society, one can neglect the words of the elders only to one's detriment, not simply because of a general idea of respect but also because those words constitute the major source of information. The only way of finding out about the past, about interpretations of the world, is from them. Clearly, there are other ways of knowing, of knowing that someone has just died because one has heard a certain phrase on the xylophone, that it is time to plant the maize because of the appearance of some insect. This is basic primary knowledge, knowledge though experience, that makes the wheels of society turn. But an interpretation of, a gloss on, this primary knowledge is often provided by the elders in the form of a history or genealogy (a 'historical explanation'), or by placing a particular incident in a wider frame ('generalization').

The idea of *tenkouri yil* is related to that of *tenkouri sor*, 'le chemin des origines' or 'way of the past' as Erbs (1975) translates it. This is both a concrete and a metaphorical expression. The road exists. It is the path leading to the 'old country', the place from which the particular clan section has come in the past, the route of migration. The path is recognized not only in speech but in sacrifice too, and it is there that one sacrifices, for example during the recitation of the Bagre, on the side of the path leading to the 'old country'. But path also means 'way' in the metaphorical sense. In the First Bagre, man is led astray by the beings of the wild, and loses the path to God (1972:275). In the Lawra Bagre, a version which includes a long recitation on the migration of the section of a particular clan (the Kusiele), not only is there a description of the path, indeed of the whole movement, but this account is associated with the story of how the clan section rediscovered the ceremony of the Bagre which they had lost. In other words, they rediscovered the 'path' (ways) of the ancestors in the course of their movements along the path their ancestors had followed.

I believe the LoDagaa would regard 'traditional knowledge' as most critically imparted in ceremonies (rituals if you like), and possibly most critically of all in the course of the Bagre when the neophytes are shut in for many hours in the long-room of the house where it is being performed while their elders (the 'Bagre elders') recite to them the long 'myth' which is partly about the ceremony itself and partly about the origin of culture and the problems of mankind. My own contrary view is that little is imparted on these occasions that is not already known to the neophytes, having been acquired, less formally, in the give and take of ordinary life. Much of the myth is concerned with the detailed description of well-known technical processes, and this whole account is repeated many times during the course of the series of ceremonies. In addition, there is also a special recitation, the Funeral Bagre, where little or nothing is imparted on a cognitive level other than a general statement of the joys and dangers of life and death (Goody and Gandah, 1981). This is the most secret of all the performances. When I at last heard it, I was told, "Now you know all". In fact I knew little more than when we started. What I had been revealed was a 'secret' – heavily loaded with emotion, as are many funeral chants – but almost nonsense from the semantic point of view. An alleluya, an helas, an amen.

One aspect of this knowledge is a certain similarity, in the setting of its transfer, to the way that written knowledge, and knowledge of writing, is transferred in that central institution of literate culture, the school itself. The neophytes are separated from society by being enclosed within the walls of the long-room, where they are kept cooped up for several hours at a time. Some of the participants in the ceremony, the Bagre elders, take on quasi-kinship roles; there are the Bagre fathers and the Bagre mothers, who, as is made explicit in the recitation, take over the roles of the domestic father and mother. Seniority of entry supersedes genealogical status. Note that the use of kinship terms was characteristic of early Sumerian schools, where the monitor was known as 'big brother', conjuring up an Orwellian vision of the past.

Not only was there separation and enclosure, and the substitution of metaphoric-kinship for kinship authority, but there was also repetition, by the Speaker as well as by the neophytes, who repeated his every phrase. Again the LoDagaa often think of this repetition as making for 'perfect' reproduction. In fact there is a good deal of creation, judging by the variants, large and small; as we see in chapter 8, there is little evidence of exact copying, of verbatim reproduction.

But there is one important source of knowledge which supplements that coming from the elders (*tenkouri yil*) and that coming from our own immediate experience (what I have called 'primary knowledge' but which one could perhaps call 'information' rather than 'knowledge', though the former is interpreted in terms of and transformed into the latter). I refer to the knowledge that comes from beyond the human universe, directly from spiritual agencies, and especially from the beings of the wild (*kontome*), a type of spirit or genius (in the Roman sense of that word) that mediates between God and man.

In appearance, in some of their actions, the beings of the wild are not unlike the dwarfs, fairies, trolls of the European tradition, who were no doubt to be taken more seriously before they were pushed aside by God as the consequence of the dominant position He played in Christianity, just as *djinn* may have been demoted to folklore in parts of the Islamic world. Among the LoDagaa, these beings have to be taken very seriously indeed, because they constitute an important source of cultural (not simply magical) knowledge, in the past and in the present, and hence a channel by which culture may extend itself beyond 'traditional knowledge'.

In the First Black Bagre it is the beings of the wild who show man how to cultivate, how to make iron – who show him everything except how to speak and how to create (or procreate). The creation of the first child takes place in front of God; it is creation rather than procreation, for later on procreation (as distinct from creation) is separately shown to woman, who then shows man, being revealed by animals, by snakes, by the natural, rather than by the supernatural. Apart from accounting for, in the sense of being responsible for, a great deal of traditional knowledge, the beings of the wild have another part to play, for they continue their revelatory role into the present. Their revelations are partly direct, showing man the secrets of the natural world (such as the virtues of plants and the powers of the roots of trees) just as they had originally shown him the major features of his cultural order – at least at the technological level. They reveal this knowledge not in an institutional way, but by direct communication to individuals. It is also they who reveal to diviners what offering their clients should take to what agency. Typically a client consults a diviner after a bad dream, but he also does so when illness or misfortune strikes. The diviner himself holds in his left hand a small version of a sleeping mat as he calls upon the beings of the wild, shaking his bell and his rattle to put himself in touch. Revelation is associated with sleep, trance possession itself playing little or no part in the life of the LoDagaa, although I have come across a case where an epileptic was thought to have been taken over by the beings of the wild. Indeed any form of 'madness' is linked with these spirits and is seen perhaps as a form of unsuccessful communication.

More successful communication is established by those humans who acquire knowledge, about new shrines for example, by journeying to the places of the wild, the hills, the river banks, the woods themselves. These are the dwelling places of the beings of the wild, whose livestock are the animals they hunt. They are the complement to man, the revealers of knowledge, frequently to the more deviant members of the community (if I can use that term for my acquaintances: for Zuko who drank no beer and for Bechaara, who spent much time at the river's edge, moved his house nearby, and was eventually drowned there trying to rescue Nimidem, the Master of the Earth.) For there is in fact no direct communication with God, the Creator God. One cannot speak to Him, that is, pray to Him. "The pot doesn't know the woman who made it. The field of millet doesn't know the sower. The cloth forgets its weaver" (Erbs 1975:9).

Among the LoDagaa, then, as among other African peoples, there are two recognized paths to knowledge, apart from that by which 'information' is acquired, which is practical life itself. One path leads to the relatively codified knowledge passed down by elders, the other to the more individual, creative knowledge derived from other powers, whose acquisition is linked with dissociation, with madness and with inspiration (or possession). At this stage, the terms of the analysis may appear to bear a resemblance to Victor Turner's 'structure' and 'anti-structure' (or *communitas*') (1966); if so, it is simply because the poles of his dichotomy are all inclusive, while my inquiry is more specific, at least from the standpoint of content. We can extend the geographic range of our observations by briefly pointing to the widespread distribution of these two paths of knowledge, and particularly to the important role of the beings of the wild, among other West African cultures.

Among the Asante certain new medicines are revealed to man by those brave enough to immerse themselves in the woods, whose secrets are disclosed by the *mmoatia*, beings described in a very similar way to those of the LoDagaa and equated by Muslims with the *djinn* (the Gonja *alejina*) of the Middle East where they are mainly founts of magical knowledge and power for mankind. Knowledge, therefore, can be acquired in various ways, but there is also some recognition of a growth, or at least change, of that corpus.

As we noted in the first chapter, interesting institutional forms of these different ways of acquiring knowledge are found among the Ojibway of North America, where two kinds of 'shamanism' emerge, shamans being essentially the recognized transmitters of special knowledge. First, associated with the Midéwewin association for 'medicine' or 'curing', there is a type of what has been called 'tutorial shamanism', which used a graphic system (a system of so-called pictographs on birch-bark scrolls) as mnemonics, or rather as 'prompts', for accounts of tribal migrations, of the other world, and so on. At the same time, knowledge of the same general kind could also be acquired directly in the course of the widespread vision quests of the North American Indians; the 'visionary' shamanism, possibly of earlier origin, supplements the tutorial shamanism which depended upon an individual becoming a pupil of a senior member of the society and handing over a large amount of wealth in exchange for instruction by means of the scrolls. Indeed in the 1930s, when the Depression made initiation too costly (James Red Sky Senior reckoned he paid $10,000), there was a return to the cheaper and more direct visionary forms; as in southern Nigeria and Melanesia, a sequence of initiatory rites, involving high contributions by the prospective members, was associated with an acephalous but nonetheless wealthy society. The relative emphasis on tutorial or visionary shamanism responded in some measure to variations in the amount of wealth circulating in the society.

The general situation in 'traditional' societies bears some resemblance to the present position of the indigenous priesthood among the Agni (or Aowin) to the west of Asante, described by Ebin (1978). On the one hand there are the priestesses of the state cult who proceed through consultation and sacrifice. On the other we have a more marginal set of priestesses who are transported into trance-like states and who reveal the words of those by whom they are possessed. Both of these roles were formerly performed by men, but given the increasingly peripheral nature of the local cults, men have moved into the arena of medicinal cures where local practices happily mix with imported drugs. It is an area at once more profitable and more adapted to the new social order. As in many African countries, it is possible to become a registered practitioner of traditional medicine, a possibility not open to the priestesses who suffer competition from churches, old and new.

The growth of knowledge

I have spoken of the growth of knowledge by the search, the quest, the journey, the sojourn in the woods, all common themes of oral recitation. I am concerned to stress that oral cultures are not simply incessant reduplications of the same thing, the model of perfect reproduction, a pre-literate photo-copier. There is some change in knowledge, sometimes perceived as growth by the actors.

From one standpoint the growth of knowledge is clearly limited. Changes come slowly, certainly in the technological field. Indeed that is one of the major characteristics of pre-modern societies. But there are other areas in which the changes in knowledge, knowledge about the world, come much more rapidly. I refer principally to ideas about the world that we, from our post-modern standpoint, call supernatural beliefs. The evidence of such changes in ideas and cults is of two kinds. First, the pantheon is often in considerable flux, not fixed or unalterable as we wrongly imagine the Greek schema to have been because of the way it has been set down and arranged in writing. Of course among the LoDagaa, as elsewhere, there are fixed points, Heaven and Earth, the ancestors and the beings of the wild. But there is also a whole set of deities, gods, shrines, call them what you will, who change in emphasis and in actuality. I have argued that this change is related to the kind of internal contradiction that is generated by much human thought about the universe, whether utopian in a secular sense or millenarian in a religious one. It is the problem of the God who failed, the problem of evil, and on the more specific level of cures, the built-in obsolescence of patent medicines, from whatever source they come. Disappointment generates the search for new shrines, new curing agencies (possibly in an attempt to resolve cognitive dissonance) and these new forms are never simply repetitions of the last. A new cult may, for example, introduce a new prohibition (or taboo) on some food or action, which (if we may refer to the structural analyses of oppositions and analogies) will modify to some degree the classificatory schema of the society, forbidding what was otherwise allowed.

The second type of evidence comes from the Bagre recitation. If one looks at the recordings from different villages, different times and even the same reciter on different occasions, it is clear that important variations are arising, variations that elaborate or slim down certain aspects of cultural potential, the ideo-logic, to use Augé's expression. Once again, though this can be seen as a transformation of similar patterns, it is more than a simple transformation, more than bringing a potential into being. A creative act is involved. Something new is born, an idea which may well conflict with other ideas, though I would not claim (for reasons that will become apparent) that there is the same clash, the same contention of ideas, in non-literate societies that some have seen as the critical factor in the growth of knowledge in our own, or in Greece. In oral societies such contradictions are more easily swallowed up, as I have elsewhere argued is the case with scepticism. They are not absent, certainly, but neither are they explicitly transmitted.

Three modes of acquiring knowledge

There are then, grossly, three modes of acquiring knowledge among the LoDagaa, and these seem widespread in oral societies. There is the basic knowledge that men and women require to carry on their daily round. Although this knowledge is 'traditional' in one sense, and some of it enters into the Bagre recitation, basically it is acquired in interaction, largely within the house and peer group, by participation in the events themselves, by experience. It is in this way that the bulk of LoDagaa culture, the sum total of learned behaviour, of communal knowledge, is acquired.

Secondly, there is the rather specialized form of knowledge, *tenkouri yil*, which anglophone West Africans often designate by the word 'deep', and which is transmitted in the bounded situation of the Bagre (at least so the LoDagaa often think) as well as in the course of other ceremonies such as funerals, the Night Cow (with the bull-roarer), the Cleansing Ceremony (where the houses are painted white), and so forth. But it comes largely from participation in ceremonies and in discussions with elders. It has to be said that some of this knowledge, certainly about the problems of man's relationship with God and with death, is a knowledge that one has been deceived, a verbal parallel to the revelation that it was not a mysterious monster (the Night Cow) making that bizarre noise, but the bull-roarer, a piece of wood with a hole in the end.

Thirdly, there is the knowledge that is not mediated by humans, either informally or formally, but comes direct from powers, spiritual forces, agencies (I do not know what other expressions to use), who alone seem to have the ability to reveal to man the secrets of his universe. It is in a way extraordinary that man should allocate to the beings of the wild and other agencies all the responsibility, both the glory and the blame, for having introduced into his world not only himself but virtually the whole of his cultural apparatus, old and new. We are a far cry from the "Man Makes Himself" of the historian and pre-historian. Durkheim would see in this dependence, man's dependence on society, which is the kind of truism, at the verbal level, on which the social sciences flourish. Going beyond the mystification of the obvious, the problem is why the recognition of the omnipresent social factor should take this particular form. But this is not the place for a more detailed enquiry into the sociology of fairies, nor into that of cosmological structures. It is sufficient to insist upon the external nature of sources of knowledge, even about oneself.

Literacy

Among the Ancient Greeks, and it is time we turned back to literate societies, there was an analogous division, at least as far as the transmission of a certain type of knowledge was concerned. I refer to the distinction between those who recited Homer or other works (the *rhapsodes*), and those who were 'inspired' in the literal sense, received the breath, the anima of another, and created new knowledge (the *aoidoi*). However a new dimension has emerged. In the spheres of music and in literature the distinction between artist–creator and artist–performer is largely a function of the introduction of writing. It is then that exact repetition, associated with the reproduction not so much of the anonymous, but of the named, personalized contribution to culture, is differentiated from the act of creating, often still conceived, at least in the fields covered by the Muses, as inspired from outside, the signed, attributed work of these creators of culture that weighs down our bookshelves and fills our gramophone cabinets. Creative activity in the field of the arts still continues to come from outside, whereas other forms of knowledge get transmitted, modified and increased in the context of the school, of book-learning.

Creative knowledge gets written down in books, just as in pre-literate cultures it can get incorporated into oral 'tradition'. But books themselves are a double-edged weapon. First they serve as stores of knowledge, to be copied exactly (physically so in the days before printing), as in the splendid calligraphy of the Qu'ran or the exquisite workmanship of the medieval Books of the Hours. Later on they are copied mentally as text-books. The whole process of literate education becomes a matter of absorbing abstracted knowledge through mediators, either directly from books or indirectly from teachers; it is as if the initiation of Bagre were prolonged so that it took over virtually the whole instead of only a fraction of the life of each new entrant into the culture, teaching him about the world in which he lives by a series of verbatim exercises as a prelude to action and possibily as a prelude to making a creative contribution to knowledge. Knowledge here has been separated off from 'artistic' activity, which continues to be associated more with inspiration, with dissociation, with direct communion with the forces of nature, than with the bookish learning of the schoolroom.

As an example of what now happens as far as the wider acquisition of knowledge is concerned, let me turn to the curriculum of the temple school near the Step Pyramid of the ancient Memphis, dating from the sixth century BC. From the crumpled fragments of papyri in rubbish dumps surrounding the temple buildings, it is possible to reconstruct the learning process:

The poor apprentices began with small demotic groups, and graduated to the chore of paradigms such as the "I said to him; he said to me" type. The next stage was perhaps month-names, or artifical sentences. One scribe informs us dutifully that dogs bark and cats miaw, and it must be admitted that there is a "postillion struck by lightning" note to many of his model sentences. Lists of names may be dull, until we recognize that they are arranged according to something very like an alphabetic scheme; the height of this is reached with a remarkable text in which alphabetic birds perch on alphabetical bushes before heading for suitable destinations. It is as if we recited "the crow perched on the chrysanthemum and flew away to Croydon". The scheme is certainly strange: it begins with the letter "h" but Plutarch tells us that the first letter of the Egyptian alphabet was an ibis. The Egyptian word for this began with "h" and the ibis was the bird of learning; and Plutarch was a watchful man (*Quaestiones conviviales* 9, 3.2). Once released from such tasks the scribe was free to copy literary texts. (Ray 1978:155)

Now what is happening here is that in the first instance a great deal of textual material was learnt 'by heart', that curious expression which means verbatim, word for word, and which is very difficult to accomplish, without a written text, a written text that is in itself a formalization of speech,

the crow perched on the chrysanthemum ... amo, amas, amat ...

Essentially one is not ingesting or conveying any information about the world outside or the world within; one is 'learning to learn', acquiring the techniques of the written word, of written composition, which are so different from speech. One is learning to order words differently and for different ends.

And after all this has been achieved, the scribe "was free to copy ... texts". Note the use of 'free' in juxtaposition to 'copy'. One was freed from one automatic task so that one could accomplish another, copying, so essential to written culture before the advent of printing and of its present rival, the photo-copier, one of the great academic money-spinners of all time.

The modes of acquiring knowledge affect the nature of that knowledge and the way in which knowledge is organized. In Scotland, with the fall of the Dalriadic Kingdom in the eleventh century, Norman feudalism played a centralizing and unifying role, partly politically (the organization of sheriffdoms), partly economically (the organization of royal boroughs), but also through the reform of the church, the institution of bishoprics, the plantation of abbeys, the introduction of European 'rule'. "For the first time there was an organized body of literate intellectuals in the country, men of one common purpose to whom the location of their dwelling place . . . was almost irrelevant" (Smout 1969:26).

Contrast, perhaps too starkly, the acquisition of sacred knowledge in the earlier period. One old Norse story, represented on stones in Manx and Iona, relates how Sigurd killed a huge dragon, and toasted its heart over a fire. In doing this he touched the hot dragon's heart, and, burning his finger, put it in his mouth, with the result that he immediately became possessed of "all the knowledge of the two worlds" (MacLeod 1930:7).

With the rise of "an organized body of intellectuals", we also get its complement, the differentiation of ideas into ideologies, the fragmentation of the world view, the conflict of ideas.

What is the relation of knowledge to ideology? A widely accepted definition of knowledge is "justified true belief" (Quinton 1967: iv, 345), a definition which presents problems not only for philosophy but for comparison as well. An ideology, according to Gellner (1978:69), is a system of ideas or beliefs, not any system but one that attracts and repels (and hence must surely be 'partial'). From these partial systems, ideologies, Gellner distinguishes the social construction of reality, the inclusive "central belief system of a society", the "total vision of reality". For this reason, he concludes, it is "pointless to include pre-literate, tribal religions within the class of ideologies" (p. 81). "Ideology involves doctrine; ideological conflict arises when doctrines, not men and shrines, are in opposition" (p. 82).

Once again it would be patently untrue to claim that there was *no* conflict of doctrines in the pre-literate societies to which Gellner refers, *no* differentiation, *no* fragmentation. But the sharpness of the challenge, which is intrinsic to his discussion, does seem to be (like the sharpness of the conflict of ideas in the growth of knowledge) a function of the use of writing.

I want to comment on some aspects of this change that affect the accumulation, transmission, sources and nature of knowledge. The first has to do with the change in God–man, and hence man–God communication. The world of Islam is very definite about the nature of God to man communication. Chapter 96, vv.3 – 5 of the Qu'ran (the organization is highly literate) runs "Read: for your Lord is the Most Generous One, who taught by the pen, taught man what he did not know".

In oral societies, too, God, or some other category of spiritual being, teaches man what he did not know. For originally he was simply a poor bare forked animal who knew nothing. But when writing appears, God shows the way by means of the book or tablet, the tablets that were shown to Moses, the golden ones revealed to John Smith and other Mormons, and the books which were written under the instruction of God and which then became holy to man. Ever since man himself became literate he has assumed, as Chadwick said of Crete, that the gods were literate too. Hence the stuffing of written words into the cracks in the Temple Wall at Jerusalem, the recourse to written talismen in Ancient Egypt and in contemporary Israel, as well as our own letters to Father Christmas.

Once writing was introduced the voice of God was supplemented by His hand; scriptural authority is the authority of the written (scripted) word, not the oral one. Written religion implies stratification. The written word belongs to the priest, the learned man, and is enshrined in ritualistic religion; the oral is the sphere of the prophet, of ecstatic religion, of messianic cults, of innovation. For it is one of the contradictions of the written word that at one level it restricts and at another encourages innovatory action. The two different paths to knowledge we noted in oral societies become increasingly separate; the conflict between priest and prophet, between church and sect, is the counterpart of the fixed text and the fluid utterance.

Two paths to knowledge as social control

The opposition between 'learned' i.e. booklearned, and 'unlearned' i.e. unschooled, is not only a matter of individual roles; it divides the whole society and the whole culture. For most of the history of civilization, by which I mean no more than the history of towns with writing (in one meaningful sense, there cannot be a 'history' of any other towns), people who were taught by literate methods i.e. in schools that removed individuals from the primary productive processes, formed only a limited percentage of the population. Not that the rest of society was uninfluenced by the presence of this additional means of communication. Far from it, for apart from all else, it encouraged (in places introduced) a radical differentiation within culture, a differentiation between the 'high' culture of the consumers of books and the 'low' culture of those confined to the oral register; between the audience of Chaucer and that of a singer of ballads. The 'two cultures' (to borrow a phrase from the waspish controversy between Snow and Leavis) interacted, and each clearly contributed to the other, but they were also distinct, and defined themselves in opposition to one another. What was high was what was not low: the low set aside the high, at least in the form in which it was offered. The non-literates could of course have the works of Bunyan or the books of the Bible read out to them. They could watch the plays of Shakespeare and listen to the sagas of Icelandic bards. But they had to do so through intermediaries and in this area of culture they were essentially a category of receivers rather than transmitters, let alone creators.

Of course at one level this statement applies with similar force even in societies where literacy is quasi-universal, that is to say, in certain industrial societies of the last 100 years. The difference is that in the earlier situation, the non-literate were unable to contribute to written culture (they were unable by definition to do so) or to communicate (e.g. by letter) as other men did. They were unable to operate one of the major channels of communication, and hence were in that sense 'deprived', though it was perhaps a deprivation that did not make itself really felt until the advent of printing vastly increased the availability of books and reading matter (e.g. the printed almanack).

The differentiation into high (derived from the written) and low (primarily oral) was not simply a division of the kind of cultural activity, it was also a matter of the division of labour. Some jobs (the scribal, bureaucratic, academic jobs) needed literacy; for many productive jobs, especially in the rural areas, it was far from essential. The kinds of knowledge involved in the first set of activities was increasingly valued more highly than the 'practical' knowledge, knowledge by experience, the knowledge of the bricoleur, as well as of the craftsman, which was acquired by some form of participation, apprenticeship, family labour, servanthood. But with compulsory schooling there is an increasing tendency at the popular urban level to see proper knowledge as coming from books alone; it is they that tell the truth, not the knowledge we obtain from our parents (i.e. the elders) or from our peers, nor yet directly from nature itself. If I may take refuge in personal experience in default of a more systematic enquiry, in the house where I grew up there was an encyclopaedia called *The Book of Knowledge*, especially for children wanting to know (or more exactly, for children needing to answer questions set by the school and for parents to answer those posed by their children). Knowledge was in a book, or in the head of a bookish person like the teacher (who, though we did not then know, had consulted the book the night before) rather than in the head of mere parents, whose role in 'education', in 'upbringing', did not involve the passing down of anything except fringe subjects, often practical knowledge about cooking and cleaning, cycle repairs and electrical failures

I have now seen the other side of this process, my children learning botany from a book and getting to know the flora without knowing the trees and flowers, though admittedly some urban environments take pains to keep nature as far away as possible – flowers are patterns on plates, designs on material, even bunches of blooms collected in a vase.

It is clear that most of our knowledge does not come to us directly from the outside world. It is mediated by books, magazines and newspapers. The study of botany is carried out by means of textbooks that explain verbally and diagram visually the structure of a flower. In biology the dissection of the dog-fish follows months, perhaps years of learning about the respiration of fishes. The source of knowledge, for both pupil and teacher, is the book, the text-book, whose contents are memorized the night before the lesson, the weeks before the exam. An 'authority' may even be a book, or someone who has read it studiously and can explain its message to others; it is not even necessary for him to make his own contribution to knowledge. He is the recognized mediator.

When the bulk of knowledge, true knowledge, is defined as coming from an outside, impersonal source (a book) and acquired largely in the context of some outside, bounded institution such as the school, there is certain to be a difference in intra-familial roles, relations with the elders, compared to societies where the bulk of knowledge is passed down orally, in face-to-face contact, between members of the same household, kin-group or village. There the elders are the embodiment of wisdom; they have the largest memory stores and their own experiences reach back to the most distant points in time. With book cultures, particularly with mass cultures of the printed word, the elders are by-passed; they are those who have not 'kept up', attached to the old way rather than the new.

Mass literate cultures are the product, even in the most developed of nations, of the last 100 years, with a few minor exceptions. This was the time when determined efforts were made to spread school education throughout the population. The result is to spread the devaluation, including the self-devaluation, of knowledge and tasks that are not gained through the book but by experience. It is not my intention to take this analysis into the realm of socio–political action, although the implications are obvious and the possible solutions limited in number and utopian in character. But intrinsic to any effort to change the situation is a revaluation of forms of knowledge that are not derived from books. Not a return to 'savagery', but a modification of one's concessions to the civilization of the book.

Conclusions

Some of the most significant differences between the societies I have studied in Africa and those I have experienced in Europe relate to the changes (and I put the matter quite deliberately in a developmental framework) that have occurred, and are occurring, in the means, modes, and accumulated results of communication. But the nature of these shifts is far from simple, far from unidirectional, as we can see from the stress placed on different pathways of knowledge.

Oral societies such as the LoDagaa conceive of knowledge as of different kinds. *Tenkouri yil*, traditional knowledge, is explicitly associated with ceremonial contests but it is in fact mainly transmitted in more general ways, in the same contexts of social life in which 'practical' knowledge is passed along. There is no specific way of designating this latter knowledge, except that it is usually excluded from the category of 'traditional'. Both are set aside from the kind of knowledge acquired by direct contact with spiritual agencies, and specifically with the beings of the wild, a form of knowing that allows for innovation in apparently static cultures. Innovation is authorized by outside agencies.

In literate societies, we still emphasize inspirational access in the arts and in one segment of religion but we no longer deem this 'knowledge' in the usual sense, even though the imperialism of the school tries to transfer its training to the classroom from the workshop or the family. Of course, book-learning has its inspirational figures, its gurus, but it is their teaching rather than their 'knowledge' which displays this quality. The paths to knowledge in the more restricted sense become more sharply differentiated into the bookish mode and the practical one of empirical action, largely acquired by oral discourse, even though in many cases an outcome of bookish activities. Indeed 'knowledge' and 'science' have become almost synonymous with book-learning, to be distinguished from most productive activities which are largely learned by apprenticeship, by imitation, by participation. With the establishment of schools among the LoDagaa, as throughout the world, it is this second dichotomy that is imposing itself upon the first, a dichotomy that is value-laden (the high and the low), not only on the general level of the assumed quality of 'knowledge', but also in relation to the nature of the jobs to which such training leads. Schoolteaching is high, farming is low (although as I note earlier there are reversals under certain conditions). Massive world-wide emphasis on literate education, the largest part of the budget of most developing countries, has certain clear concomitants, leading to a devaluation of non-literate, even food-getting, skills, of learning by experience, as well as of occupations essential to society (though these were sometimes already devalued). In Africa the result is the emergence of what, in another context, Djilas (1957) called the New Class, the class of literate bureaucrats, politicians, school-teachers, and so forth, with the non-literates filling the lower positions. In Europe, facing the problems arising from universal scholarization, the valued jobs become scarce, the devalued ones unwanted. So that *gäst-arbeiter*, Turks in Germany, Algerians and Portuguese in France, Indians and West Indians in Britain, are imported to do the jobs the indigenes have been educated to regard as unworthy. Having imported them, society then attempts to train them for higher, scribal jobs. The reduction of structural unemployment must depend in part upon a revaluation of our paths of knowledge, our ways of knowing as well as the content of that knowledge. I do not suggest that a consideration of the LoDagaa or other oral societies provides the answers. But it does at least bring the problems to the surface.

Memory and learning in oral and literate cultures: the reproduction of the Bagre

In the last chapter I considered types of knowledge in oral cultures contrasting this with literate forms. Here I want to examine the processes of learning themselves. I have referred in earlier chapters to my work on the recitation of the Bagre, recorded among the LoDagaa of northern Ghana. I begin by commenting upon this in greater depth, then go on to consider some aspects of the learning process in oral and literate cultures and finally try to link this discussion with ideas about memory and schooling, picking up the themes of the last two chapters. The study of the 'myth' of pre-literate societies is a seemingly arcane subject, having little apparently to do with wider intellectual problems, or even those more vital questions that concern educationalists, psychologists or sociologists. Here I try to indicate its relevance for such interests, pursuing a line rather different from the dominant anthropological trends in the study of myth. Since the discussion focusses upon the process of reproduction, it is concerned more with the structures of recall utilized by the participants than with the 'deep structures' posited by observers. It is an approach more related to praxis, but not for that reason less productive of fruitful theory; for the argument is closely linked to discussions of oral transmission by Parry and Lord, to analyses of early literate cultures of the Near East by Kramer, Gardiner, Oppenheim and others, as well as to the results of psychological work of a more than monocultural kind.

Memory and the Bagre

In writing of the first version of the Bagre I recorded, I made the following comments on the way in which it was learned:

167

The memorizing of these myths is enjoined upon the new initiates and rewards are offered to those who succeed in this task. Apart from the prestige that accrues to him, a Speaker is given special allocations of food, beer, and money. The neophytes are encouraged, when they become members, to go and watch other Bagre performances, outside their own lineages and settlements, so they may get to know how to recite (The White Bagre, 1.5209). Yet it is clear that more systematic methods are needed to learn a work of these dimensions, some 12,000 'lines' in all. Such instructions were in fact given, but essentially on a household basis. Benima told me how he had been the favourite of his grandfather, Napii, who had taught him the Bagre line by line. When the sons of the late chief of Birifu, Gandaa, returned home in the school holidays, the old man would call his younger 'brother' Yinkwo to assemble the boys in the rooftop hut and get them to repeat whole sections, line by line. Then he would test them, one by one, to see what they had learned. (1972:60)

Since then I have recorded other versions of the same perform-ance, which lead me to modify my view of the learning process. In a word, the differences between these versions are so great that if the Bagre were taught by the deliberate methods I suggested, they can only be described as a staggering failure. I do not doubt the information I was given about the learning of Bagre in the house-hold. But such instruction must have been very rare, as well as being very partial. The desire for a correct or 'true' version (*yil miona*) was certainly present, but I failed to make clear the latitude permitted under the term 'correct'. The reasons are several. First, given the speed and context of the recital, there is the difficulty of correcting anything perceived as 'wrong'. Secondly, there is the prior difficulty of perceiving and establishing anything 'wrong', even if correction were possible. Finally, there is the possibility that exact repetition is not given the same value as in many written cultures, where there is a necessary distinction between performer and composer (Finnegan 1970).

I have no knowledge of other instances of this kind of instruction apart from the two reports I quoted. Certainly the results of the comparison of the versions of Bagre suggest that verbatim learning, rote memory, learning by heart, plays little part in the reproduction of the myth. If no formal teaching takes place, how then does one learn? Mainly if not entirely within the context of the recital itself, as is indicated in the original published version:

If there's a small boy
among you
who has some sense,
and goes
to someone's Bagre
and sits,
it's not for food you go.
You will go
and sit
and look
and listen
how it is
they perform.
Bagre
is all one;
nevertheless
the way it's performed
is different.
If you hear people
reciting Bagre,
you'll adopt
their way
and one day,
when you recite
the Bagre,
you'll include this.
When you recite,
you include that in your Bagre.
You do so,
then greet
their elders
and their distant ancestors.
You will greet them,
greet their guardians,
greet their Earth shrines,
then recite Bagre.
If you leave
the Bagre room,
you will go
outside
and pray
to the Earth shrine
and then return.
You'll find
you're able
to speak (Goody 1972:186–7).

What happens in performance is that the Speaker recites, the audience listens and one or more individuals respond by repeating his words. However Speaker and respondents are not working from an original that both have learned; the chorus repeats exactly what the Speaker says, and they are in no position to question him. It is he that has the authority of the 'stool' on which he sits; his words *are* the Bagre. He recites rapidly and cannot be interrupted unless he himself calls upon someone else to take over. It is true that on the next occasion the recital takes place, another Speaker may choose to ignore some form of words, some order of incident, that his predecessor used. But since he does not explain that he thinks his predecessor was wrong, the audience now has (at least) two differing models in front of them. Indeed new models proliferate all the time.

It is not simply that there is an absence of sanctions against deviation from the original, but rather that the whole concept of an original is out of place. For even if people were trying to reproduce and correct a recital of this length and complexity, they would be unable to do so because they cannot set utterances side by side. It is quite different with texts where writing gives the work an external spatial dimension. A detailed comparison of successive verbal inputs of this length and rapidity is quite beyond the capability of the long-term memory of individuals in oral societies. Since there is no one authoritative speaker or authorized context (lodges exist in many settlements), versions proliferate.

There are several pieces of evidence that we may draw upon to strengthen these conclusions:
1 the variations in the myth, even of the most standardized part
2 the discussion of right and wrong versions when such an evaluation is deliberately 'elicited' in ways that I shall describe
3 the why and where of rote learning.

I have examined some aspects of the variations in the recorded versions of the Bagre myth (1951–2 and 1969–70) elsewhere (Goody and Duly 1981), though much remains to be done. Here I will only summarize the results, which are necessarily preliminary as further versions have since been collected (1974–5, 1976–7, 1978–9). The Bagre, as recited in Birifu, is divided into two parts, the White and the Black, the first being the equivalent of the 'ritual texts' of the Ancient Near East and elsewhere, the second being narrative and speculative in kind. While the actors call the recitation by the same name as the one they give to the association with which it is linked, that is, the Bagre, and while they see both the rite and recital, both the visual and verbal action, as being enduring elements of their culture, the Black Bagre varies very considerably with time, place and with speaker. Thus while in most contexts the actors speak of versions of the Bagre as being one and the same, in fact these differ very substantially. The White Bagre, being tied to ritual, to a set of standardized visual acts, varies less than the Black. Nevertheless the order in which the ceremonies are presented differs from recitation to recitation around this external norm and even the words of the formal invocation, which everybody knows 'by heart', vary significantly from speaker to speaker, without having any outside reference to act as a check and a correction.

The second type of evidence concerning the variations in the Bagre and the light they shed on the learning process comes from an examination of the way the myth is recalled and the nature of the prompts given when a pause occurs. My interest here is in structures of recall and how they stand with regard to the relational structures of the semantic structuralist. By the relational structures I refer to the outcome of an analysis, say, by Lévi-Strauss of South American myth (1964) or by Greimas of the novels of Bernanos (1966). By the structures of recall I mean the aspects of a myth or other complex standardized oral form (SOF) that an individual (or plurality of individuals) grasps when he reproduces this utterance. But having made these general statements of interest, we need to raise the more particular questions. What is the structure that emerges from a 'structuralist' analysis? Putting the matter at its simplest, the output is phrased in terms of the relation (usually binary) between categories. As examples, the reader may take Greimas' concluding formula in his analysis of Bernanos (1966) or he may take the 'triangle culinaire' by means of which Lévi-Strauss summarizes his perception of the semantics of cooking (1965).

How do we get at structures of recall? It would be possible to devise an experimental situation in which individuals were asked to reproduce a novel (or other genre) in a limited space–time and to

analyze in broad terms the elements they selected, whether narrative, characterological, thematic, relational, etc. My own material
derives from an unintended experiment brought about by the use of
a tape recorder. Normally the Bagre is told in an 'authoritative'
situation. The Speaker recites one line which is repeated by those
present and he normally continues until the Bagre is finished or
until he himself indicates that someone else should take over from
him. In other words he is not interrupted during the recital, and
there is no opportunity for others to point out that something has
been omitted or wrongly included. However, in one set of performances which were especially arranged for my collaborator,
S. W. D. K. Gandah, by his kith and kin, the recitation was stopped
at various points to allow us to change the tapes on one or other of
our two machines. When this happened, the participants often
discussed what should follow and their words were recorded on the
second machine that was still running.

What then is the framework within which people recall a long
recitation of the Bagre kind? Are they similar to our structures of
recall, either recall for reproduction or simply recall for comment,
when we hear a play on the radio or read a novel? What is chosen
for comment will depend to a large extent on pre-programming,
more so than recall for reproduction. In the latter case at least, we
can say with some certainty that the structures of recall do not
appear to resemble the structures of 'structural analysis'. The
framework of reproduction consists mainly of large-scale incidents
and events, such as ceremonies, accounts of activities or set-piece
narratives, punctuated by formulaic phrases that often enable the
Speaker to mark time while he sorts out what follows. For the White
Bagre, the framework is provided by the sequence of ceremonies,
for which the recitation is both cue and cued. Comparing the
different versions of the sections dealing with a particular ceremony
in the long sequence, we find both constants and variables. There is
variation if only because the ceremony is much more complex than
its 'description', which is a resumé rather than a mnemonic; what
is chosen to be included is not always the same. There are constants
in the shape of standard narrative elements embedded in the
account of the procedures. These narrative elements are three in
number. First, there is the story of the fruit bat who quarrels with

his mate about sex, goes off to find food and comes across a shea nut which he refuses to share. But he drops it on the ground where it is found by a farmer who realizes that the Bagre ceremonies must now begin, for the ripe fruit of the nut is forbidden to the neophytes. The nut itself is needed (verbally at least) to make the 'oil' (in fact, whitewash) that is used to mark the bodies of the new members. At a later stage, there is a similar narrative about a guinea cock and his mate that signals the start of the Ceremony of the Bean Flower. And there is a third story about a passing trader who comes to sell the salt needed for the main ceremony, the Bagre Dance.

When discussing the order of the recitation, or what has been omitted, the actors refer to large incidents of this kind, to the next ceremony or to sequences such as the building of a house. If these have been included, then the recitation is adequate, whatever else there is by way of unnoticed omission or unremarked addition. It appears, then, that the framework of recall lies neither at the surface level, by which I mean the level at which verbatim memory operates, nor yet at the level of 'deep structure' as discerned by many mythologists and literary critics. On the contrary, the important role seems to be taken by narrative and by other 'event structures'. I take narrative as being a special case of an event structure, namely reported or imagined events linked by common participation. Common sense would dictate that it is easier to retell stories than to give an account of a series of ceremonies, because the plot, the logic of the narrative, the thread of common participation, acts as its own prompt. The series of ceremonies is in turn easier to deal with than a series of taboos or philosophical speculations, since there is a chronological structure to hang on to. Nevertheless the structure of ceremonies does not have an overwhelmingly compelling logic, which is why mistakes are made and the performances are sometimes introduced in the wrong order during the course of the myth. This occurs when one is talking *about* rather than talking *within* ceremonies, which are therefore dissociated from all the cues of season, group confirmation, and so on, that operate when the sequence is acted as well as uttered.

Verbatim memory in oral cultures

My third point has to do with the role of memory, specifically verbatim memory, in cultures generally. It is not always easy to understand much of the discussion, observations and experiments on memory and recall in 'other cultures'. In all societies individuals clearly keep a great deal of information in genetic store, in long-term memory and, temporarily, in the working memory. In most non-literate cultures, and in many segments of our own, the accumulation of items in memory store is part of everyday activity. One learns to weave not by listening to a set of 'instructions' that are 'committed' to memory, but by watching and doing. While such activity is intentional in the sense of goal oriented, the intention is not to 'memorize'. There is no specific development of a rehearsal procedure of the type involved in repetition, copying, recital, which mean 'committing' things to memory. A young child, for example, learns sounds, words and syntax in order to communicate and in the process of communicating with others; at this level rehearsal procedures operate, but directly, in the context of communication.

Since the memory store is involved in all cultural activities, what do anthropologists and psychologists mean when they talk about societies or individuals displaying different capacities for recall or memory, having 'good' or 'bad' memories?[1] In common speech we know what we mean. If we are walking along a road and come across a plant with purple berries, I might ask, "Tell me, what's the name of that plant? I can't remember". To which you might reply, "It's deadly nightshade. What a bad memory you have. You've certainly seen it before". Such differences between individuals may be attributed to different abilities or alternatively to different interests. If it turned out that I live in the city while you are a country dweller, a gardener or a botanist, we will not bother to attribute the differences in recall to differences in ability but rather to differences in experience. You hear the word twenty times a year, myself one in ten. In addition, there is the factor of motivation. You need to steer your children away from a dangerous plant, while mine stand in greater danger from wheeled vehicles.

It is not this generalized type of memory to which anthropologists and psychologists usually refer. The first are impressed with the ability to reproduce long strings of names of the kind we find in the opening books of the Bible. "Now the sons of Jacob were twelve: The sons of Leah; Reuben, Jacob's firstborn, and Simeon, and Levi, and Judah, and Issachar, and Zebulon: The sons of Rachel; Joseph and Benjamin: And the sons of Bilhah, Rachel's handmaid; Dan and Naphthali: And the sons of Zilpah, Leah's handmaid; Gad and Asher" (*Gen.* 35:22–6). However among the Nuer, as origi- nally in the case of the Bible, the string of names is not merely a pedigree but a genealogy that represents existing social relations, that is, the disposition of the 'tribes' of Israel or the relations between segments and individuals (Evans-Pritchard 1940).[2] In other words these genealogies are not the result of precise instruc- tion and rote learning; since they fit closely with contemporary social relations, they are also acquired directly in the ordinary processes of communication and not by the deliberate exercise of memory skills. Or alternatively anthropologists are impressed with their ability to recite long poems or myths, but there is often very little evidence about the exactness of reproduction.

Psychologists on the other hand are generally concerned with situations that involve the deliberate learning of special tasks in a particular context, and with the repetition of this material back to the one who taught it. It was this second model that I originally thought relevant to the reproduction of the Bagre, a model based upon verbatim learning, the exact recall of deliberately transmitted information. I now think that such learning took place only to a negligible degree in the context of Bagre and that it is very rarely found in any sector of LoDagaa life. I refer particularly to conscious memory tasks, which are removed from specific operations such as telling someone the way to a particular village. These contexts are few, and fewer still if we concentrate on operations that are primarily auditory like the recitation of Bagre. Finding the way is largely a visual task, especially when one is dealing with territory that has been already explored; and one of the functions of visits to the maternal home or of the Australian 'walkabout' is precisely to establish an area of 'already explored' territory. So, too, giving directions is primarily a matter of recalling and specifying visual cues. Indeed, exact recall of auditory cues seem to be rare, for most occasions when such recall is required are in fact recollections of transactions where auditory cues are embedded in a 'total situation'; of such a kind for example is the activity of a witness to a set of marriage payments, or of a widow or widower who has to recount the debits and credits of the transactions that had been made with the dead partner. One of the few exceptions I know of occurs in the centralized state of Gonja in northern Ghana, where the divisions of a country are listed for ceremonial or other purposes, and even here there is a geographic basis for remembering. In all these situations, the recall required is of an extremely limited kind when compared with learning a long 'myth', and in any case aural cues would be stongly reinforced by cues of other kinds.

I do not wish for one moment to deny that in non-literate cultures some standardized oral forms are memorized in exact form. Clearly songs are committed to memory in just this way, as well as some longer pieces. On special occasions the *kuntunkure* drummer of Gonja recites a series of verses which encapsulate the past of the West African kingdom and are sometimes referred to in cases of dispute about chiefship; the preservation of earlier speech forms ('deep Gonja') gives them a sibylline character which makes the meaning difficult to unravel and capable of a variety of interpretations. An oracular pronouncement is difficult to dispute. The utterances themselves do appear to have a certain stability over time, no doubt helped by their rhythmic form and drum accompaniment. The verses of the Yoruba divinatory system known as Ifa are also memorized as part of the initiation into the profession of diviner, though they certainly vary from individual to individual (Bascom 1969). In Ruanda some court poetry is said to have been composed as early as the seventeenth century, and to have been handed down by dynastic poets (*umusîzi*) who were both composers and reciters. Organized into corporations, these poets were taught in 'schools', rewarded with beer and privileges, and encouraged to preserve their poems word by word (Coupez and Kamanzi 1970:159), the evidence for which consists of little more than the archaic character of the language used.

Evidence for exact repetition of longer pieces does exist, though its reliability is limited by the absence of 'texts' (transcribed utterances) gathered at different times. It may be significant that in each of these three cases mentioned above, we are dealing with specialist reciters who play important roles in centralized political systems; the same would be true of the historical recitations of the 'spokesman' among the Akan or the drum histories of the chiefly houses of the Mossi states. But by and large in the simpler societies exact repetition of standardized verbal forms, whether narrative or not, whether short or long, is rare.

One reason for this situation is the difficulty experienced in repeating information unless there is a fixed model, first to initiate the task, and secondly, to serve as a corrective. Of course, items of limited length, both teacher and pupil can retain in their short-term memory for long enough to repeat, check and store. This can be done more easily with 'memorable speech' (to use the phrase with which Auden described poetry) than with the more pedestrian 'prose' of everyday life. And in theory it can be done even with longer utterances like the Bagre if these are broken down into a series of smaller blocks. But this possibility begs the question of how the longer utterance was stored in the first place, whether in precise verbatim form or whether as a 'structure', a series of cues, which leaves much space for individual elaboration. And it also assumes a mode of learning by repetition which seems to be rarely employed in oral societies.

Most people find difficulties in verbatim recall from long term storage unless they adopt explicit rehearsal procedures. Learning by heart is a very deliberate process of repeating sequences several times until one has them correct. This can be done relatively easily by reading a text, turning away the eyes, repeating as much of the content as possible, then returning to the text to correct what was remembered and continuing from the corrected section.

Deliberate repetition is an attention-focussing device that attempts to exclude other inputs; hence the resort to closing our eyes and putting our fingers to our ears when we are trying to 'learn' something in this way. Simply hearing it several times, as a member of the association which listens to the Bagre myth, and repeating each phrase after the Speaker, is normally insufficient to store even limited sections in verbatim chunks. The same is true of ordinary reading, except perhaps for some exceptional individuals with 'photographic memories'.

If oral cultures place little emphasis upon repetitive learning, this is partly because of the difficulty of transmitting an exact copy and partly because such a mode of activity is rarely called for. Indeed the product of exact recall may be less useful, less valuable than the product of inexact remembering.

Let us set aside the 'objective' difficulties for a moment. George Miller has pointed to the value of recoding for increasing the amount of information we can deal with, over and above the magical number seven. The most customary kind of recoding is translation into another verbal form. "When there is a story or argument we want to remember, we usually try and rephrase it 'in our own words'" (Miller 1956:95). This was certainly what Bartlett discovered when he asked his subjects to reproduce more complex material, such as a story or an argument. Here he found that accuracy of report was the exception. His subjects appeared to reconstruct the material rather than remember it, a process that was particularly evident when they were asked to recollect after a long interval of time. What remained was "isolated but striking details" which fitted with the subject's preconceptions. When the subjects tried to recall stories, they eliminated parts, made them more coherent, but not necessarily shorter; for there was invention as well as recall, what Bartlett called "constructive remembering". The individuals themselves were often unaware they were inventing, for the part they had created was frequently the part which pleased them most and about which they were most certain. This led Bartlett to place less emphasis upon the memory trace, upon recollection, and more upon reconstruction within a schema, "an active organisation of past reactions, or of past experiences" (1932:201).

I did not begin with a hypothesis derived from Bartlett's work. This omission was somewhat surprising as we had already discussed his book on *Remembering* in an earlier paper on literacy (Goody and Watt 1963); his work not only fitted with theories on memory then emerging from the Durkheimian school but he was also in touch with research on 'other cultures' through Rivers and other Cambridge social scientists of the period. Looking back at some earlier notes, I found I had taken a different view about the incidence of rote learning in simple societies, thinking it was essential in the absence of pencil and paper as an aide memoire. But I would now extend the idea of generative reconstruction in oral cultures from complex events to many simple ones; the situations involving the necessity of rote learning or the making of the lists that were so common in early literate cultures (and involving the record keeping which Whorf (1956) saw wrongly but characteristically as a feature of Standard Average European) are rare. Outside school, we don't often come across the type of learning situation that is modelled in so many psychological experiments. As a group of psychologists have themselves remarked, "A memorizer's task in the psychological laboratory is to learn how to produce a particular sequence of noises that he would never make ordinarily, that have no significance, and that will be of no use to him later. Rote serial memorization is a complicated, tricky thing to learn to do, and when it is mastered it represents a rather special skill" (Norman 1969:102). This quotation clearly indicates the reason why we find little of this type of learning in oral cultures and in everyday life generally. It errs, I think, in under-rating both the skill and the psychological experiments based upon it, not because these latter are reaching into the human mind, but because they are getting at a procedure intrinsic to our educational processes, to the literate tradition itself. On the other hand, there are distinct advantages of the oral mode in the 'literary' or 'mythological' sphere, and these are illustrated in that always suggestive corpus of material collected in Yugoslavia by Parry and Lord.

In one paper Lord compares the words of some songs in Parry's collection with those written down by Vuk Karadžić in the early part of the nineteenth century. Thirteen songs were recorded from one singer and all but one were represented in the collection made 100 years later.

The Parry songs can be divided into three categories: A, those that appear to be 'independent' of the earlier tradition; B, those influenced by the written text; and C, those that follow the text word for word. Significantly the examples Lord chooses from categories B and C are both songs sung by literate singers, some of whom have modified the texts in relatively minor ways. These modifications do not become part of the general repertoire since the next generation of singers goes back to the written 'original'; variations are 'individual' not 'social', matters of performance rather than creation, resembling the variations in performance in an interpretation of a concerto. On the other hand, the example of the 'independent' text comes from a non-literate singer who gives a version of 'Naheod Simeun' considerably different from the song with a similar title in the earlier written text. It contains 305 lines compared with the earlier 197 and it tells "an entirely different, though related story" (Lord 1967:1205). The differences are indeed very remarkable; for instance, in one case the hero is guilty of incest, in the other not. Here the singer, like those who precede him, has given expression to the 'creative habits' of oral poets, whereas the other two have been constrained, in greater or lesser degree, by the written texts.

The difference here is between exact recall (what psychologists often mean by 'memory') and creative reconstruction, which does not involve verbatim learning or even imitation, but generative recall. This kind of recall is not amenable to the usual forms of psychological testing, but is nevertheless the basis of much creative literature.

Let me put the problem in another way. If verbatim learning were widespread in oral cultures, we would expect to find developed there a number of mnemotechnical devices of the sort described by Frances Yates in her well-known book on the *The Art of Memory* (1966). Certainly mnemonic devices were available to pre-literate cultures, though the repeated recourse to the quipu of the Inca as an example might suggest that these were not so common as is sometimes supposed. But, more significantly, the elaborate systems discussed by Yates, appear to have been invented by a literate society. "Few people know" writes Yates, "that the Greeks, who invented many arts, invented an art of memory which, like their other arts, was passed on to Rome whence it descended in the European tradition" (1966:xi). The invention is vividly described by Cicero in his *De Oratore* when he is discussing memory as one of the five parts of rhetoric. Writing of the discovery of Simonides, he says:

He inferred that persons desiring to train this faculty (of memory) must select places and form mental images of the things they wish to remember and store those images in the places, so that the order of the places will preserve the order of the things, and the images of the things will denote the things themselves, and we shall employ the places and images respectively as a wax writing-tablet and the letters written on it. (quoted by Yates 1966:2)

The author of the major Roman textbook on the art of memory writes in a similar vein. "For the places are very much like wax tablets or papyrus, the images like the letters, the arrangement and disposition of the images like the script, and the delivery is like the reading" (quoted by Yates 1966:7). Even the oral techniques are likened to writing and reading.

This form of artificial memory appears to have been practised for 'things' rather than 'words'. In memorizing verse, for example, the author says it is still necessary to learn it by heart in the usual way. Or sometimes words might be remembered by means of "shorthand symbols or *notae* ... by a kind of inner stenography, the shorthand symbols were written down inwardly and memorized on the memory plates" (Yates 1966:15).

It is not difficult to see why the use of mnemotechnics for words rather than things was difficult, partly because of the large number of possibilities, partly because of lesser concreteness, partly because of the complexity of meaning. But it is just as important to note that both of the techniques suggested for learning words are dependent upon the use of writing; in the first case writing enables the learner to go over a text several times, in the second it helps to reduce words to shorthand symbols. Indeed since the whole system depends upon locating visual cues, in a building, theatre, etc., speech must first be reduced from sound to visual elements before any storage can take place, and writing is one way of doing just this.

So *memoria verborum* is associated with the existence of writing, as these authors suggest. The image of the wax writing-tablet seems to be more than an analogy and it is no accident that the invention is attributed to the Greeks, the inventors of the full alphabet. But what about *memoria rerum*, the memory of things? There is no similar reason why this technique should be tied to writing. In oral cultures, it need hardly be stated, people remember things and words without any great difficulty, and in many cases learn to improve upon nature by 'artificial' means. Yet the kind of development that is claimed for the poet Simonides can be plausibly seen as associated with writing for two rather different reasons.

The first of these has to do with the insistence upon order. While the idea of the deliberate spatial location of objects is not confined to literate societies, it is certainly promoted by the increased recourse to graphic arrangements, as I have argued is the case with lists, tables, matrices, systems of columns and rows. The analogy with the table and the alphabet is again no mere simile. The ordering involved in written lists seems to promote a feed-back effect that reacts upon the definition of categories, in some contexts, by making them more visible, though this consideration may be irrelevant if the informational input that one is trying to remember cannot be ordered on any 'abstract' basis.

The second reason has to do with the aim of the game and relates to the means by which literate knowledge was transmitted in schools and scriptoria; at least in the four and a half thousand years before printing, reproduction was largely through one scholar copying the work of another.

Schools and memory

Schooling and writing are inextricably linked from the very beginning of both (which makes it difficult to separate them for analytical purposes). In the last chapter I gave an example for Ancient Egypt. Similar features are found in Mesopotamia. "The Sumerian school system" writes Kramer, "was the direct outgrowth of the invention and development of the cuneiform system of writing" (1956:3). Even among the very first written documents discovered at Erech (*c*. 3000 BC), among the 1,000 or so small clay tablets inscribed with economic and administrative memoranda, several contain word lists for study and practice. In Shuruppak, some 500 years later, we find a considerable number of school 'textbooks'. But the great expansion appears to date from the following 500 years, a period from which we have tens of thousands of clay tablets, mainly administrative and covering every aspect of Sumerian life. At this time, the production of scribes must have been considerable; they were differentiated into junior and high scribes, royal and temple scribes, scribes who were specialized for particular categories of administrative activity, and ones who became leading government officials (Kramer 1956:3–4).

From the first half of the second millennium, records about the schools themselves become available, because schoolmasters wrote about their occupation. The main aim was to provide professional training, but the school gradually became "the center of culture and learning in Sumer. Within its walls flourished the scholar-scientist, the man who studied whatever theological, botanical, zoological, mineralogical, geographical, mathematical, grammatical, and linguistic knowledge was current in his day, and who in some cases added to this knowledge" (1956:4). It was also the centre of creative writing.

What started as a religious institution in time became largely secular. Most students came from the wealthier families of urban communities; and they were all males. In terms of organization too, there were close parallels to later European practices. The head was known as the 'school father' and kinship terms were also appropriated to describe the pupils, the 'school sons'. 'Big Brother' was the teacher who wrote tables for the students to copy, examined their work and heard them "recite their studies from memory" (1956:5).

In ancient Babylonia, in Sumerian times, boys attended 'the tablet-house', where they were apprenticed to the master ('father'). After learning the signs of the complicated cuneiform script, the students "quickly moved on to copy lists of words, synonym lists and vocabularies, and to extracts, written from memory rather than from dictation . . . In this way a student copied more than 30,000 lines and most of the standard literary and other forms of text before qualification as a specialist". Examinations were given in a variety of topics, calligraphy, grammar, translation, vocabulary, phonetics, epigraphy, as well as for special studies in accountancy.

There is much evidence that schooling, from its earliest moment, encouraged memory tasks. In Mesopotamia from c.3100 BC, and soon after in Egypt, Anatolia and Elam, there are records of scribes in the main centres of government. From the beginning, schools were equated with the urban environment and with the withdrawal from manual tasks. They were also high status, though not necessarily of the highest, and they were often under priestly control. In the third millennium it is generally assumed that Egyptian schools were controlled by the priests whose primary aim was "the preservation of 'the word of god', of 'divine words' – the sacred writing" (Wiseman 1970:33). Manuscripts were kept in the scriptorium or 'house of life' and from this store copies and selections of standard texts (the Pyramid, Coffin Texts or the Book of the Dead) were made. The scribal tradition was inherited, being passed on from father to son, but in the context of scribal schools.

The bureaucracy of the Middle Kingdom led to the establishment of government schools to supply the growing number of secretaries and clerks required . . . The students first learned the hieroglyphic and hieratic scripts and then moved on to exercises and extracts from traditional texts . . . The memorizing and copying of lists of the names of deities, professions and places (*onomastica*) were included. (p. 36)

The verbatim tasks encouraged by schools in the course of the transmission of knowledge, for the purpose of which artificial techniques of memorizing were well adapted, are the verbal equivalents of the central routine of the budding scribe from earliest times, namely copying. With early tablets – the so-called school texts, a junior teacher, Big Brother, writes a passage on one side and the pupil copies on the reverse. The teacher then corrects the pupil's work in the same manner that teachers have always done with 'copy-books', meting out punishments to those who do badly and rewards to those who do well (i.e. copy correctly).

We have here the institutionalization of the written equivalent of verbatim memory, namely exact copying (an idea reflected in the meaning of 'literal', 'to the letter', where the very alphabet seems implicated in compulsive precision), a procedure which in schools has its oral counterpart not only in specific memory tasks, but also in the tutorial question and answer where pupils are asked to give back to the teacher what they know he already knows.

The whole process of removing the children from the family, placing them under special authorities, can be roughly described as one of 'decontextualization', formalization; for schools inevitably place an emphasis on the 'unnatural', 'non-oral', 'decontextualized' process of repetition, copying, verbatim memory. A recognition of this tendency will help us to understand the contrast with oral societies, where we get little emphasis on repetition, rather upon re-creation, anyhow in most of the area of cognitive activity with which I am dealing. It helps us to understand the problem of variation in myth, as well as the so-called invention of memory procedures in classical times; it was not altogether an invention, since we find such procedures in oral cultures, though they then underwent a very particular development. But what we should also understand, lest we too readily fall into lamentations for the loss of creativity in schools (anyhow in written activity as distinct from other early graphic activity where the child has more freedom) is that, especially before the age of printing, it was essential to copy correctly because the resulting text came to form an individual's own textbook which, as in the case of mathematical tables, was often useful in later life as well as in the classroom. As in medieval universities, school provided the means of building a library; manuscript reproduction is necessarily manual and therefore singular, whereas printing is multiple and relieves individuals from this aspect of the copying task (Febvre and Martin 1958). That is, relieves them potentially, for in many schools of the Third World, and even in poorer areas of developed countries, a lack of text books is likely to lead to a greater emphasis on making copies. Under these conditions the suppression of creativity, the suppression of freedom of expression, is necessary for the reproduction of culture. It was necessary not only for its reproduction, but also for the generation of new incremental activity. A central difference between an oral and a literate culture lies in the modes of transmission, the first allowing a surprisingly wide degree of creativity but of a largely cyclical kind, the latter demanding repetition as a condition of some incremental change.

In discussing the differences between oral and literate cultures with regard to memory tasks (or more precisely, the effects of changes in the means, modes and content of communication), we need to steer a line between those views asserting that all men have the same abilities and those others that, implicitly or explicitly, pose some great divide between 'them' and 'us'. An explanation (even if partial) in terms of changes in these patterns of communication helps form a bridge. For writing, like language, is a cultural tool that enables the possessor to perform certain tasks in a revolutionary manner. Not only in the obvious sense that the external visual store substitutes for the internal auditory one, but in relation to the internal organization of cognition and memory.

Soviet investigators, including Vygotsky, have pointed out that memory is elementary and direct only in relatively rare cases, and that as a rule the process of recall is based on a system of intermediary aids (or codes) and is thus indirect in character. So recall is a complex active process, a form of mnestic activity determined by motives, the task, and appropriate methods or codes "which increase the volume of recallable material, increase the time during which it can be retained, and sometimes . . . abolish the inhibitory action of irrelevant, interfering agents which . . . lies at the basis of forgetting" (Luria 1973:286). The process depends upon the way in which incoming stimuli are organized into successive or simultaneous structures, and it is here that writing intervenes.

What writing does is to provide auditory information with a visual, and hence a spatial frame. In fact it changes the channel of communicated language from an auditory to a visual one. You hear speech and see writing; speaking with mouth, listening with ear; writing with hand, reading with eyes. To the channel mouth-to-ear is added the channel hand-to-eye. This process has a number of cultural implications. It makes possible the study of grammar, of the structure of language, since it is now possible to organize auditory stimuli into a simultaneous rather than a successive structure (or pattern), so that a sentence can have a synchronic character as well as a diachronic one. It does the same for argument, leading to the development of formal 'logic' (Goody and Watt 1963).

What does this switch of channels do for recall, for memory? Clearly the relationship between the spoken and the written word or sentence, between utterance and text (Olson 1976), continues to be close. In order to direct the pen one uses the silent language, to misappropriate E. T. Hall's phrase; one formulates and then translates into muscular movements of the hand. In reading, one usually retranslates into the auditory channel, again silently, although for some individuals muscular movement is a necessary accompaniment. Rehearsal is largely auditory; that is to say, it is probably easier to remember by repeating the words to oneself than by reading them over the same number of times if only because one can exclude interference (by closing one's eyes). What then does writing do to change the methods of storage and recall? If the codes of language can, as Luria claims and as commonsense confirms, assist in the organization of memory traces, does writing have a similar effect on the organization of mnestic activity?

Despite the apparent advantage of visual storage, writing is largely translated into the auditory channel for storage purposes. It affects storage and recall in three main ways. In the first place, by making possible the greater ordering of the world, it is doing the same kind of thing for cognition and memory that Bruner and Luria assign to language, but in a higher degree. That is where tables, lists and formulas come in. Secondly, while it does not substitute visual for auditory storage, it adds a visual, spatial and even motor element to the recall of linguistic acts. Thirdly, it facilitates rehearsal procedures by making it possible to refer back to a continuing stimulus, the text, which enables one to check as well as to repeat.

I have discussed the first point in an earlier study (1977). Writing permits not only the recording but the reorganization of information. One can operate on the representations. What we find here is a shift away from a perceptual base for sorting. Psychological work cited by Bruner (1966:28) indicates that children up to the age of eight or nine also prefer perceptual bases; "non-schematized imagery is highly characteristic of early intellectual operations". When a child uses abstract terms like animal, according to Brown, "he does not usually possess the full category but only applies the term to some restricted subclass of the whole" (1958:277). What writing does is to increase the visibility and definition of classes, hence increase the part that hierarchies play in social life and in mental processes. It increases too the sensitivity to boundary phenomena, of the kind discussed by Mary Douglas and others. But it could mean that an individual is more likely to reclassify material according to formal, 'decontextual' criteria. The greater visibility of 'formal' classes is perhaps indicated in Luria's experiment concerning farm instruments, where the hierarchical classification of the man on the collective farm is contrasted with the 'contiguity association' of the traditional thinker. But as Scribner and Cole later point out (1981:10), a number of other factors were involved in this situation.

In discussing the role of writing in adding a spatial element, providing a spatial frame, to speech (just as other graphic forms can provide different kinds of spatial frameworks), reference needs to be made to Bruner's discussion of "the uniqueness of a spatial framework" in relation to cognitive growth (1966:15). A spatially defined perceptual locus, which is intrinsic to vision, enables the brain to analyze simultaneously information that is present serially, successively. Representation, he argues (following Lashley), must be in the form of serial or 'atemporal' representation (p. 18). For behaviour to become more skillful, it must become increasingly 'freer' of immediate or serial regulation by environmental stimuli; this freedom, he suggests, is achieved by means of a shift from response learning to place learning, which makes possible the organization of behaviour in more flexible ways.

An extension of this mechanism is achieved by writing, and the more efficient the writing system, the greater the extension. Writing provides, *inter alia*, a spatial coordinate of language, giving it an atemporal dimension which makes it possible to subject a speech act, a sentence, a chronological record, a list, to greater, more context-free, manipulation. The organizing matrix is temporarily shifted from an internal representation to an external one, with the advantage of greater concreteness, the danger of reifying the unreal, of formalizing the ambiguous, of taking one's creations too literally.

With regard to the third point, I have suggested that the kind of rehearsal necessary for verbatim recall may be encouraged by the existence of writing, first because there is a fixed text to copy, then to use for correction (self-correction if necessary); secondly, because such procedures are needed in the learning of scripts, whose units (graphemes), unlike the basic units of speech (phonemes), can easily be learnt at a later age; thirdly, because verbatim copying is essential to the reproduction of written materials under certain conditions; before the advent of print one needed the scriptoria of Medieval Europe, the Middle East or of Ugarit where perfect copies of the *words* were accorded great value and where reproduction was easily characterized as right (exact) or wrong (different).

It is also possible that these procedures may be encouraged by reading. For reading usually involves a subvocal rehearsal of the speech equivalent of the print on the page. Indeed this procedure provides an obvious memory mechanism, as Sperling points out. For when asked to write down letters briefly exposed, all of his subjects reported that they used subvocal rehearsal, while some actually spoke the words out loud. If asked to wait before writing down, they repeated the letters to themselves and thus refreshed the auditory image as it was fading. Such a procedure assumes that the sound image of a letter can enter auditory memory directly from subvocal rehearsal without actually being converted into audible sound and passing through the ear (Norman 1969:65).

Conclusion

Starting from the tardy realization that variations of the Bagre suggest that it could not have been deliberately learnt (or taught) by verbatim methods, I argue that there were in fact very few (if any) occasions in LoDagaa society where such methods were utilized for the storage and recall of utterance. I suggest this is generally true of oral cultures which had neither the developed techniques nor the developed requirements for rote learning. Since there is not one original that could be studied as a text, nor a single keeper of the oral tradition, the Bagre expands, develops and contracts with each ceiling, in a 'generative', 'creative' way that characterizes much oral activity of a 'literary' kind.

It is rather in literate societies that verbatim memory flourishes. Partly because the existence of a fixed original makes it much easier; partly because of the elaboration of spatially oriented memory techniques; partly because of the school situation which has to encourage 'decontextualized' memory tasks since it has removed learning from doing and has redefined the corpus of knowledge. Verbatim memorizing is the equivalent of exact copying, which is intrinsic to the transmission of scribal culture, indeed manuscript cultures generally. After the advent of printing, with its mechanization of reproduction, and its elimination of the necessity of copying that existed when every student had to make his own textbook, and when his arithmetic tables were not printed on the back of his copybook, verbatim memory became less imperative for storage, though it was still valuable for rapid retrieval; by memorizing the phone number instead of looking through the book, one gains speed as well as power. The technique has obvious limitations of scale. Nevertheless the bounded separateness of school, its specialization for literate instruction, the type of information it imparts, still places great emphasis on memory tasks; for mental storage is still seen as bringing disparate knowledge into meaningful relations.

In contrasting the generative recall of the Bagre with the verbatim recall often demanded by schools, I do not wish to downgrade the latter, which seems to me a condition of our cultural elaboration, and which anyhow has different implications for 'scientific' than for 'literary' activity. This is not the place to pursue the point, but it is worth while recalling that the Speaker of the Bagre is in the position of being both reciter and creator; he fills the roles that we (or rather writing) have divided into composer and performer, dramatist and player, author and publisher. One of these roles requires a faithful adherence to the text; the other is therefore freer to invent.[3]

9

Writing and formal operations: a case study among the Vai (with Michael Cole and Sylvia Scribner)

The present chapter reports a kind of 'experiment' in the field of literacy in West Africa, made possible by the 'experimental anthropology' of my co-authors, Michael Cole and Sylvia Scribner among the Vai of West Africa.[1] It also serves to link the socio–cultural concerns of the previous chapter with the more individual, internal, 'psychological' direction of the next, although this 'boundary' needs to be treated, as Vygotsky insisted, with much caution.

In earlier discussions with Michael Cole I had suggested that the uses of any newly invented script would be likely to include listing procedures that re-contextualized verbal material and made it possible to subject the word to new cognitive operations. On a visit to Liberia in 1975 we went in search of Vai texts and with the help of one of the participants in the Vai Literacy Project came across a cache of just such material. These writings fell within the Muslim tradition I discussed in chapter 6 but were in the Vai script and served original ends.

The Islamic brotherhoods common in North Africa take a variety of forms south of the Sahara, but even at the very fringes of Muslim penetration the great orders such as the Qaddiriyya have a part to play in the lives of the believers. One function they have is to bring adherents back to what members of the order see as the essential tenets of the faith, to purge practice of the inevitable compromises made with local 'pagan' cults, and to increase the solidarity of the congregation of the faithful.

The Tijānīyya *ṭarīqa* is one of the two main Islamic brotherhoods found in West Africa, having spread from Fez at the death of the founder Ahmad b. Muhammad al-Tijani (1737–1815) and having

191

been given a great boost by the conquests of Al-Hajj 'Umar Tal
(1794–1864), whose activities began in a Tukulor empire in the
Fouta Jalon area of Guinea and led to the conquest of the Bambara
kingdoms. Although lineally descended from the Sufi
brotherhoods, there is very little of the original mysticism to be
found in these orders south of the Sahara. Affiliation means adding
certain litanies to daily prayer and enjoins mutual obligations
between members, though the Tijānīyya also stress prohibitions on
smoking, drinking, lying and corruption, as well as being more
hostile to local magico–religious associations like the *bori* of
Hausaland. The leader of an order (*shaikh*) appoints local agents,
generally called *muqaddams* (and sometimes *khalīfas*) who
organize religious compounds with sections for the family, disciples, pilgrims, a mosque and school. Ritual is centred around a
dhikr, a form of individual and collective praise for God and the
Prophet, which differs with each brotherhood. Saintly power is
passed down by means of a chain of authority which links the village
cleric with the founder by way of the *muqaddam* under whom he
has studied.

In the mid 1930s, a Tijānīyya marabout known as Al-Hajj
Mohammed Ahmad Tunis was preaching in Fairo in south-eastern
Sierra Leone and exercising considerable influence on the surrounding population, including some of the Vai in neighbouring
Liberia, an ethnic group split by the international boundary and
closely related (in cultural terms) to the Mende and Kono of
southern Sierra Leone. He crossed the borders into Liberia where
one of his students was Braimah Nyei (b. 1899, later Al-Hajj) who
in turn influenced two members of a business partnership, Braimah
Kemokai (now Al-Hajj) and Ansumana Sonie (d. August, 1959)
who were at the time engaged in commercial ventures including
cash farming and trading between Monrovia and Cape Mount
County (a Vai area).

According to the accounts given to us by Kemokai and Nyei in
June, 1975, the three men became closely associated in 1923, two
years after Sonie's return from Europe. Nyei's role in the business
side was less important than that of the other two men, who had
both had previous experience of commerce and had dealt with
Europeans in various transactions. Nyei however belonged to a

scholarly family and had had a more profound religious training, during which time he acquired the ability to read and write some Arabic. Muslim commercial concerns in West Africa often have their religious facet, and it was on this side that Nyei's contribution mainly lay.

In 1937 word reached Nyei that his teacher and spiritual leader, Al-Hajj Tunis, had died on his return to Sierra Leone. At the same time he was told that Tunis had left instructions that Nyei become the leader (*muqaddam*) of the Tijānīyya in Liberia. As a result Nyei called a meeting of a group of followers, including Kemokai and Sonie, in Misila, a small township in the Gawula chiefdom in Cape Mount County which was built when their natal town was abandoned some years earlier. The men met together and prayed all night to honour their dead teacher, in the special manner that marks adherents to the Tijānīyya brotherhood. It was agreed to start an association along the lines of those which appear to have been already established among the Mende of Sierra Leone; known by the same term of *Malodi* (Arabic *mawlid*), and which are described by Trimingham in the following words: "They have a great feast on the birthday of the Prophet, they help the family with funeral expenses, as much as ten pounds being provided, and wear small black badges with an Arabic inscription. Each member has to pay regular subscriptions, and if a member dies in default they will not help at funeral rites – the kind of discrimination characteristic of Creole Christians" (1959:223). The aim of these Mende associations was to promote self-help, education and Muslim solidarity, performing the role of a 'friendly society' as well as fulfilling specific religious functions. 'Insurance societies' of this general kind are common throughout West Africa, from Sierra Leone to the Yoruba, in 'pagan' as well as in Muslim groups, and they offer some protection against misfortune through the collection and redistribution of the contributions of the members. Another feature common to Muslim West Africa is the celebration of the birth or circumcision of the prophet by a ceremony (Arabic *mawlid*) such as the *Damba* of Gonja and other areas influenced by the Mande, which draws people together into some central place.[2]

The model for the Malodi association[3] of Misila existed already. But in the hand of Nyei, who became the Imam, and of Sonie, who became the 'president' (or 'chairman'), it developed its own character. One important aspect was the series of records kept by the chairman, which we were shown when we visited Misila in the company of Mohamed Nyei, son of Braimah, on 18–19 June 1975. These books consisted of lists of members, lists of dues paid and owed, lists of expenses, and a copy of the constitution of the association.

These records were kept almost entirely in the local Vai script and the local Vai language (though they used European numbers and included some Arabic dates). Since here, as throughout the Islamic world, Arabic is the language of the Qu'ran and hence the language of prayer and of all religious instruction in reading, this resort to a local script and a local language requires some explanation.

As in other West African areas, with the exception of a few Arabic speaking desert tribes, traditional Muslim education takes place in the language of the Book, Arabic, rather than in the local tongue. By and large, 'learning book' means being taught to find the rough phonetic equivalents of Arabic letters so that individuals can memorize verses of the Qu'ran, the meaning of which may be explained by some learned man who has actually acquired some Arabic or who has memorized a translation of a commentary. Achieving a learned status means acquiring a second language, Arabic, by methods which are primarily directed towards verbatim memorizing rather than towards language acquisition, and then pursuing a lengthy series of peripatetic studies, visiting scholars in different towns and different countries, in order to learn about particular books mostly of a religious character.[4] Alternatively it means learning by heart not only the text itself but the translation as well. Both of these are formidable tasks, given the lack of aids to literate achievement which the cultures provide and it is surprising that we find any scholars at all of the calibre of Al-Hajj 'Umar of Salaga, who know enough Arabic to compose anything more than simple letters or copies of Muslim charms. Such scholars were not unknown, though it is significant that in Al-Hajj 'Umar's case he learnt fluent Arabic as the result of an extended pilgrimage to Mecca. But it is also significant that the areas where Islamic scholarship was most strongly developed, namely among the Fulani kingdoms and in Hausaland, were the very areas where, despite the pressure to retain the language of the Book for religious purposes, the mother tongue was later written down in Arabic script and became an important medium of literate communication. However the use of Arabic itself was relatively restricted not only because of its religious context, but also because the number of people who could decode the meaning (i.e. read) as distinct from decode the sound was very limited.

In the case of the Vai, restrictions on knowledge of Arabic were no hindrance to record keeping for organizational purposes. At least since the middle of the nineteenth century, they have been using an indigenous, syllabic script for the kind of transactions required by the operation of the Misila organization.[5] Over the course of time the Vai developed a rough division of literate labour in which religious matters were handled in Arabic, secular matters in Vai, and some transactions outside the group in English, the national language of Liberia and the medium of school instruction. And each of these languages had its particular script. The acceptance of Vai was not without its difficulties. Al-Hajj Kemokai told us of 'fortune tellers' from Guinea and Mali who in their preaching claimed that a book of 165 characters (i.e. the Vai syllabary) would harm the book of 28 characters (i.e. the Arabic alphabet). He went on to add: "In Africa we need Arabic to help us to go to Heaven and we need English to improve our standard of living",[6] and we need Vai, he might have added, because it is our mother tongue and we can use it for pragmatic and cultural activities.

Certainly the Malodi association adopted a division of labour among its founders which paralleled this general division in the uses of Vai and Arabic. The Imam, Braimah Nyei, was responsible for the proper religious observances which were conducted in Arabic. The president, Ansumana Sonie, was responsible for keeping the financial records, distributing assistance to those in need and possibly for adjudicating those disputes among members which fell within the organization's purview. All of these latter activities were conducted in Vai and the records associated with them kept in the Vai script. It is this corpus of Ansumana Sonie's writings which we now examine as evidence of the ways in which this script was used and the kind of operations that were involved.

The writings of Ansumana Sonie

These writings consist of a set of copybooks, a few with hard covers, extending over the years 1926 to 1959, the year of Sonie's death. The first of the books differs from the others in that it contains personal records of business transactions over a short period as well as of some important family events. The remainder are all records of the Malodi association, which begin with a membership list started in 1937 and include a written constitution (dated 1941) as well as several ledgers of dues and expenditures.

In looking at these books, our concern is not to convey the details of their content and structure. Rather, we select for special attention aspects which illustrate operations of a specifically 'graphic' character and which draw attention to the implications of the change from an oral to a literate technology for the recording and manipulation of information.

1. A business ledger and family almanac

According to his partners, Nyei and Kemokai, in the early 1900s Sonie was engaged in commerce in the area of Lake Piso, at the mouth of which the old trading centre of Robertsport is located. Subsequently he was employed as a steward by an English prospector in whose company he travelled to Nigeria and England. It was upon his return that he entered business with Kemokai and Nyei and it is from this period that we find the earliest of the documents.

Unlike many of the later documents, which were written in small copybooks, this early set of records was in a hardbound foolscap volume which dated back to 1926. Here we find detailed daily accounts for a two-week period, listing sales of cloth, singlets, thread, kerosene, medicine, soap, shirts, trousers and pomade. The number and price of each in pounds, shillings and pence was listed and totalled up both by row (i.e. sales of particular items) and by column (i.e. sales for the day), enabling Sonie to keep track of stocks and takings, and presumably of income.[7] It would seem unlikely, though possible, that this record was unique; in any case it illustrates certain of the possibilities opened up by record-keeping in columns and rows, enabling individuals to enter into economic transactions that are increasingly complex and extensive.

A limited amount of the kind of information Sonie recorded here can be held in memory store. But it cannot be subjected to the same kind of checking and addition that is possible when it is preserved in graphic form. In particular, it is difficult to see how he could otherwise keep track simultaneously of sales by type of goods and by date of sale. These bookkeeping operations, however, were critical to the expansion of Sonie's commercial activites. They enabled him to deal with a wider range of goods and to make a finer calculation of profit and loss. Such calculations were critical because on the one hand he was buying imported produce from European traders and on the other, he was buying farm produce from local cultivators. He was thus acting as middleman for a variety of transactions and a variety of customers in a manner somewhat different from the usual kind of 'pre-literate' trading activity, which tends to concentrate upon a single item or a limited range of goods with relatively fixed prices.

The earliest book contains a further set of data which is of equal interest, namely family records concerned primarily with the dates of important events. These events are a rather heterogeneous collection, mainly the births of children and grandchildren kept in a combination of Vai and Arabic (at least for days of the week). Sonie notes when one of his sons "killed a leopard", thereby achieving adult status; he gives the dates of his daughters' marriages; and he records the fact that he paid the expenses of the marriage of another man. What we find here provides the rough outline for a family history, or for his own biography; it is the establishment of a personal chronology with reference to the Common Era. But there are two other aspects connected with this enterprise, which deserve attention. The first has to do with the continuing concern for dates which is still manifest in his family: individuals frequently quote dates, which is unusual for West African societies, even Muslim ones, except among those who have attended European-type schools. Secondly, Sonie himself is led to 'play' a number of 'games' with these figures; we mean by this that he sets about manipulating the figures in ways which are not immediately 'utilitarian', i.e. relevant to the particular situation.

These entries remind one of the kind of operation children are constantly called upon to perform in school: number games for their own sake. For example, in 1958, the year before his death, he used the fact that he married his first wife in 1909 and divorced her in 1913, to calculate the number of years between the time of that divorce and the time of her death, in other words thirty-seven years. He also worked out the time that had elapsed since he married her.

2. *The constitution*

Written in 1941, the constitution of the association is an interesting document from several points of view.

In content, it shows the close affinity with the Mende Malodi associations referred to earlier. The bulk of its twenty-eight articles specify the duties of the members to ensure the proper burial rites, their obligations to support one another in need, and the consequences of noncompliance.

In form, the constitution is interesting as a written document. It occupies a separate copy book with the date 10/2/41 written at the top, and the phrase, "What we have to do in this organization" on the first line. This phrase, together with the remainder of the document, is written in Vai script, with the exception of the English numbering (e.g. No. 1) of each article, which is indented, i.e. spatially set aside, on the page.

Two aspects of the constitution suggest that while its contents are doubtless derived from the rules and procedures of the Malodi associations among the Mende, the articles were still being subjected to the kind of reorganization that writing can facilitate. When we examine the sequence in which individual items follow each other, there seems room for further re-arrangement that would bring items associated according to general criteria into proximity with one another. Such a conclusion is fraught with difficulties, but a consideration of a subset of articles will illustrate the point. Articles having to do with burial obligations occur as 2, 5, 9 and 14. These are separated by ones dealing with such topics as marriage rules, prohibitions against drinking and adultery, and the performance of the *mawlid* ceremony. There are several neighbouring articles that concern women (18–23) but these seem to be related by a specific chain of association rather than by a more general principle of inclusion; in any case women also enter into articles 4 and 5.

This line of argument receives some support from a note in the margin of page 1 to the effect that article 23, which states that no unmarried woman may join the organization prior to the menopause, should be moved up to article 2, the burden of which is to specify the limitation of membership to Muslims. It seems later to have occurred to Ansumana Sonie on inspection of the written text that the 'logical' position for article 23 is with the others that deal with eligibility for membership. 'Logic' comes into play when one can regroup the elements of study.

One reason for the present order of items in the constitution may be that it was not recopied and reworked. At least we have no evidence of this. The only copy we have was written down in 1941, four years after the association was founded. It does not appear to have been circulated among members but was kept in the hands of the president of the association. As we shall see in our examination of the remaining materials, the existence of a recopied text, of which we have the original, is an important source of light on the way writing permits the re-ordering of information according to more general, 'logical' principles.

3. The list of members and dues

The first membership list begins with an entry of names dated 22 September 1937 and continues with two or more dated sets of entries each year until 1958. The names of approximately 450 members are listed over this twenty-one year period, the initial entry including the men who founded the organization. The successive entries are listed in chronological order, each new set being headed by the date of admission written in Vai on the centre of each page. The number of entries on a given date varies from one to two dozen or more, but there is no indication of the occasion the dates refer to. These presumably include the celebration of the *mawlid* and the performance of funerals, which were both mandatory for members and were times when new members could be recruited.

This chronological listing is supplemented by seven books in which the same basic list is used for specialized purposes. A book covering the years 1941–44 contains entries of the following type. For the year 1941 those attending the *mawlid* celebration are listed by geographical area and 'clan', the two groups being separated by several pages in the copy book.[8] Following the 1941 grouping by clan, there are additional entries for new members recruited in the years 1942–44. There are also notations indicating the grand totals of the membership. Sonie kept track of totals by writing down the names of new members and striking out those who had died. At or near the end of the entries for a given clan we find subtotals giving the number of members of each sex and their respective contributions. For example an entry for the Vai Kohnee chiefdom for the year 1942 reads:

Men	41	6/-	12– 6–0
Women	19	3/-	2– 8–0
			14–14–0

This notation is not only economical of space, it assists Sonie to multiply, incorrectly in the latter case, instead of adding sums of 41 and 19 items individually.

Books of dues for other years illustrate further ways in which Sonie used geographical and social categories to organize information about the membership and income. The roll book for the 1951 celebration in Misila is arranged by geographic area, clan name and town name, since a single clan, e.g. Kiazodi, may be represented in several towns. This classificatory scheme is made visually salient by a numbering system that starts again whenever the clan or area changes.

An innovation in 1949 and 1950 was the creation of a ledger book with the members of each sub-unit (usually a town) listed on the left hand page of the copy book, with spaces for contributions for the years 1949 to 1951 on the right. By scanning the right hand side of the page, it was possible to see immediately if an individual was in arrears.

At least two books, one for 1947–48 and one for 1961, list the members owing money to the association, specifying the exact amounts in each individual case. As in the previous books of dues the lists are organized by geographical area and clan, which presumably relates to the system of collection.

The 1950–52 period was the occasion for another variation in the listing of the membership. In one book members were frequently entered according to the first two syllables of their name. For example, on page 1 he listed sixteen men called Mɔmɔdi followed by a single Mɔmɔlu. Page 2 contains those named Bai and Bale. Not all the pages contain lists of this kind, but the incidence is far too high to permit any doubt that Sonie intended to compile lists based upon phonetic similarity.

Finally, we call attention to a small book of summary information on the membership that apparently represents another kind of abstraction from the original roll book. The first section gives an estimate of the total membership in the years 1939–53. A second section gives a summary of the number of deaths of members and a third (apparently written in 1957) summarizes the total active and inactive (i.e. not paid up) membership at that time.

Taken as a corpus, these lists of members and dues illustrate several of the features of information coding and re-coding emphasized in other papers (Goody 1977b). But before discussing their implications further, we want to consider another part of Sonie's writings, his ledger books on expenditures.

4. The ledger books

Like the lists of members and dues, the ledger books containing the outlays of the association take on added significance for the reason that Sonie produced more than one book to cover any one period; for example, there was an initial entry for outlays covering the period (1944–1946) and a second book which subsumes the first (1944–51). The first book is clearly more haphazard than the second in the way the entries are noted; for example, entries are made in the margin or on the facing page. But Sonie was sufficiently systematic to enable the reader to trace the relations between the two books, and so discern the summarizing principles at work, a process that was made possible only by the fact that this information was written down i.e. given a visuo-spatial dimension.

A comparison of the first few dated entries for 1944 illustrates the main points. In the initial ledger there are three entries for the date, 24 March 1944:

Kiash (cash) to M. Sonie
Kiash (cash) to F. Tomi Fayein Tombe
Thread

When these same entries are located in the second copy book, we find the following alterations: the entry for cash to F. Tomi has been expanded to include the reason for sending the cash, namely that fire had damaged the town. The item for thread is missing altogether for this date, but we find it listed instead under 14 August 1944. The reason for moving the entry becomes apparent from an examination of other items under this date. In the first book we find that on 14 August there are entries for expenditure on cloth to make the badges of the association (also used in the Mende case) as well as on a messenger sent to "buy copy books". In the second book, the thread is listed as "thread for badges" and the messenger is listed as the man sent to get the thread and the material. There may be some doubt as to the true date of the expenditures in question, but what seems clear is that in recopying the material, Sonie has chosen to regroup the expenses according to their common function, the making of the badges.

An entry for 23 February 1945 contains an instance of re-organization of a rather special sort. In the first book we find a heading showing that the entries are for food for the *mawlid* celebration; the first two entries are for two chickens (*tiyɛ*) costing eight shillings, and for 'meat' (*suyɛ*) at five shillings. In the second book these two entries have been combined in a single entry labelled 'meat' (*suyɛ*) at thirteen shillings. This appears to be a case where two subordinate terms have been grouped under a superordinate in a straightforward manner. What makes the case unusual is that in Vai the word *suyɛ* is not the superordinate that subsumes both *tiyɛ* and *suyɛ*. Rather the term *luafe* should be used in this case. This reclassification is clear evidence of Sonie's knowledge of English, no doubt derived from his experience as a steward, as well as for the combination of separate items into 'like' categories when copying from the first book to the second.

In the preceding sections we have analyzed certain aspects of the writings of one individual covering a period of some thirty years, along with a brief account of the circumstances under which this corpus came into existence. Why should this material be of more than a parochial interest to social scientists?

The writings of Ansumana Sonie provide evidence concerning the organization and functions of Muslim brotherhoods in West Africa, and the spread of the Malodi associations from Mende into the neighbouring Vai, including a statement of the rules, or constitution, of one such association.

While the documentary value of the writings is clear, we are primarily interested in their value for assessing the implications of a literate technology for individuals and for social groups.

At several points we noted that use of a writing system had enabled Sonie to engage in a number of activities which would otherwise have been impossible (or at least improbable). These include the compilation of the long lists of members which form the bulk of the materials, as well as the elementary bookkeeping of his own early ledger and of the accounts of the Malodi association. They include the 'games' to which we have referred, apparently 'non-utilitarian' activities that can lead, for example, to the establishment of personal and family 'histories'. But it is also the case that activities which have their 'functional equivalents' in non-literate societies, such as the methods of collecting contributions from members of an association or from those attending a funeral, may also be changed by the fact that they are recorded in writing.[9] In the sphere of broader economic activity, trade (even over long distances) is a common feature of non-literate societies. New operations in this sphere were rendered possible by Sonie's use of writing for his ledgers, operations which assisted him to cope with a number of different types of goods and transactions with customers, producers and merchants. Though written records are not intrinsic to trade, they appear to be essential for transactions of a varied and complex nature as those in which Sonie engaged.

Let us consider the collection of the contributions to the association and the impact made by Sonie's detailed recording. In the first place the amount of money which passed through his hands was large relative to the income of individual members. For the decade of the 1940s the average income to the organization amounted to approximately $200.00 per year. During this same period, the cash income of individual members of the organization was probably in the neighbourhood of $20.00 a year. Thus Sonie not only had to deal with a relatively large amount of money which, while certainly not impossible without writing, would have been very difficult to keep track of in such a systematic way. He had also to use a system that would bridge both time and space, for the reckoning of debtors was not limited to the occasion itself, namely, the celebration of *mawlid*. Instead, an individual's debts were written down in the record book, which meant he could be pursued for payment of dues over a long period, and his standing in the society depended not simply upon an initial membership fee, not purely upon a subsequent attendance contribution, but upon an annual payment which fell due even in the absence of any specific action on his part; membership was 'decontextualized' from overt events such as attendance at funeral or ceremony. It is in this sense that members were kept track of, in a general way, over time and space; belonging did not depend upon continued residence in the local area nor was it an automatic result of entering and participating in a specific event. It depended, *inter alia*, upon the continued payment of dues to a central figure, the 'president' of the organization.

The results of this arrangement were multiple. As several writers have argued for literacy in general (Goody and Watt 1963), this application of the Vai script went hand in hand with the depersonalization of social activities which had previously depended upon face-to-face interaction backed by normative rules whose interpretation was open to negotiation.

In the second place, written recording of information established Sonie as an 'honest man', a fact upon which all those whom we met insisted. Such a reputation was essential for the continued inflow of contributions and for the continued survival of the association. Thirdly, Sonie's systematic bookkeeping placed strong constraints upon members to pay dues, and particularly arrears of dues; delinquents were singled out for inclusion in special ledgers.

These rules and the financial success of the organization led to a great deal of power being concentrated in an individual who was not a member of the traditional or modern 'elites', either political or religious. Because of the accumulation of capital and its power to call upon the services of members, the association was able to build mosques and meeting halls in a number of villages. Some of this expenditure, at least, fell in the category of 'conspicuous consumption'; in Misila itself, which was a small township, there were two mosques and two meeting halls, one for the 'town' and one for the association. It is difficult to be certain whether the existence of Sonie's records affected the size or complexity of the organization since we have no adequate comparative evidence. Clearly the existence of the Vai script would enable the leadership to keep in touch with members and vice versa, although the documents we collected did not in fact include letters of this kind. But if it cannot be shown to affect size, writing certainly affected centrality and control.

How does the kind of material illustrated in the writings of Ansumana Sonie relate to wider theories about the implications of 'literacy', or more generally 'writing', for intellectual processes, a subject that has been part of our on-going discussion (see Goody and Watt 1963; Luria 1976; Olson 1975; Scribner 1969; Scribner and Cole 1974, 1981). These discussions, whose lines of argument differ markedly in their details, acknowledge that writing has repercussions not only for the society into which it is introduced, but also for the organization of intellectual activities in the user. The line of theory developed by Vygotsky (see Luria 1976) maintains that when an individual comes to master writing, the basic system underlying the nature of his mental processes is changed fundamentally as the external symbol system comes to mediate the organization of all his basic intellectual operations. Thus, for example, knowledge of a writing system would alter the very structure of memory, classification and problem-solving by altering the way in which these elementary processes are organized to include an external (written) symbol system.

In the context of this discussion, we want to draw particular attention to the importance of studying recopied texts in order to analyze the kind of operations that writing facilitates or makes possible. At several points in our discussion of the materials themselves, we were led to remark on the special significance of the reworking of the written data: the note suggesting the reordering of an article from the constitution, the rearrangement of goods purchased for the Malodi organization (putting thread with cloth, meat with chicken) and the repeated use of various classificatory schemes (sex, clan, etc.) for reordering the lists of members and of dues.

In each of these cases we are provided with data roughly analogous to what psychologists obtain when they ask subjects to classify common objects or pictures of objects. But the analogy is a rough one and closer examination suggests that there may be less in common between the two tasks than one might suppose.

When psychologists have set these tasks, they have done so in the specific context of an experimental situation. Thus the context (and presumably the goal) of the activity is markedly different from Sonie's attempt to reorder the membership lists of the Malodi association. As we have seen, some of his efforts at reorganization entailed the use of major categories of persons in the society (e.g. male and female) in order to specify the source of dues. That is, reclassification was not the goal of the activity; rather, classification was the means to particular ends.

At other times, as when he reclassified members by their first names, the ends were certainly less easy to specify; he was playing a 'game' with the recorded information of a kind that is perhaps closer to the task set by the psychologist. But even here can we accept the assumption that these classifying activities are equivalent from the standpoint of social or psychological theory? This assumption is implicit in much psychological research, which assumes that experiments are indicators of generalized abilities. It allows the generalization from laboratory-style studies of classification to 'classification' abilities in general. Far from accepting this assumption, we have suggested (Goody 1977b; Cole and Scribner 1974) that the generalization of skills exhibited by an individual in one realm of activity to other spheres is open to doubt. There is, then, danger in using the results derived from the analysis of Sonie's writings to draw conclusions about generalized competencies, if only because of the difficulty in specifying such qualities.

Nevertheless the analysis of Sonie's writings may help as a guide to further experimental research if it convinces investigators that they should look for evidence of intellectual abilities in wider and more 'natural' contexts than those usually sampled in psychological experiments which concentrate upon the classification and manipulation of static properties of objects. During our brief period of joint field work we applied the suggestion (obtained from Sonie's writing) that social categories would be prominent in recall if the right subject matter and framework of elicitation were provided. When we asked an informant to tell us the names of the various Vai clans ordinarily represented at funerals in his town we not only obtained an impressively long list, but the grouping of clans according to their respective chiefdoms was a prominent feature of the order of recall. Although such a result may appear trivial, it stands in sharp contrast to the many experimentally contrived situations in which populations such as the Vai fail to demonstrate conceptually ordered recall (Cole and Scribner 1974).

In any use of this evidence for discussing the role of literacy, we would also have to be careful to avoid generalizing the specific competencies we have been discussing from Sonie to the Vai as a whole. Few of the latter are as 'literate' in their use of script as was Sonie himself; besides which, Sonie was an unusual man with unusual experiences, which certainly affected the thoroughness and extent of his record keeping practices. The average user of the Vai script would be unlikely to duplicate his achievements.

Moreover, even among those Vai who have a reasonable 'fluency' with their own script, their literate activities are devoted to different ends with different consequences. Some, like Sonie, keep records. The vast majority use the script for family correspondence, and occasionally for business letters as well. A few have employed it for 'literary' purposes (writing down stories and proverbs), while others have used it to deepen their understanding of religious dogma.[10]

Here again there are implications for further experimental research. Our analysis leads us to ask what kinds of intellectual operations each of these different forms of literate activity require. We cannot provide a detailed answer to this question, but it is obvious that writing a letter to one's sister about an impending wedding and keeping business records are not identical activities. To understand the implications of such facts we must inquire further into the relation between different kinds of literate activity and specific intellectual processes. If we pursue this approach, we may help to clarify more general problems in understanding intellectual abilities, in addition to furthering the more immediate goal of understanding the changes wrought on individuals and societies by the introduction of writing.

IV

Writing and its impact on individuals in society

10

The interface between the sociological and the psychological analysis of literacy

Achievement in the Vai script

The last chapter presented an account of the joint work we carried out in Liberia based on the analysis of the records of Ansumana Sonie. Note how their general shape corresponded to the kinds of literate production characteristic of early Mesopotamia. There were records of transactions, both personal and on behalf of the 'company'; there were membership records; there was the constitution of the company and finally the records of family dates with which the writer 'played' in the manner of a cross-word puzzle. Of these documents the constitution was the only one that used sentence-like forms, though obviously letters and stories, which were part of the output of Vai writing, also have a similar syntactic structure. The rest of his writing took the form of lists, tables as I define them, which consisted of names and payments (membership lists with dues) and objects and prices (ledgers), in other words they consisted of combinations of single words plus numbers. The literacy was closely involved with numeracy.

Very similar but simpler forms of writing, the 'elementary forms' one might say, are widely found in West Africa among cooks and petty traders. The first make out shopping lists to which they add the costs of their purchases, the second attempt to account for incomings and outgoings by keeping simple records of objects, numbers and prices. In this low level use of writing, numeracy is as important as literacy. In combination they fill a gap in the activities of those who have no or little schooling, some members of transitional societies, cooks, traders, as well as craftsmen of various kinds, in Africa, India and in South America. The same is true of

211

membership lists. While working in a slum area of Accra, Ghana, in 1966 Hart was recruited by his host to keep the books of a Frafra benevolent society of a vaguely similar kind to the Malodi association among the Vai. These records, which consisted of members' names, dues paid, and sums disbursed, had been previously kept by his host who had worked as a cook and so acquired this basic grapho–linguistic ability.

In principle a system of graphic representations capable of recording objects (or names) and numbers is not difficult to construct. For objects one has pictograms, plus a simple numerical system of strokes or dots. In contemporary West Africa there is certainly some pressure from below in favour of a simple system of reckoning. In Birifu (LoDagaa) the Young Men's Association recorded the receipt of dues, and schoolboys were pulled into funerals to 'book' the gifts brought by kith and kin. In the same way, I have suggested, there was evidence of pressure towards a more accurate system of time-reckoning, for I was continually being asked how many moons would there be till harvest. But despite the pressure towards the elementary forms of writing, despite the relatively simple calculus that is required, these minimal types of reckoning usually seem to be found as fragments of more inclusive, more developed systems. In Sonie's case, his use of ledgers occurred within the overall framework not only of the complete syllabic system of the Vai script but also of English writing. Moreover, he himself had been a cook and may have already been familiar with some elementary bookkeeping.

That does not detract from his achievements; and whether he invented or borrowed the system of accounting, writing was necessary either as a pre-requisite for its emergence or because bookkeeping formed part of the written tradition. And bookkeeping in its turn required that objects be reduced to monetary (or unitary) terms, promoted the use of a generalized medium of exchange or abstract units of account so that one could add up the total gains and losses, and calculate the balance.

Before referring to the specific psycho–social activities of reclassification involved in reviewing written information, let me turn to one other aspect of these documents which, while dependent on writing, was not an automatic result of turning on the tap of literacy. I refer to Sonie's use of dates based on the Common Era.

Although it is not inconceivable that oral societies might develop a 'progressive', linear mode of reckoning the passage of years, I do not know of one. Such societies are sometimes said to have a cyclical rather than a linear concept of time. This contrast is a matter of emphasis rather than of binary division; all societies operate with cycles (for example, with annual festivals and developmental cycles) as well as with linear progression. But greater emphasis is given to the latter when one is able to fix a point in time and then start numbering consecutively from that base line; the result is a universalistic system of counting in years (instead of a personal reckoning linked to 'summers'), which requires a line to be drawn – a graphic act – followed by a graphic representation of numbers as the basis for carrying out the calculations.

Sonie used the annual count to record family events, as did others in the region, setting them down in a notebook in the way that Europeans used the Family Bible. But the calculations he made on the basis of these dates were not simply 'utilitarian'. As in some of the notebooks where information on membership was re-ordered, he seemed to be 'playing' with the figures in a way that was at once pointless and puzzle-solving in the 'decontextualized' way that characterizes many of the kind of problems set at school. As such, the 'pointless' activity was potentially generative, displaying features of those cognitive operations that psychologists search for in looking for growth.

The same was true of the attempts in the notebooks to reorganize information in more useful, more 'logical', sometimes simply different ways:

1 accounts are re-ordered for the daily or annual statement. Quite apart from the more obvious utilitarian aspects of the enterprise, Sonie brought together purchases made on different dates on the basis of their longer-term ends. We also find him changing some categories, bringing 'chicken' under the category 'meat' which was customarily excluded, being a lateral counterpart.

2 membership lists are re-ordered to make retrieval easier. The chronological order of entry into the society is set aside in favour of one based on the initial syllable, sex, and clan/chiefdom affiliation. These forms of re-ordering information, as we com-

mented, are activities that psychologists often look for in oral
societies but fail to find by means of their particular testing
procedures.

3 finally we concluded that the numbered items in the constitution
would probably have been re-ordered in a more logical manner
when the constitution was next copied out.

Vygotsky and the psychological analysis of Vai literacy

This study of Sonie's writings in Vai clearly gave some support to
ideas about the positive relation between literacy and achievement,
both of a cultural and of a personal kind. On the other hand the
more extensive study by Scribner and Cole that emerged from the
Vai Literacy Project, entitled *The Psychology of Literacy* (1981),
has been interpreted as in some sense rejecting the general hypothesis. Although the authors would deny this interpretation, the
work contains statements about their early disillusion with the idea
of finding any "general cognitive consequences of literacy among
the Vai" (p. 158, elsewhere the word 'cognitive' is sometimes
omitted), a disillusion which forced them to re-think their strategies
in the course of the research and to turn from the quest for general
cognitive abilities to that for special skills. In this chapter I want to
try and resolve the apparent contradictions between these two
studies, a venture that will lead to comments on psychological
experiments in the context of the social history of cognitive
processes.

There are two preliminary points, discussed by the authors, that
need stressing. The first concerns the use of systems of writing
among the Vai. In the summary presented in Table 3 (see p. 223),
the authors divide their results according to the type of 'literacy'
with which the respondents were most familiar. The situation they
are dealing with is culturally complex, since while with Vai script
there is a fairly direct relationship between sign and sound,
between script and maternal language, in the case of English and
Arabic, the Vai have to learn the language before they can read the
script. Of course, there is another sense of 'read' which means to
produce the sounds without understanding the words, as I can do
with any language written in the Roman script, especially if I had

been taught the phonetic equivalences relevant to the particular tongue. But this has little to do with reading in the sense of knowing the meaning of what has been written. The category of Qu'ranic 'readers' includes those with the ability to memorize a text without comprehension. In this case reading involves no communication, unless somebody who also knows the meaning of the text provides the 'reader' with a parallel translation and the latter picks up some visual clues about the beginning and end of certain 'bits' of text (verses, surahs, paragraphs, sections, chapters). Although in a few cases readers have adequate understanding, much Arabic 'literacy' in West Africa is of this kind. In learning to read English, on the other hand, pupils are subjected to intensive, long-term, systematic language-learning in the full sense of the word, an enduring process which takes several years for any individual or class.

Secondly, there is the context of the written tradition to consider. In both English and Arabic texts a considerable amount of knowledge has been stored and to this one has access by reading a new language. In comparison very little knowledge has been written down in Vai script, although this transcribes their maternal tongue. In this study all the tests were conducted in Vai, so that we do not know what performance in English and Arabic was like.

I mention these differences because they mean that the learning of each of these scripts and the associated languages will have different implications over the longer and shorter terms. Indeed it was to test the specific effects of different scripts and languages that halfway through the study the authors redirected the search from general abilities to specific skills. If we are examining the consequences of learning to read English or Arabic in the full sense of the word, the potentialities for increasing our understanding of the world are enormous since the acquisition of these skills opens up whole bodies of texts that deal with so many aspects of that world. By reading Darwin I may reshape my view about the creation of the world and about the categories of beings therein. Nor is such understanding simply passive but may also involve practical action. By reading the Qu'ran I may be motivated to set out on the long pilgrimage to Mecca in order to get to know the centre of that world. Each of these activities involve cognitive processes but not ones that are likely to be brought out in the usual psychological tests, however ingeniously constructed.

Let us first try to attack the heart of the matter. A consideration of the effects of literacy on general cognitive abilities takes us back to that important figure, Vygotsky. In the last chapter we summarized the theory he developed in the following words; "when an individual comes to master writing, the basic system underlying the nature of his mental processes is changed fundamentally as the external symbol system comes to mediate the organization of all of his basic intellectual operations. Thus, for example, knowledge of a writing system would alter the very structure of memory, classification and problem-solving by altering the way in which these elementary processes are organized to include an external (written) symbol system" (p. 205 above). This summary points to an area of serious theoretical misunderstanding. Despite his willingness to cross the internal–external boundary and to consider historical factors, Vygotsky gives little weight to the mediation of the whole set of cultural and historical processes, adopting a basically mentalistic view of intellectual operations or cognitive skills, which in turn leads to a simplistic causal nexus. It is the position discussed by Scribner and Cole (1981:239) when they write that the Vai material does not fulfill the expectations of those social scientists who consider literacy a prime mover in social change. "It has not set off a dramatic modernizing sequence; it has not been accompanied by rapid developments in technology, art and science; it has not led to the growth of new intellectual disciplines" (1981:239). The same theme crops up anew in their modification of the statement that "becoming literate profoundly changes what people know about their language and how they think about it" (p. 134). Again, "More radical is the claim that mastery of a written language affects not only the content of thought but also the process of thinking – *how* we classify, reason, remember" (p. 5), a claim that would justify us in speaking not only of literate and preliterate societies but of literate and preliterate people. The view they wish to modify implies that we should find all the cognitive implications of literacy everywhere and immediately. The notion is that of the chemist. Mix two ingredients together and you will get a specific result which can be tested by means of a litmus paper, producing instant literacy. In this view, psychological tests of, for example, syllogistic reasoning are the equivalent of the litmus paper. If respondents who can decode the script of any language, regardless of whether or not it is their own, fail to pass the litmus test, then writing has no effect, leaving aside for the moment the question of whether we describe that effect in terms of cognitive abilities, capabilities or skills – as psychological, cultural or technological.

Varieties of script and varieties of tradition

Given the implications of these claims it is not surprising that Scribner and Cole are led to conclude that there are no "general cognitive effects as we have defined them" (p. 132), a statement which at another point is phrased as no "general cognitive consequences" (p. 158). The question they are getting at is illuminated in the earlier chapter entitled "*social* correlates of literacy" (my italics), where the authors write that "we failed to find a discrete dimension of Vai life that could be labeled 'literacy'" (p. 107). Since commonsense tells us that such a dimension is obviously involved in the very presence of writing or at least in the ability to read books and write letters, this statement is likely to be misunderstood. Its meaning is elucidated in the following sentence. "With nearly 30 percent of our male correspondents having some reading or writing skill in some script, we were nonetheless unable to discover any attribute other than sex which related to *all types* of script knowledge" (p. 107, my italics). That is to say, their factor analysis of social correlates did not show any general characteristic attaching to all those who could read or 'read' one or more of the three scripts. Given the diversity of forms of writing and written traditions, the conclusion is hardly surprising. Does it really justify the statement that "Our evidence for the specificity of literacy knowledge among the Vai has several consequences: one, primarily theoretical in nature, suggests the need to revise some of the leading speculations about literacy and its social basis and functions" (p.107), a theme taken up again in the last chapter? Surely the proper conclusion is that the initial model with which they started was over-simplistic and that the notion of literacy (as a general ability to read/'read' any language in any script) having a direct, precise, immediate and unmediated effect on general cognitive abilities in a specific psychological sense is a non-starter. The authors consider the fault with this contention lies in technological determinism, but that is not the only problem. It is psychologically over-determined and it is historically and sociologically naive. I have myself spoken of writing as a 'technology of the intellect' and some commentators have seen this phrase as reflecting a species of technological determinism. Their conclusion would make it impossible to talk about the influence of any 'technology' on the human condition without being so accused. Whether one is correct to speak of writing in the sense of a script as a technology, or, as I did, of literacy in the sense of acquiring access to a body of writing (one that provides, for example, a lever on cognitive operations by means of the syllogism) as a technology of the intellect, these usages do not assume, whatever other questions they may raise, a one-to-one causal relation, certainly not of the immediate kind involved in the theories that Scribner and Cole are initially testing before they give up the search for general cognitive abilities in favour of specific cognitive skills.

My own view would be that most specific cognitive skills have also to be related to particular socio–historical situations. Let me take an example in the area of problem-solving. I have spoken of the cross-word puzzle as encouraging a particular type of cognitive skill. It is not that in some mysterious way writing gives birth to a general ability permitting literates to solve cross-word puzzles. The puzzle is a specific invention that arises out of other types of writing activity (the graphic representation of linguistic units in columns and rows). It involves a type of skill which may be limited in its distribution as well as in its transferability to other situations. But even if the skill allows one person to go on to invent another type of puzzle, to write a detective story or to construct a computer, then that activity has some further cognitive consequences both for him and for the society. As for the present, these particular skills may be so specific that they are detectable only by giving literates and non-literates a cross-word puzzle to solve. The result will be predictable but not altogether negligible. By this I simply mean that one important feature of literacy is that it enables people to read books and the consequences of this achievement may not always be visible in 'psychological' procedures, that is, in tests which substitute for the particular activity itself, immediate and unmediated consequences, and draw too sharp an internal–external boundary around the psyche, separating what I can consult in my head from what I can consult in my diary (or even in other people's books). This contention raises a more general question about cognitive processes to which I will return. Let me pursue the problem of the confusion to which the testing of Vygotsky's hypothesis, as it has been stated or interpreted, seems to give rise. I take the case of the link between writing or literacy and 'logical' or 'abstract' reasoning.

Logic and logical reasoning

In the preamble to the presentation of their tests on logic the authors note: "the Greenfield–Bruner thesis explicitly maintained that schooling pushes cognitive growth to new levels; and Luria, Goody, Havelock, and others claimed that literacy is linked to abstract and logical reasoning" (1981:114). Leaving aside the possible claims of Luria, Havelock and others, what Goody and Watt suggested with regard to 'logical reasoning' was highly specific. They maintained that the procedures constituting the Greek study of 'logic', procedures of inference of inductive and deductive kinds such as the syllogism, were dependent on the prior existence of writing. In our first paper (1963) we looked upon these procedures as a consequence (in the sense of 'following from') the alphabet, but in various subsequent publications over the last twenty years I have suggested that similar procedures, less formalized, less explicit, were available in Mesopotamia and in other written cultures, thus attempting to rectify the ethnocentric bias of much of the argument about the alphabet (Wang 1981:234).

Logical reasoning in the general sense was never at stake. Similar procedures of an even less explicit kind are found in oral cultures. We rejected Lévy-Bruhl's contention that primitive mentality was pre-logical, but were trying to find an explanation of one point that the author seemed to be getting at. We did not see the primitive or savage mind (for which read 'oral' man) as being incapable of logical reasoning or of perceiving contradiction as he contended;

that was completely contrary to our personal experience, our theoretical claims and our individual preconceptions. What we did argue was that oral man lacked not logical reasoning but certain tools of intellectual operation that defined the Greek notion of 'logic', a notion which is shared by contemporary philosophers, practised by some members of the society, ignored by the many, although fed back in watered-down ways in schools through books such as Stebbing's *Thinking to Some Purpose* (1939) and its more recent equivalents. The same can be said for contradiction, the notion of which is associated with 'logic'. Our argument, developed in the context of ideas about the past, was simply that the presence of documents enabled one to lay side by side different accounts, emanating from different sources, different times and different places, and so perceive contradictions which in the oral mode would be virtually impossible to spot. A similar argument was used about scepticism when discussing the way in which writing not only promotes a kind of critical attention to a text read that would be impossible to apply to an utterance heard (that is, in an oral society, not in one that has other means of recording utterance), but also permits the accumulation of sceptical knowledge as it does of logical procedures. Such texts are in turn capable of being fed back into the mental storage system of any individual but they also exist independently as an actual or potential resource. Some of these forms of 'logic' or contradiction can be used as discovery procedures, as methods of 'proof' or inference. As such they are not simply parts of the static field of 'logic' but devices that enable individuals to make 'discoveries' which may profoundly influence the shape of socio–cultural systems.

Watt and I were not arguing along the same lines as Vygotsky. His position was embodied in the experimental assumptions behind the work carried out by the expedition to Central Asia in the 1930s led by Luria. Here the investigators compared groups of 'traditional' farmers with other residents of the same village who had gone through brief literacy courses or who had participated in short teacher-training programmes. On various tests to do with reasoning and categorization, they found graded differences depending upon exposure to literacy (that is, to written traditions rather than to script *per se*). These are the results that Scribner and Cole were trying to duplicate, unsuccessfully in their eyes.

However when we wrote in chapter 9 of Sonie's achievements with the same Vai script, we were talking about tasks that writing *"facilitates or makes possible"* (p. 205, my italics). That is to say, we did not expect the "mastery of writing" (of whatever form) to produce in itself an immediate change in the intellectual operations of individuals. There may well be a few activities that do turn out to be widespread if not universal consequences of an immediate kind (even a positive statistical association already carries explanatory implications) and the study by Scribner and Cole points to some of these. By widespread here I mean widespread among societies, for 'individuals' in a society will always vary in their exposure and reaction to writing. But if we are referring to an operation like syllogistic reasoning, the expectation that 'mastery of writing' in itself would lead directly to its adoption is patently absurd. The syllogism, as we know it, was a particular invention of a particular place and time; there were forerunners of a sort in Mesopotamia just as there were forerunners of Pythagoras' Theorem; nor on a more general level is the process of deductive inference unknown in oral societies. But we are talking about a particular kind of puzzle, 'logic', theorem, that involves a graphic lay-out. In this sense the syllogism is consequent upon or implied in writing. However its use as distinct from its invention does not demand a mastery of writing. Once invented it can be fed back into the activities of individual illiterates or even non-literates just as the same individuals can be taught to operate the arithmetic table or, as Scribner and Cole point out, to decode rebus writing (pp. 184–5).

Mediated and unmediated implications

We can put the point another way (and I hope not too mislead-ingly). We can speak of the *unmediated* and *mediated* consequences or implications of writing, though once again it is necessary to distinguish what kind of writing system we are dealing with. Does writing involve language learning? Or, rather, to what extent does it do so, for the written language always diverges from the oral in some degree and hence the school-child has to learn new forms (syntactical, lexical, semantic) even when learning to write in what is basically his maternal tongue? To how much of the written tradition is one gaining access? It is perfectly possible for us to learn to read without being introduced to the syllogism, although the general type of formal reasoning involved may reach us through the practice of teachers.

It would be possible to describe *mediated* consequences as 'cultural' rather than 'individual'. If this particular description has any meaning, it is obvious and not very helpful, except in reminding us of the problem with Vygotsky's approach and the way we should interpret the occasionally pessimistic comments of Scribner and Cole. Because what we need to look for is not a generalized blanket description of the way that 'culture' intervenes, but a specific account of the mechanisms by which writing can encourage changes in categorization, for example. Such changes occur, I have suggested, either by means of the decontextualizing procedures involved in producing a written list of, say, trees, which provides a definite beginning and an end to the category, or else by the kind of reorganization of written material in more 'logical' ways that was demonstrated in the activities of Ansumana Sonie. It is the written 'tradition', the accumulated knowledge stored in documents as well as in the mind, whether over a few years as in Sonie's case or over a millennium as with Islam, that provides an intervening variable between mastery of a skill and cognitive operations.

A list of trees may be adopted as a standardized 'cultural' product to be taught in schools, so becoming part (but not the whole) of that system of categories. The reorganization of information, making lists more 'logical' by regrouping the items, is a continuous possibility in many types of rewriting activity that do not entail the verbatim copying that is sometimes demanded for religious or other purposes; Sonie would not have attempted to reorganize the surahs of the Qu'ran in the way he did with his lists. Learning to read the Holy Book and to copy its words does not lead to creative reorganization, though it often encourages exegesis (Scribner and Cole 1981); the text is sacred but the commentary is not. In the first case the written reproduction of the text (so essential an undertaking before mechanical means were available)

Broad category of effect		Type of literacy			
		English/school	Vai script	Qur'anic	Arabic language
Categorizing	Form/number sort	▨	▨		▨
Memory	Incremental recall			▨	▨
	Free recall	▨			
Logical reasoning	Syllogisms	▨			
Encoding and decoding	Rebus reading	▨	▨		
	Rebus writing	▨			▨
Semantic integration	Integrating words	▨	▨	▨	▨
	Integrating syllables		▨		
Verbal explanation	Communication game	▨			
	Grammatical rules	▨	▨		
	Sorting geometric figures	▨			
	Logical syllogisms	▨			
	Sun-moon name-switching (Because of ambiguities in this task, we include only those literacy effects appearing in more than one administration.)	▨			

Table 3. Schematic representation of effects associated with each 'literacy'

does not permit reorganization; in the second it does. Contrast the process of reciting the Bagre where one set of comments, the Speaker's, actually gets incorporated into the utterance and then becomes the current version of the recitation.

Literacy effects in the Vai study

Let us now return to the results of the major Vai study itself, the positive findings of which are summarized in Table 3. Despite the great diversity of script use and potentiality to which I have drawn attention, there are, surprisingly, some skills which appear to be found across the whole range of these writing systems. "Rebus reading and writing tasks suggest that prior experience in constructing meaning from graphic symbols in all scripts is helpful in semantic interpretation of other symbols" (Scribner and Cole 1981: 184). While rebus writing can be taught to non-literates, learning is definitely enhanced by having worked with a script. Again the ability to repeat and make sense out of a 'degraded' (that is, slowed down) sentence composed of words (an auditory integration task) may be enhanced by all forms of literacy, providing the units are semantically meaningful. Those familiar with Vai script were better able to handle syllables as the units of communication because of the syllabic nature of the writing.

Given the fact that the Vai use these different scripts to write three different languages (one of them largely unlearnt), it is surprising to find any cross-cutting features at all, because the systems are complementary rather than alternative. Arabic is the language of the Holy Book, English is the national tongue and Vai the maternal one. Moreover since fluent Arabic is known only by few, most claims to know Arabic 'Book' do not indicate literacy in any substantial sense; the level of knowledge required to get into the Arabic literate category (3 and 4 levels of achievement, 50.3 per cent of the readers) seems to be fairly generous, especially as the use made of this script is small compared with the other two (pp. 64, 72). So most of the possible links are between those literate in Vai and English. Here we see some positive results. Table 3 is a matrix, a "schematic representation of effects" associated with each 'literacy'. Arabic language literates show four positive features, three of which are shared with Vai and English readers. Two we have discussed; the third effect is demonstrated by a categorizing test (a form/number sort). It is not surprising to find that the fourth characteristic, shared only with Qu'ranic scholars (those who don't know Arabic), is a memory task, that is, incremental recall, encouraged by the nature of the process of learning the Qu'ran by heart, verbatim.

English and Vai readers also scored positively on rebus reading (characterized as encoding/decoding) and in two verbal explanation tasks, the 'communication game' and 'grammatical rules'. English alone is associated with positive performance in the following tasks: free recall, syllogisms, sorting generative figures, logical syllogisms, sun-moon name switching. These tasks all showed effects on more than one administration.

What Scribner and Cole were initially looking for were results that would confirm or reject Vygotsky's hypothesis about the immediate (unmediated) effects of any form of writing (script). This point has to be understood when they write that non-schooled literacy does not produce general cognitive effects (p. 132), a result that "precludes any sweeping generalizations about literacy and cognitive change". Leaving aside the epithet "sweeping", such generalizations (that is, definable trends) are surely still possible if one does not assume immediacy of effect. When they speak of the absence of a general 'literacy' phenomenon, they are talking of unmediated responses, generalized throughout a population, and assessable by 'psychological tests'. It is therefore perhaps misleading to begin (p. 119) the discussion of the first results on abstraction (geometric sorting tasks) by quoting Havelock as maintaining that ordering events and doings to "'topical groupings and categories' (1963:189) is contingent on the development of a written language which identifies and names the headings and categories", since his contention surely does not imply an unmediated effect. Certainly in my own discussion of changes in categorization I have pointed to the creation of conceptual lists as one intervening mechanism, and I would argue that its effects are limited to particular contexts, for example, in insisting we make a binary choice in locating the ambiguous tomato among the fruits or among the vegetables. It is difficult to deny the influence of writing on classification if we look at the constant attempts to order and reorder items found in Ancient Greece (Lloyd 1979), in the Renaissance (Ong 1974; 1982) and in a minor way in the activities of Ansumana Sonie himself. To reconcile these historical facts with the statement that, overall, the results on taxonomic classification "discourage conclusions about a strong influence of literacy on categorization and abstraction" (p. 124), we have to bear in mind the unmediated nature of the literacy variable being tested.

The second task was one of memory, to which I will return later.

The third had to do with 'logic' and the discussion of the results begins by referring to the contention of Watt and myself about writing being a precondition for Aristotle's invention of the syllogism and the emergence of the discipline of logic (Scribner and Cole 1981:126). Like Havelock we were not predicting any immediate effects unless the acquisition of writing goes hand in hand with a written tradition that embodies Aristotle's invention (or someone else's replication). This point is brought out in the link the tests show between such practices and English schooling (and it would no doubt hold true for some forms of Arabic, Chinese and Hindu instruction). The fourth test had to do with 'language objectivity', in discussing which the authors begin by quoting a statement of mine that "writing *may change* an individual's perception of the relation between words and their referents"; when it is put down on paper, "the written word becomes a separate thing". Scribner and Cole invent an ingenious experimental task involving a change in the names of the sun and the moon; once again there is a positive effect with schooling (as with Vai/Arabic literacy) but the test does not take into account the fact that in speaking of the word as a separate thing I referred not only to words and meanings but also to the separation of words from sentences when they are incorporated in lists, that is, to the non-syntactic use of language. Such separateness ocurs in the individual act of writing down the word LOVE on the blackboard, as well as in the historical, cultural phenomenon of grammatical analysis or dictionary definitions.

The shift from abilities to skills

Looking at the results as a whole it is perhaps not the general effects of 'literacy' that need reassessing as much as the way of measuring those effects. In the first place there are other tests that could have been given which might have provided evidence of abstraction, assuming that is a definable notion. For example, if one considers nominalization as an aspect of abstraction, one can examine the use of nouns and verbs in the speech of readers and non-readers. Scribner and Cole have themselves called attention to the need to shift our level of analysis from abilities to skills, whose generalization is questionable (Cole and Scribner 1974; Goody 1977b). In our joint work reported in chapter 9 we referred to the difference between the experimental tasks and the actual goal-oriented activity itself. Future investigators were advised to look for evidence of intellectual abilities in wider and more 'neutral' contexts. "When we asked an informant to tell us the names of the various Vai clans ordinarily represented at funerals . . . we not only obtained an impressively long list, but the grouping of clans according to their representative chiefdoms was a prominent feature of the order of recall" (p. 207). Although such a result may appear trivial, we commented, it stands in sharp contrast to the many experimentally contrived situations in which populations such as the Vai fail to demonstrate conceptually ordered recall. There could be no stronger statement about the limitations on testing procedures that involve the attempt to mock-up certain kinds of actual activity.

The Vai project followed up its attempt to test the unmediated effects of learning to read on general cognitive abilities with more specific tests of their respondent's metalinguistic knowledge about the Vai language (though not initially on the school population). First, the language objectivity, 'names and things', test was repeated using the names for sun and moon. There were some positive results in which all three 'literacies' were implicated to a modest degree (p. 140). A fascinating light was shed on this test in the subsequent discussion when one influential man, who clearly realized the separateness of names and things, asserted that God's names for the things of creation could not be changed (p. 141). The will of God or Allah was final, indicating one effect of religion (in this case written) on categorical systems.

The influence of writing in separating the 'word' from the sentence was clearly brought out in the next series of metalinguistic tests. The authors note that Vai has no concept of a word but only, as I have also noted for the LoDagaa, of a 'piece of speech'. This is understandable as Vai writing is not logographic but syllabic with no word division. Asking respondents to give the longest 'word' produced spotty results, partly because of this very ambiguity; in the replication study no more than half offered single words. However, by giving learned respondents an actual text, it appeared that Vai script literates can analyze the written language into semantic segments but the basic units are meaning-carrying phrases (p. 149).

Word definition tasks were given to non-school respondents in the metalinguistic survey. This task excluded the use of a dictionary and was not given to schooled adults; again there were no positive results.

The next task was grammatical. All groups pointed out ungrammatical sentences. But it was the Vai and English readers who could explain what was wrong. In other words, reading had the effect of making explicit what had been implicit, a result that on replication was stronger with the English readers and relatively weak for those 'literate' in Arabic.

It will be recalled that in the major survey of cognitive abilities, only schooling improved performance generally. Scribner and Cole now returned to the syllogism from a new point of view. They remark that most contemporary psychologists would argue that the tendency to react to syllogisms empirically (and thus give the wrong answer) "is not so much a sign of the inability to reason logically as it is an indication of how people understand this particular verbal form" (p. 155). This is the very point Watt and I were trying to make, although we assumed that understanding this verbal form had some implications for the formal notion of proof. The authors go on to test responses to syllogisms from the standpoint of 'logical relations to propositions', and then the respondents were asked to explain the answers they gave. On this occasion there was little positive to report, casting doubt on hypotheses "that implicate literacy *directly* in the acquisition of metalinguistic knowledge about the properties of propositions" (p. 156, my italics), though there is some evidence to show that 'discourse context' affected how the task was understood. The latter finding would seem to be in keeping with the notion that unless people were specifically taught about this bizarre literate invention, they would hardly be able to explain it. But while the result may say something negative about the *direct* effects of instant literacy, it says nothing about the cultural–historical relation of the syllogism to writing. So that while we may agree with the authors when they conclude by saying that "Our results furnish little support for speculations that literacy is a precondition or prime cause for an understanding of language as an object" (p. 157), the historical, cultural hypothesis rests on more than this kind of evidence. In the case of instant literacy, one can assent, but one has only to think about the influence of grammarians like Pāṇini (or later equivalents) to understand that their task (a cognitive task if ever there was one) would have been impossible without the aid of writing, and it is through writing that their work is fed back into more general spheres of social action by its use in schools. Grammar schools, in Britain and the United States, were not so called without good reason.

As we have seen, in the second part of their study the authors shift from looking for general abilities to looking for the generalization of skills, a course that eventually leads them to adopt a more optimistic view of their results. They first examine the question of whether the ability to read one script helped with the ability to read others. They found this to be the case for rebus reading and writing with both English language and Vai script readers, and with writing alone for Arabic literates. At this level the authors discerned a "'common literacy' effect" (1981:184). On auditory integration tasks, the ability to make sense out of a slowed down sentence composed of words was again a common feature. What was impressive to the authors was the fact that the Vai literates were especially capable of handling syllables as units of communication which, because the capacity varied according to experience, did suggest a "causal interpretation of script literacy" (p. 185). The suggestion is also made that these skills (activities) in the written language may effect "comprehension and memory of *spoken* languages"; "Practice in reading may promote the development of specialized skills for linguistic analysis in the auditory mode" which "may differ for different scripts" (p. 186), a suggestion that is critical in discussing the implications of writing for the development of grammars and grammarians. This point is taken up in Reder's linguistic section of the Vai study summarized in the following chapter of their book where the results give support to the case for the historical connection between the work of Pāṇini in India and the advent of a script, alphabetic in that case. And the conclusions for grammarians of language are not perhaps so very different historically for another sort of grammarian, the grammarians of reasoning we call logicians.

The next problem tackled by Scribner and Cole is that of communications skills, 'making meaning clear'. Trying again to get nearer to the specific cultural context in these tests, they take into account not just the 'mastery of writing' but two other factors I see as necessary in considering the implications of literacy. The first of these is the form of a script, its relationship to the spoken language and the specific role of that script with regard to other scripts. The second is the interaction between skills and a specific product of writing itself, namely, letter-writing, which is one of the main uses of literacy in Vai.

In an interesting analysis of this last feature the authors explain that "Vai letters are more than talk written down; they are a new, written form of discourse" (p. 204). In the first place the letters take specific forms, which like Cherokee letters (and like letters from the Ancient Near East), "indicate that the communicative exchange is framed in conventions of writing rather than speaking" (p. 202). There are formulaic expressions to open and close; the letter itself is "addressed not to the 'medium' or 'messenger' but to the recipient". Basically letters deal in transactions (rather than information); many are written by 'scholars' rather than by the originator of the message, and while they are generally addressed to individuals that are known to the 'writer', they have on occasion to provide a fuller explanation of the situation than would be needed in face-to-face communication (p. 204).

Scribner and Cole set out to test the consequences of this pressure for 'elaborated meaning' by setting up a task that implicated "the same kind of communication skills" that were attributed to letter-writing but which did not privilege literates (p. 204). For this purpose they taught all the respondents a board game, asked them to explain it to another person, then to write or dictate a letter explaining it to someone at a distance. Secondly they asked the respondents to write (or dictate) a letter giving directions to get to their farms. Note that in both these latter cases all the respondents were asked to compose a letter rather than simply give an account.

The results showed that, while the schooled population did better, Vai script literates had an advantage over Arabic literates which was consistent and related to proficiency in certain instructional tasks in the larger communication study, especially with regard to two features, the amount of explicit information and of expository (descriptive or orienting) statements (p. 217). These literates were not alone in attempting to assess the information needs of the recipient, although Vai literates did it better; it is not so much that they had greater capacity to take the other person's perspective, but that writing provides special techniques to meet the informational demands of the situation. These techniques of description consist of extracting information from the flow of narrative and presenting it in an expository (static) mode. '*Characterization*' of the game in general terms also helped since it was a way, in which the schooled were especially good, of "organizing and presenting information outside of a narrative sequence" (p. 219). The authors summarize this evidence as suggesting a 'causal role' for Vai script literacy in fostering effective instructional communication. However they are inclined to see Vai literacy as a 'surrogate' for schooling, which has yet a greater effect, thus again defining literacy in opposition to English schooling. Arabic literacy on the other hand does not help (though it is more 'schooled' than Vai) and the authors ascribe the difference to the fact that Vai is used for letter writing, Arabic apparently not. In this case it is also surely a question of the lack of fluent linguistic knowledge of Arabic, for elsewhere Arabic is widely used for this task. But more generally I would suggest that writing and the written tradition are preconditions of schooling as we know it, for most of its procedures are directed first to the acquisition of literate skills and then to probing literate sources of knowledge.

On another, more ethnographic, level, Scribner and Cole had become impressed with the common practice of arguing about the content of letters and applying criteria of communicative adequacy. They gave prepared letters to a series of Vai readers to compare and found the criteria of adequacy very similar to their own. So that in addition to letter writing, Vai script literates "have created a practice of criticism and standards for writing" which they apply to their own performance as well as to that of others, suggesting "useful consequences for other communicative exhanges in which learning takes place" (p. 220).

While the sending of letters is not in itself a spontaneous development of writing, it comes near to being a universal feature.

Letters were widely used in Ancient Egypt from an early period (on papyrus in the Sixth Dynasty, *c.* 2250 BC) and their composition taught in schools. We find many personal as well as official examples and in one case a scribe criticizes another for writing an unintelligible letter, in other words, for communicative inadequacy (James 1979:117). When literacy arrives, so the letter-writer follows, offering a service to the illiterate, making use of books of sample letters which lay down the form these communications should take, modes of address, ways of making a request and transmitting information, methods of marking the conclusion. But what I want to emphasize in the Vai case is that even if there were no "consequences for other communicative exchanges" and even if there were no differences in test performance on related, mock-up activities, writing would have had important implications in making letters possible, with consequent effects:

1 on speech, through a feedback of formulaic patterns
2 on communication at a distance, with all that this entails
3 on creating a social and practical difference between scribes and non-scribes.

The possibility of communication at a distance, of getting one's thoughts across to someone without meeting him or her face-to-face (and vice versa) potentially alters man's cognitive capacities; this is accomplished by the act itself, irrespective of any halo effect. If one is worried about privileging literates in tests, this alone provides clear recognition that they have an advantage in being able to perform certain tasks, an advantage that one can best assess by looking at the activity itself.

The last of the series of tests discussed by Scribner and Cole had to do with memory and hence concentrated upon the differences between Qu'ranic students and others since so much rote learning was involved in their instruction. The first study consisted in giving respondents three sentences to remember and then, after a delay, presenting them with a longer series, the task being to recognize those statements that had been included in the original set. One of these items was plain wrong, another a true inference, another a false inference. All groups tended to recognize true inferences although the investigators had thought that Arabic literacy might make exact recall more important than sense.

The next task tested serial recall (already done in the initial survey) but used pictures of common objects to test serial anticipation, that is, when picture one was presented, the respondent had to name the second. In this Arabic and English language students (the schooled) showed superiority over Vai script readers and non-literates.

Finally they turned to a task closer to Qu'ranic learning itself, which used an incremental procedure of recall. This involved a trial with a single element, then element one plus two, then one plus two, plus three, and so on. A count was made of the maximum number of words recalled in the correct order; then they made the same calculation with no missing items (that is, perfect recall of a segment). On these tasks Qu'ranic scholars showed consistently better performance than non-literates. When the study was extended to other literates (in a slightly different way, using oral plus visual cues), this procedure not only produced superior results all round but, while maximum recall itself displayed no difference, the Arabic group did best in the tasks involving maximum recall with order and with perfect recall of a segment, followed by the English school group, then the Vai script readers, although in a replication study the school group did not stand out. Story recall, however, showed no difference (except that unschooled children were less competent), from which the authors conclude that there was no general 'memory ability' related to the forms of writing in Vai country.

This conclusion is undoubtedly correct for the results of this kind of test. But note that the use of combined oral and visual procedures produced better recall in the incremental tasks and as the tests got closer to Qu'ranic practice, so too the results of those scholars stood out. Take the process a step further and construct an even more realistic test. Add not only procedures of learning the book but the book itself. There one has an instrument of recall, a form of storage, that enables individuals to master vast areas of knowledge as well as to recall events of their own past. The point is obvious but intrinsic. It is one of the consequences of literacy that we have less need of memory for some purposes, but it is not true that we store less material. And we have not only memory store but the library as well.

Secondly, there is the question of verbatim recall. Had we not wished to privilege literates (thereby possibly neglecting the power of the written word), we could set up the following test. Take an unknown poem of 250 lines. Give the literates a written version and the others an instructor who repeats the poem continuously. Give both groups three hours. Then test for verbatim recall. There is little doubt who would win out. On the other hand test for creative reinterpretation and that is likely to be the inverse of verbatim recall (almost by definition). This difference would be even more marked if one were to give no instructions except of the kind "I want you to recite this poem after three hours practice". Giving this freedom of action to the respondents one has to ask (following the observations of Lord and others) whether the oral reciter would wish to recall anything of this kind in a verbatim manner. For as we have seen, only in special circumstances is that activity required in oral cultures and then there is usually no mechanism for saying if the result of such an attempt is exact or not.

Memory and writing

A good deal of attention has been paid to the question of memory and recall in relation to literacy, giving rise to psychological testing in the form of lists as well as to claims by anthropologists for the outstanding memory of oral poets. It is obvious that any culture requires a good deal from its members by way of internal storage. Some of this clearly has to be precise, as with phonemes. Deviate slightly and you won't be understood. On the other hand, much in the way of knowledge can afford to be less exact, and this was the case with sections of the long Bagre myth of the LoDagaa (chapter 8). Writing, on the other hand, makes it possible to store linguistic material in an exact form over long periods, in principle to infinity. Instead of having to recall the Bagre, one can read it out. I do not memorize Milton, except for the purposes of examinations. Otherwise I consult the text.

What is interesting about early schooling is that at the very moment when memory could be dispensed with for certain purposes, precise, verbatim, recall came into its own. There is no need to memorize the Qu'ran or the Bible in order to 'know' it, but many people do just that. Indeed schools seem to specialize in this kind of memory activity. Now schools are essentially instruments of written culture. One can just imagine literacy without schools (Vai literacy is now like that), but not schools without literacy – unless you want to extend the term to so-called 'bush schools' associated with 'secret' societies in Africa and elsewhere. But whatever view one takes of these marginal cases, there is obviously an intimate connection between formal schooling and the acquisition of writing.

When we include in the implications of literacy, those aspects of a written tradition that are critically dependent on writing (some aspects are more so than others), then the content and transmission of that tradition cannot easily be separated from the presence of writing itself. The two overlap. If we assume that even in an attenuated form, the practice of certain tasks such as operating logical syllogisms or sorting geometric figures influences the content of a particular curriculum (e.g. in English language schools), then we should expect Vai students at these schools to do better at these tasks than those students at Arabic ones. At other 'modern' types of school such tasks may be omitted, possibly because of the level of teacher education or of new ideas about what to teach. Children in these different schools would obviously differ on mediated as distinct from unmediated tasks, though we have also to allow for different 'unmediated' effects depending on the scripts they use and the relations between the spoken and written languages.

The effect of schooling is stressed throughout the Vai study. "English school stands out as an important influence on perform-ance across a wide spectrum of tasks". But the results make up a chequered pattern. School obtained the highest ranking in "expla-nation of sorting, logic explanation, explanation of grammatical rules, game instructions (communication), and answers to hypo-thetical questions about name switching". All of these are 'talking about' tasks – skills in verbal exposition, what Olson calls "skills involved in the logical functions of language" (pp. 242–3). But schooling also exerts some selected effects on story recall and on behavioural measures in tasks taken to indicate higher-order skills, that is, abstraction, as indicated by the choice of form or number as a sorting principle, and correctly solving logic problems. However the results did not show any greater use of taxonomic clusters in free recall nor any preference for the grouping of objects by class membership, findings which were out of line with studies that have been carried out elsewhere, indicating perhaps the different selection of written tasks in different schools.

Schools

Let us turn from contemporary test performance in schools to the nature of the schools themselves as revealed in the records, since this may shed some light on the practices we are considering. To many brought up on liberal principles, especially those based on psychological theories about learning to learn, the nature of the activities in the early school, indeed in the majority of schools throughout the history, comes as a shock. In Ancient Mesopotamia the great importance placed on memory tasks is evident in the way students had to turn over the clay tablets and reproduce there what was inscribed on the hidden side. That is to say, they had to internalize the words in short-term memory before writing them down. Even today it is still felt by some that knowing a poem, for example, means being able to recite it. So too in many religious traditions real knowledge was internalized knowledge, a copy of the book imprinted verbatim on the mind. The Lord's Prayer has to be 'learnt', and learning is memorizing. This process had two effects. It placed a great deal of importance on the exact words that had been written down, whatever those words were. And it tended to standardize category lists and other written forms by feeding them back as received knowledge, which did not destroy but tended to dominate the more contextually variable oral forms. That is, the written form tended to become the orthodox one.

Let us turn to a specific example of the role of memory in Ancient Egypt, where there is evidence for schools at the end of the third millennium. In later periods reading and writing were learned by copying, and probably reciting, classical literary works. Traditional texts were transmitted for millennia and from the New Kingdom on (1550 BC) this handing down probably occurred in the "House of Life", a scriptorium attached to the temple and where there were also students. But proficiency in writing, as James remarks (1979:96), was not easily acquired. Pupils in scribal schools were asked to copy well-known literary works, especially the *Book of Kemit*, a didactic piece partly devoted to annunciating moral principles and partly to extolling the profession of scribe. They began by writing in an archaic script before developing their own handwriting and going on to copy model letters, mathematical exercises and lists of technical words, place-names, etc. It is interesting to note two points. First the importance of copying and possibly of reciting, that is, internalizing written texts in precise form. Where the latter occurs, and this is also the case in Islam, in India (e.g. Mehta 1984) as well as with much Bible 'reading' in the West, verbatim memory becomes a more important factor than in oral cultures (though now irrelevant from a strictly functional point of view); an appreciation of this point does something to account for the discrepancies that some have perceived in the thesis of Lord and Parry (Lord 1960; Smith 1975; Goody 1977b; Baines 1983). Secondly, such scriptoria become yet more important "when written and spoken languages had diverged a long way" and when access to elite culture had narrowed, contributing to later images of Egypt as "a land dominated by priests" (Baines 1983:581). Hierarchical and specialist variants of linguistic usage are of course not unknown in oral societies, but writing adds quite a new dimension by creating 'dead' languages that are still living or capable (like modern Hebrew) of resurrection – whereas in oral societies they are truly dead. In this way it gives rise to a new axis of 'class' differentiation based on knowledge of the texts. Moreover with the accumulation of texts over time the diversity between their language and that of current literary usage (and yet more with speech itself) increases, bringing with it the need for study, for grammarians, for scholarship, if these earlier texts are still to form any part, however, peripheral, of the contemporary repertoire. The disparity between written text and oral utterance was of course present from the beginning, even if we assume exact transcription without transformation. For example, Baines notes that Egyptian texts give no expression to dialects, though we know that these existed (p. 581). Written languages have to select out one of many speech forms and the consequences are important. "The standardized written form aided communication over the country, but must have been for many at best half-way to a foreign language ..." (p. 581). Whatever the feedback of written forms on patterns of speech, this discrepancy remains a fundamental handicap in the process of literate education, especially for children whose families do not equip them with a form of speech that approximates to the written construct.

Schools teaching Sumerian cuneiform were found in the city state of Ebla, although the local language was Western Semitic. For the third millennium all the schools we know of before Ebla were located in southern Mesopotamia, Uruk, Ur, Fara, Abu-Salabikh, Kish, Adab and Nippur. They were places where scribes were taught to draft administrative texts but also, as in Egypt, where the cultural patrimony was processed and preserved. Myths and poems were put in writing, literary and religious compositions were created, and knowledge catalogued in lexical texts (Pettinato 1981:230). Such an academy acted as a magnet over a wide area. Pettinato writes of a teacher of mathematics who was a 'visiting professor' from Kish. Other scribes paid visits from Mari. One of the first signs that a school existed in Ebla was the discovery of a text that listed popular personal names arranged by the scribe on the basis of formative elements of the name itself. It was a school text used for practice that isolated, then ordered, names in a list, an activity very similar to that found in the writings of Ansumana Sonie. This was not the only example. One room of the Ebla archives turned out to be a library with the tablets arranged on wooden shelves according to "modern archival standards" (p. 231). Among the texts there are lists of cuneiform signs, syllabaries, dictionaries and vocabularies (again using homography, ordering the words according to the initial formative element). We find so-called 'encyclopaedias', that is, lists of words arranged by subject; these include lists of animals (two of birds), of fishes, of precious and non-precious stones, lists of plants, trees and objects of wood, lists of metals or objects of metal. In addition there are rolls of geographic names, personal names, lists of professions, "all exhibiting the same characteristics of methodicalness and arranged according to the principal of acography" (Pettinato 1981: 238). While many of these lists derived from the Mesopotamian tradition, some like the geographical terms were of local origin and were even recopied in Mesopotamia. Apart from indicating the intensity of cultural exchange, these lists show the ways that information is ordered, formalized and categorized in order that it can be 'rationalized' and retrieved.

I am insisting here on the mixed character of scholastic activity. On the one hand memory tasks are linked to the storage, reorganization and retrieval of information. But there is also the problem-solving element that I have elsewhere discussed in relation to the potential questions raised by the categories when they are laid out in lists. We find a yet more direct example from the archives of Ebla where the scribe of Kish presents a mathematical problem in the following form:

> 600 large
> 3,600 large
> 36,000 large
> 360,000 large
> 360,000 x 6 large
> not done;
> the problem
> of the scribe
> of Kish,
> Išma– Ya   (Pettinato 1981:239–40)

Problem texts of this kind are found in the Old Babylonian period at the same time as mathematical tables. "They either state a problem by giving the basic facts and figures, prescribing step by step the way to the solution of the problem, or list large numbers of problems without indicating any solution" (Oppenheim 1964:30). We find 200 or more problems arranged in increasing order of complexity. In this way, mathematics was developed beyond its utilitarian use and became "a vehicle of scientific creativity", the same process that occurred in astronomy a millennium later at the time of the rise of Greek mathematics initiated by Euclid. The later change represented a shift of interest and methods among the scribes observing the sky and consisted in the application of well-known mathematical methods to the data they had collected. An essential constituent of these developments was the collection of observations in writing; the discovery of the regularity of the eclipses, which may have lessened their astrological interest as it increased their astronomical value, depended upon accumulating and recording such a series. In this way it became possible to predict specific calendrical events (of a longer and less obvious kind than the appearance and revolution of the sun and moon) and to work out certain relations between them.

The relative emphasis given in schools to one activity as against another varied from place to place. But the great stress on exact recall was not only typical of the scribal schools of the Ancient Near East. The contemporary Indian writer, Ved Mehta, gives us another example in a vivid description of the educational experiences of his grandfather, Bhola Ram. Belonging to one of the three Hindu families in the village, at the age of nine or ten he went to study informally at the mosque with the *maulvi*, the Muslim 'priest', who was also the wise man of the village. Exhorting him to give up temporary pleasures for permanent achievements, the *maulvi* "taught the boy to read and write Urdu and, with the help of primers . . ., gave him a little instruction in Persian and Arabic. But the child's education consisted mainly of memorizing the Koran and, to improve his calligraphy, copying out passages from it" (1984:16). At the end of the day the boy would join the company of the singing girls whose quarters lay just outside the village, where he would learn to play the sitar. Hearing of this, the *maulvi* reprimanded him, saying "It is written that dance and song have no place in Islam." "From that day on, the boy shunned the company of girls and redoubled his study of the Koran."

The description is instructive on several counts. First there is the opposition, stressed by the teacher, between the study of books (and in a wider context, school) and worldly pleasures which have to be set aside in order to achieve mastery of the written word. The particular sentiments are no doubt specific to the type of Islam, but they represent a wider set of attitudes that see an education based on reading and writing as moral (partly because they provide access to sacred texts) and at the same time as involving a heavy sacrifice. Such a sacrifice is especially heavy in a community where schooling is not universal, partly for the parents but mainly for the child who sees others 'playing' while he is 'working'.

Secondly, the nature of that education is telling in various ways.

It involved reading and writing not primarily one's own language but Urdu, a specifically 'constructed', written language, and later Persian and Arabic; music and dance were plainly extra-curricula.

Thirdly, the initial stages of learning were essentially ones of memorizing and copying. As we have seen, in principle memorizing had been rendered superfluous for many purposes by writing and later the process of copying by printing, nevertheless learning consisted in storing written material internally and in copying it externally, notions that have not altogether vanished from contemporary Western education, and for which there are, up to a point, sound reasons. One must, for example, memorize the alphabet in a specific order before one can use a dictionary.

Fourthly, there are the appeals to the authority of the sacred text (even where that text has nothing to say on the specific subject); "It is written . . ." says the *maulvi*, which is sufficient justification for the statement that follows. For it is the Qu'ran that has to be memorized verbatim, before Arabic is understood, and then copied exactly.

Mehta's account of the early education of later members of his family is not very different, so that the Qu'ranic teaching among the Vai does not seem unusual. Indeed, lest one should think that European schools were much different, let us look at the case of France. Examining the relation with literacy in Aquitaine under the Ancien Régime, Butel and Mandon show that schooling did not always lead to the acquisition of writing, even at the level of the signature. On the eve of the Revolution this capacity remained rare in a large triangle in the west running from Brittany to the Landes, while in the north and east, as well as in Languedoc and Provence, there was a considerable increase in the eighteenth century.

This increase was partly due to the pressure of the Counter-Reformation after the Revocation of the Edict of Nantes. A royal declaration of 1698 envisaged the establishment of primary education (*la régence*) in every parish in the kingdom, although reality fell well short of intention. Schools were unequally distributed. In this some socio-ecological factors were involved. The towns were relatively well provided for. Otherwise schools were scattered along the coast and the main rivers, which were also routes of commerce. Richer rural areas were better equipped than poorer ones, or those where family labour was needed on the farm.

Wooded and mountainous areas tended to be less well off. But the failure to provide schools was also due to the indifference of the inhabitants and the hostility of the nobility, and even of the bourgeoisie. In 1833 the mayor of Medoc proclaimed that the region "needed vine-growers, not readers, a peasant who knows how to read becomes a restless cultivator, idle and argumentative" (Butel and Mandon 1977:19). In the previous century one administrator had protested that those who went to school no longer wished to bend to the plough, as a consequence of which the family was scattered and paternal authority flouted (p. 20).

The ordinance of 1698 linked education with the eradication of heresy; that is to say, as with many earlier Islamic and Hindu schools, the aim was to encourage orthodoxy rather than 'cognitive growth'. The 'regents' were in effect auxiliaries to the clergy, paid for by the parish; they had to instruct children in the catechism and take them to mass as well as teach them self-control (note that men taught boys and women, girls, especially under Colbert): "In the countryside primary education was above all religious, instruction in the catechism counting for much more than that of reading, writing and arithmetic" (p. 23).

Often, after teaching the alphabet, the regent proceeded to teach Latin; even when this was not the case, the language of instruction was French rather than, say, Occitan in the south. Moreover reading was separately taught from writing and arithmetic: "The dissociation between reading and writing was an essential feature of education in the modern period" (p. 29).

Combined with the mediocrity of the teaching, the mobility of the teachers and the irregularity of attendance, this 'restricted literacy' helps explain the low rate of signatures on marriage certificates compared with the numbers attending school. It was made worse by late marriage which meant that literate skills had been forgotten by the time the registers had to be completed. Add to this that the teaching of writing involved acquiring a manual dexterity with unusual tools (pen, ink and paper) which stressed the gap between reading and writing (pp. 30–1). As for the former, "It is the reading, or even the learning by heart, of the Holy Book which is essential and this knowledge of religion could take place without any knowledge of the French language" (p. 32; Compére 1977:63).

There is a general correlation in eighteenth-century France between levels of literacy and prosperity (Jeorger 1977:117) as well as with status, sex and urban residence. While levels increase over time, there are some interesting examples of backtracking. The advent of the textile industry around Rouen led to such a disruption of society that (as in Lancashire, according to Stone, 1969) we find a drop in literacy rates in the second half of the eighteenth century. Perhaps this was due to the fact that both children and parents were working, perhaps to a general pauperization of the area.

In this system of education the insistence on memory tasks (the internalization of the book), the devotion to a dead or foreign language, the religious aim of most instruction, all these features recall the uses of literacy in early Mesopotamian and many contemporary Arabic schools. It was predicated upon a radical separation between the ecclesiastical culture written in Latin and French, and the lay culture spoken in 'patois'. Protestant schools were not so different in practice, except in the use of a wider range of teaching materials (Compére 1977:52). Yet the presence of so many Protestants in the Montpellier area was one factor in the higher rates of literacy in that part of Languedoc (p. 92).

These comments on school education in the distant and the recent past apply in some measure to the present, helping us understand the differences between the results of the schooled and unschooled in psychological tests and other activities. They also emphasize the critical role of schools in relation to memory tasks; if you don't know (i.e. remember) the alphabet, you can't read; if you don't know (i.e. remember) your tables, you have difficulties with sums (until the advent of the pocket calculator). More significantly if you don't have books or access to libraries, you have either to internalize the information yourself or to consult an elder who has done so. The limitations are obvious.

The discussion of contextualized memory tasks and the importance assigned to schooling as a variable led us to an extended consideration of the relation between memory tasks, schools and literacy in a variety of cultural situations. But the shift of direction in the Vai study from a search for general abilities to specific skills also raises questions about the nature of these analytic categories themselves.

The experimental method

In turning to this question we need to reconsider some other points that arise out of the attempt to account for the differences in the ethnographic and psychological reports on Vai literacy. The first has to do with natural experiments in skills and the fact that man's cognitive activities, especially in a literate society, are not limited to internal, 'mental' processes alone. For example, if, following my suggestion concerning the separation of 'words', I gave two groups of LoDagaa, one non-literate, one literate, the task of defining the word *yelbir*, the first might talk in terms of 'bits' of speech, the second in terms of the gaps in writing; there is no way the non-literates can do the latter. Indeed a literate may reach behind him, take down a dictionary and read the definition it contains. Or he may point to the spacing of print upon a page. Those would be proper, natural, responses to my question. The occasional use of 'dictionaries' in this way is a characteristic of advanced literate behaviour. This resource affects our understanding of the world and its use can be counted as a cognitive skill available to literates. But it is one that employs a feature intrinsic to literate behaviour, that is, the use of 'tools' that lie outside us, as I am now using a paper and pen not just to write with but to think with. Nothing surpasses pen and paper as being 'good to think with'.

Let me take another example, not so much literate as graphic. If I give groups of literate and non-literate Gonja the task of finding their way to Mecca (or some nearer destination), the first may find a traditional written itinerary to follow (or a map), the other has to rely on oral questioning. The speed and efficiency of the one is likely to be far superior to the other. If the literate is travelling by car, he doesn't even need to lower the window. The map, like the dictionary, is part of the potential available to literates in many cultures. It is a cognitive resource whose reading requires a cognitive skill. But it is also a highly specialized skill that may be impossible to test by any means other than itself. It may not mock-up into tests of general ability or wider intellectual skill. And it has to be tested externally, not 'mentally'.

Let me expand on this point. Maps are important not only to

individuals but to socio–cultural systems. Map-reading assisted the Portuguese and Spaniards, then other European nations, to explore (and conquer) the world and hence to change not only our external relations (both of the societies and of their individual members) in a whole variety of ways but also our perception of the world, which ceased to be square and became round. In other words our understanding of the world was changed in various ways partly as the result of the graphic procedure of map-making, though of course other factors were involved, inventions like types of ship and guns, the use of horses in America and possibly religious conversion.

The problem is that while mental maps and plans are seen as falling within the psychologist's field of vision, printed maps and plans are excluded – unless there is a situation in which the use of printed maps affects the results of a particular kind of testing. Such tests are by definition mock-ups of one variety or another. That is to say, if I want to test the 'psychology' of map-reading, I have to find a way in which that activity affects other, more general areas of performance that can be examined by means of a 'mental' test. From my point of view map-reading is already a cognitive skill (in the sense that I understand the phrase) which affects the way we operate in the universe. Not everybody has that ability to the same extent and these differences can be minimized by individuals, by sticking to territory they know, by observing written signposts (providing the way has already been marked and they can read) or by asking someone where to go (if they know the language and are willing to get out of their car).

Culture and cognition

If my separation of unmediated (immediate) from mediated implications is useful, two other points follow for assessing the usual type of testing. In the study of Sonie's work we pointed out that he was an exceptional man and the same level of activity would not be found among the population at large. In any general survey, however, his achievement would be lost in the mass of data because it would be statistically insignificant. Yet that achievement was undoubtedly related to the use of writing, had important social implications and represented a shift in the methods of processing information. The same remarks could be made for many aspects of social action (and of the action of many individuals) in other cultures. In differentiated societies (and writing always differentiates, at societal level by generating the semi-autonomous subsystem of schooling, at the individual one by providing a ladder of achievement and a choice of reading), cognitive skills are rarely to be found at the level of generalized cognitive *abilities* or generalized cultural *attainments* that reside in the totality of the population; both abilities and culture have to be understood in another way for these are differentially distributed among the population.

Secondly, if we link certain skills with a specific written tradition (which may be fed back orally through the mouths of parents), then we can see why the results of testing school-children taught in, say, English turn out as they do. For the same reason it is difficult to attempt to test school and writing as separate variables for the purposes of enquiring into the *mediated* implications of literacy, which was the aim of the enquiry undertaken by Watt and myself. When Scribner and Cole tried to test the influence of 'instant literacy' on differences in general capacities of this kind, they got some disappointing results. When they then looked at specific skills associated with the learning of particular scripts, they found some more positive ones, although few of these were unmediated, that is, few were direct results of the introduction of a script.

Abilities, capacities and skills

In this context the term 'skill' often has a somewhat superficial resonance, as if one was talking about the handling of a tennis racket, the control of a football, whereas abilities and capacities are seen to refer to more profound dispositions. We need to look briefly at the model that lurks behind much of this discussion and is of a layer cake or geological type, namely:

_____

physiological level

_____

cognitive abilities

_____

cognitive skills

_____

As far as writing is concerned, cognitive skills obviously have to be embodied in a schema that allows for interaction with cultural factors and Scribner and Cole propose the culture–cognition model in Fig. 11. The tests they use try to discriminate various features that have been suggested as the consequences or implications of literacy. However, there are some modifications one would want to suggest. Firstly, for the implicit model we need to allow for interaction between the levels (Fig. 12).

The formal separation of the three levels enables us to approach the question, more often thought about than asked, of whether and how writing transforms the mind. I approach the subject with hesitation since basically it seems more a problem for the analytic philosopher than the social scientist. Let me start from the position that the emergence of language itself appears to be related to certain changes in the structure of the brain at a physiological level as well as in terms of information processing. Already in 1948, Keith had suggested that a 'cerebral Rubicon' separated apes and australopithecines from Homo, with a critical brain volume of 700–800 cc. necessary to attain complex thinking. It would appear that the earliest type of Homo, that is Homo habilis, does display a human-like frontal lobe as early as two million years ago, whereas

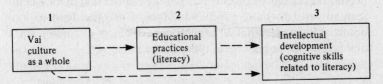

Fig. 11. A culture-cognition model (Scribner and Cole 1981:17).

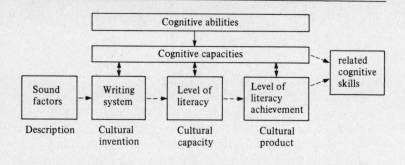

- - - ➤ precondition for

Fig. 12. A modified culture-cognition model.

more recent australopithecines retain the ape-like form. Speech appears to be associated with the earliest specimens of the genus Homo; indeed it can be seen as its critical feature. Various other skills have been suggested as responsible for human brain evolution and the growth of 'intelligence' – hunting, tool production, warfare and language. Apes occasionally do all these things except speak (Falk 1984). The human brain, in place of a groove known as the fronto-orbital sulcus, displays a particular pattern of convolutions; among these, a portion of the lower frontal lobe on the left side of the brain, known as Broca's area, processes speech, though not exclusively. But much evidence shows the superior ability of the left cerebral hemisphere for processing language (Tseng and Wang, 1984).

There is an interesting difference at the physiological level between spoken and written language. Laterality studies have shown that, while there is no simple dichotomy, the left hemisphere is superior in the recognition of oral materials, while the right is specialized for the recognition of non-verbal shapes, patterns and nonsense figures (Cohen 1973:349; White 1969); the hemispheric preferences for nominal as against physical analysis emerge in a preference for serial as against parallel processing of linguistic stimuli that can be performed either verbally or visuo–spatially (Cohen 1973:355). It is the greater capacity of the left hemisphere for finer temporal resolution that enables man to construct a language from the limited number of signals our motor-perceptual system can command by means of sequential patterning which radically extends its range (Tseng and Wang 1984): this is the duality of patterning that Hockett (1960) saw as one of the critical features of human language.

We may also note that lateralization appears to be a specifically human trait (animals are randomly left or right-handed) and probably connected with the development of language; moreover one of the major demonstrable sex-differences in cognitive processes among humans has to do with differences in lateralization that effect visuo–spatial ordering and verbal ability. These results seem to be related to the finding that, while damage to the left hemisphere is linked to the impairment of writing and reading skills (Ojemann 1983), logographic characters appear to be more efficiently recognized by the right hemisphere (Hatta 1977; 1981; Tsao *et al*. 1979). Sasanuma *et al*. (1977) claim that *kanji*, the logographic writing system of the Japanese, is vulnerable to different areas of brain injury than *kana*, the phonetic system; its preservation is better among aphasics in Japan, where there is in any case a low incidence of reading disorders (Wang 1981:234). Since reading retardation with phonetic scripts appears to be associated with the reduced involvement of the left hemisphere, such readers have to rely on the right hemisphere (Marcel *et al*. 1974). Indeed retarded readers can learn to read Chinese logograms with their English translations more proficiently than their alphabetic counterparts (Levy and Trevarthen 1976).

The obvious difference in terms of physical adaptation is that whereas language has been with human beings (some would say makes them) for perhaps two million years, writing has been there only for 5,000. While language presumably developed slowly to become a basic characteristic of all humanity, writing has only been a quasi-universal feature in any human society for little more than 100 years, although there are a few possible (Protestant) exceptions – in mid-eighteenth century Sweden for example where communion and marriage were withheld until a literacy test had been passed. The late advent of writing means that any influence on the physical structure of the brain is likely to be negligible, although there are problems to do with the brain that are clearly linked to the processing of written information in different scripts. As we have seen, while phonetic writing is processed largely in the left hemisphere, it appears that logographic coding may be equally well carried out in the right (Hatta 1977, 1981).

On the level of what we can call basic cognitive abilities, there is clearly nothing intrinsic (apart from certain widespread physiological problems associated with forms of dyslexia) that prevents human beings first learning to read and write, then learning a written tradition and becoming a member of the literate elite of this world. It is happening all around us.

If the development of language changed the physiological structure of the brain (or if they developed in interaction), then it is conceivable that in the long term parallel developments in hand–eye coordination might occur through writing. That is speculative, so let us turn to the other two 'levels'. With abilities and skills we are dealing with analytic levels that are designed to account for test results, that is, whether we find general responses to 'instant literacy', or more specific features attached to particular learning experiences. Furthermore, this dichotomy deals with the problem of the particular and the general which is intrinsic to our mode of linguistic analysis. But just because of this we have to be sceptical about the distinction. Are the abilities simply an analytic construct to group together skills?

If we take a longer-term view of the effects of writing systems and at the same time an interactive view of abilities and skills, the problem takes on a different perspective. For abilities too change in interaction, an interaction that has its developmental perspective in individual (ontogenetic) as well as historical (phylogenetic) terms, which enables them to perform new tasks over time, giving rise to different capacities and different skills. Take a non-linguistic example. No doubt the ability to drive a car is universal across cultures, though some individuals may have insufficient hand–eye coordination. But the capacity to drive a car is a socio–cultural matter that involves bringing individual and car together not only historically but in a satisfactory relationship following upon a period of practice. The institution of driving tests suggest that one can only treat that capacity or skill contextually since it presumably cannot be properly tested except in the act itself; no satisfactory mock-up is possible, though it may be feasible to test for individuals who are unlikely to learn. If you have learnt to drive a car, you probably have the capacity to fly an aeroplane, although other physiological, psychological and social factors may intervene.

Cultural resources and individual attainment

Like the motor car, the syllogism and the cross-word puzzle are also specific historical inventions, ones that are closely linked to writing and to linguistic behaviour generally. It could be argued that these activities are based on specific skills which with practice develop our capacity to solve problems of a 'logical' or 'verbal' kind, and that practice may perhaps have an indirect effect on other individuals in the community. This suggestion may get some support from the work of Johnson-Laird (1983) showing that while the ability to solve simple syllogisms is generally advanced by schooling, university students are no better able to solve complex kinds than any one else (unless presumably they are trained to do so). But two things need to be said, the general capacity, if it exists, is largely contextual, implying not a general type of 'reasoning' or 'facility with words' but a specific one, an interactive one. So that little if anything is likely to show up in a test, except in tests of the operations themselves, which is exactly what happened in the Scribner-Cole studies as far as the syllogism was concerned. If there is a further effect, it will tend to be confined to individuals like Sonie and not to show up as a general capacity.

If I want to 'test' the difference between an illiterate, a non-literate and a literate orientation to the world, I can do so either at the level of culture or at the level of the individual. There is a widespread anthropological conviction that culture is internalized, like Durkheim's social factor, in the individual members of society, forming part of their *personae*. At the level of the spoken tongue, for example, this may be true. At the level of the written word, it is clearly not the case. Illiterate members of a literate community may travel in a ship whose movements are directed by a pilot completely dependent upon graphic records and instruments for reaching his destination. At the individual level knowledge and skills are stratified and it may rest with a minority, a small minority, to widen the perspectives of a society, leading to trade, conquest, colonization or conversion.

Psychological tests and practical action

How am I to test for this cognitive skill in orienting a moving vessel on the sea towards a precise point? How am I to test for the knowledge so acquired, for the widening of the world view, in a literal sense, and for the discovery that the world is round rather than flat, that it is not a question of crossing a river into the Other World but of going up or down?

The answer is only by enquiring about the skill or knowledge itself in a way that seems too obvious even to contemplate. I can get people to draw different maps of the world they think they live in, an activity which from the very beginning privileges those with training in the use of graphic instruments. Or I can start two sets of people off from point A, give them map and compass, and ask them to find their way in overcast weather across the Sahara Desert or the Pacific Ocean. There can be no prizes for predicting the results. The skills are defined by the activities themselves, not by some abstract and general quality of 'orientation' defined cross-culturally. Indeed the general ability is likely to remain unchanged; it is the specific activity that differs. And it differs only for some of the people some of the time, although the end result may be a change in wider cognitive perspectives.

The psychologist may reply that he is not interested in such differences unless there is some more general 'mental' character to the ability, something he can measure. My comment would be that while testable internal characteristics of this kind would be important, if they could be established, they are certainly not exhaustive of cognition in the more general sense in which it has been defined. The skill we need to expand our knowledge of the world is the skill to read. That skill alone gives us a handle on an enormous range of knowledge, information and literature, but while capacities are changed, abilities remain the same. For example, I myself could not, do not, remember the telephone number of my own office. That does not stop me from calling my colleagues because I look the number up in my telephone book, store it in my short-term memory, then dial. Now that I have a new type of telephone with its own memory I don't even need to look it up. My memory skills are not engaged. Yet I have a capacity to talk to vast numbers of people on this earth at short notice.

To expect that this capacity would show up in a series of tests suffers from three theoretical difficulties. It assumes, first, that such capacities can be described, or better described, at a higher level of generality. Secondly, that this higher level of generality shows up in the 'higher mental processes'. Thirdly, that these higher mental processes go on inside the mind alone. The last sentence sounds like a tautology. But if one defines skills and knowledge as 'mental' in the sense that they are entirely contained within the mind, and have to be so tested, you quickly reach a point of no entry into the study of human interaction. The relevant boundary cannot be the human body or mind, nor yet the collectivity of bodies in a society or group. Yet that is where the study of the psyche tends to stop, not logically but implicitly and experimentally.

The internal–external problem

We are touching here upon the external–internal problem that has dogged so much thinking, in psychology, philosophy and elsewhere. On an individual level, we all have our answer. But what is the question?

Norbert Weiner asked his readers to imagine a mechanic with an artificial arm trying to repair an engine. Is the arm part of the machinery with which the mechanic is struggling, or part of the mechanic who is working on the engine? Neisser (1976) makes the critical comment that there is a similar ambiguity about the icon, that is, about the storage of the transient, high-contrast retinal pattern.

Where we locate the particular boundary, whether we define this or that as in or out, is unimportant, except in so far as it affects our notion of cognitive abilities, capacities and skills. If we have a problem with the mechanical arm, we have a similar problem with the different capabilities that are opened up to mankind through tools, through the long-handled cutters that enable us to get to the upper reaches of the hedge, through robots of all kinds, through computers and word processors. These are instruments that radically affect our capabilities, so to try and define the nature of mankind in industrial and even pre-industrial societies without discussing the tools we use, the machine that enables us to circumnavigate the globe in eighty hours or less, is to leave out a critical factor about our operations in and understanding of the world. Equally to leave out the map or the timetable and discuss only the cognitive map and nature's clock is a dereliction of duty. True, one can ask the question, what difference has literacy made to memory and then define the memory as a 'psychological' process. That is in the end to ask a rather trivial question about our cognitive operations. While there may be a discernable difference at this level, there are many more important ones that a test of this kind does not bring out, for example, those involving the storage capacities of books, archives and libraries.

Can we still talk about such interactive processes as 'cognitive'? That raises the general question about the concept of cognition. That there are innummerable definitions is itself a clue to the state of affairs. Neisser defines cognition as "the activity of knowing: the acquisition, organization, and use of knowledge". He goes on "it is something that organisms do and in particular something that people do. For this reason the study of cognition is part of psychology, and theories of cognition are psychological theories" (1976:1). Associated with the study of cognition he sees the study of cognitive processes (also known as mental processes or higher mental processes), cognitive skills, cognitive development and cognitive structure (cognitive maps), while the field of cognitive psychology studies perception, memory, attention, pattern recognition, problem-solving, the psychology of language, cognitive development, etc., a far-ranging conspectus.

Looking first at the realm of cognition so defined, it is difficult to see it as falling entirely inside psychology or being the object of purely psychological theories. Take the example of the activity of knowing, knowing about the universe, not by cognitive maps alone (as described by Boulding 1961) but with the aid of physical maps. The use of maps in exploring the world during the fifteenth and sixteenth centuries is well known. Valuable knowledge was embodied in graphic form, constructed by means of simple survey equipment; maps, logs and itineraries provide guides for complex operations. The use of maps falls within the realm of cognition defined as 'the activity of knowing', for knowing is an interactive activity which depends not only on the subject (and his capacities) but on the object. When a map or a book intervene between the object and subject, we are dealing with 'mind' out there as well as with mind inside. The capacity to read is in itself a cognitive capacity, a mental capacity, a higher mental capacity, but one we can only talk about, probe or measure when we have books.

It is inevitable, given the widespread debate it has aroused, that we should have briefly to refer to the work of Piaget on the developmental stages of cognitive growth or reasoning. The weight of my argument is against any universalistic theory, especially one that is already weakened by the prediction that individuals in "primitive societies would not develop beyond the stage of concrete operations" (Piaget 1966:309; Dasen 1972). How can we accept a universal theory that makes an exception of a large segment of mankind, unless we assume either a psycho–genetic difference in abilities or a non-psycho–genetic difference in capacities that we are failing to specify?

The question of a genetic difference is clearly untenable since the whole of mankind was once primitive and since, especially in those societies in which any earlier 'class' structure has little relevance to the contemporary situation (as is largely the case in Black Africa today), we see a remarkable transformation in the formal operations of those who, like Sonie, acquired the ability to write out of school but especially of those who have been schooled to be literate.

I earlier described writing as a technology of the intellect in order to present an alternative hypothesis. That is, basic *abilities*, in a psycho–genetic sense, remain the same, although it is possible that, as with language, these may be influenced over time by further changes in the means of communication. But writing presents us with an instrument capable of transforming our intellectual operations from the inside; it is not simply a question of a *skill* in the limiting sense but a change of *capacity*. The capacity depends upon the interaction between individual and the objects mediated by writing, and so cannot in many cases be mocked-up in ways that would test general abilities (for example, of abstract reasoning and memory) since they are highly specific skills.

This formulation of the problem is related to some Neo-Piagetian accounts concerning the sequencing of specific activities, just as it is to those increasing number of experiments on Piagetian problems that increase the element of context and tend to produce different results from earlier work. In discussing their administration of 'The Floating Bodies' task, T. and D. Carraher note an observed discrepancy between operations ("the structure of reasoning") and notions ("the explanatory concepts used by the subjects"), especially at the formal operational level (1981:67), although this is less true of the concrete operational stage. This discrepancy they tentatively link with the development of the 'scientific style' and the 'open mind'. My argument has been that while these features vary in different cultures, the very nature of formal reasoning as we usually understand it (that is, in terms of Aristotelian 'logical' procedures) is not a general ability but a highly specific skill, critically dependent upon the existence of writing and of a written tradition which helps to formalize intellectual procedures in a manner made possible by:

1 the conjunction of language and visual forms (e.g. in lists)
2 the nature of much single-channel written communication (so distinct from multi-channel oral communication)
3 the capacity to store, retrieve and build upon earlier knowledge in an incremental way (which is not to say writing is necessarily used in this way).

The joint work on Sonie's attempts to reorganize information and categories was entitled "Writing and formal operations" by my psychological colleagues in order to indicate how writing (as far as unmediated effects go) and a written tradition (as far as mediated effects go) can influence an individual's performance in the direction of formal operations, although it is unlikely Sonie would have been able to explain his actions in the Aristotelian terms that are thought by many to be intrinsic to the higher mental functions. To put it another way, such functions are no longer purely 'psychological' in one sense of that word, which makes them no less interesting to scholars of other disciplines. For literates, formal operations, including thinking itself, involve the use of pen and paper. Without such external props, one cannot express one's thoughts or communicate them to others.

Expression, communication, is an important aspect of thinking. In his book *Le Scribe* (1980) Regis Debray describes the intellectual not as "the man who thinks about the world" (*l'homme-qui-pense-le-monde*) but "he who communicates to others what he thinks about the world". The same goes for thinkers, *penseurs*. Taking his title more literally, we may add that a philosopher who does not write (or is not written about, perhaps) is hardly a philosopher as far as future ages are concerned; nor can a poet or novelist lay claim to that name without having *written* a poem or novel. Thinking alone is not enough to make an intellectual. But writing makes a difference not only to the expression of thought but to how that thinking is done in the first place.

11

Language and writing

The study of the effects of writing on human society has brought together the work of psychologists, linguists, anthropologists, historians, 'orientalists' and those concerned with graphic and oral modes of expression in words, music and even in dance and architecture. Each field has made its contribution, a contribution that has gained from the history, the techniques, and the current preoccupations of each particular area of study. But the very advantages that each brings to an enquiry of this kind can also imply certain limitations. In the last chapter I suggested that the experimental and 'mentalist' tradition of psychology made it difficult to deal with differences of a cultural–historical kind, especially those that related to highly specific cognitive skills involved in making use of 'external' aids. Anthropological relativism, which makes an uncomfortable bed-fellow with the prevailing ideology of universalism (everything is unique but ultimately the same), presents us with other problems, regarding the development of human cultures. But here I want to consider the contribution of another major field of enquiry, namely linguistics, to the question of the influence of the written word on cognitive processes.

In a previous publication (1980b) I presented a review of some linguistic material which bore on the problem. Not only do I now find that review unsatisfactory but more material has recently appeared in work by Ochs, Gumpertz, Chafe and others and meanwhile a much better summary has been given by Akinnaso (1982). However, the general points about the linguistic contribution to these studies remains important, if only because language is the medium of so much thought, so much cognitive activity;

258

language is what writing is about and so the relative neglect of this channel by linguists requires some explanation.

In his book on *Thought and Language* (1934, Engl. edn 1962), the Russian psychologist, Vygotsky, who had so strong an influence on the work examined in the previous two chapters, discusses two distinct functions of language; external communication with other human beings and, equally important, the internal manipulation of inner thoughts. I do not wish to enter into the controversy about the relation between thinking and language, partly because the definitional problems are more to the fore than the evidential ones, and partly because it is enough for my purpose to make the self-evident assumption, stressed by Vygotsky, that "speech plays an essential role in the organization of higher psychological functions" (1978:23). By this assertion he meant that while practical intelligence was clearly to be found in non-lingustic animals and in the pre-speech infant, the interweaving of the 'symbolic' (linguistic) and 'practical' (e.g. tool using) activities of the child were the very essence of complex human behaviour. The most significant moment in the course of a child's intellectual development is when speech and 'activities' converge. From there on speech not only accompanies much of the child's practical activity, but it plays a specific role in carrying it out. Social speech as well as egocentric speech, for example, enable him to plan more effectively. At a later phase the capacity to use language for problem-solving is turned inward, taking on an intrapersonal function in addition to the interpersonal one. "The history of the process of the internalization of social speech is also the history of the socialization of children's practical intellect" (1978:27).

So while language is clearly both the result and the prerequisite of communication between human beings, it is also critical for human cognitive processes in a more general sense, that is to say, for the internal as well as for the external manipulation of human thoughts, for man's understanding of the world in which he lives. And while particular languages and dialects differ in the kinds of manipulation they encourage and permit, all have an enormous amount in common in promoting classification, storage, organization, retrieval and planning, not only in a Whorfian (cultural) sense, but in a more general (structural and functional) sense

(Lenneberg 1953). In saying this I would wish to sidestep the Whorf–Chomsky debate concerning the particular or universal character of the relation between language and ways of thinking, since there are viable alternatives to both cultural particularism and genetic universality, and it is to these alternatives that Vygotsky points when he insists on the importance of the changes in the mode of communication and of the historical dimension as a whole.

If we assume some relation between language-using and the higher psychological functions, there is an *a priori* case for assuming that subsequent changes in the means and mode of communication would affect cognitive processes in parallel ways. In terms of the development of human society, and hence of human potentialities as well as achievements, the most important such change is from oral to written language, a shift which is not only many-stranded in itself but adds to rather than replaces the cultural equipment available to members of a society, just as language in its turn had added to gesture. Moreover, it is an addition in terms of individual as well as historical development; children first learn to hear, then to speak, later to read, finally to write (though in the historical sequence, the hearing and speaking, like the reading and writing, are synchronic); bringing graphics together with speech is an ontogenetic as well as a phylogenetic parallel to the convergence of speech and activity (non-verbal action).

The order is intrinsic in two ways. First, because the perpetuation of a complex human culture depends at every level upon the individual being a receiver before becoming an emitter, a copyist before being a creator. Once again, we do not need to enter the empiricist–rationalist debate, since an internal structure is obviously required before any message can be received at all, though the important question is the relation of that structure to earlier, simpler, implicit grammars the child has to operate, and the relation of these to earlier messages. Secondly, because even with the advent of script it is still in most respects a basically oral language that one is engaged in writing (though the relation varies from near identity to extreme diglossia).

Linguists and the written language

Reacting against their nineteenth-century predecessors, most linguists in this century have given their virtually exclusive attention to oral language and have tended to treat the written as a purely derivative phenomenon (for example, Bloomfield 1933). They have allowed little or no autonomy to the written channel (or register) and hence have tended to discount the possibility of its effect on cognitive processes. Anthropological theory, too, has often accepted the equation 'man = language', but avoided that which runs 'civilization = writing'; a pervasive relativism blinded them to the possibility that changes in the means of communication subsequent to the adoption of speech may have important implications for the structure of ideas, as well as for the structure of society. Consequently their analyses tend to limit the implications to the most obvious material changes alone – changes that centre around inscribing clay, stone or paper with verbal signs, and its use as a bureaucratic device, neglecting its possible effects on the organization of higher psychological functions. A similar tendency results from genetic and other universalisms; in linguistics the search for a universal grammar, while in itself taking forms that are peculiarly literate, tends to neglect the field of investigation that would look into the differences between the syntactical structures of the written and the oral registers. The assumption of a common deep structure plays down the significance of differences that lie at the level of use rather than usage, of practice rather than structure.

It is strange that a group of human beings who probably spend more time reading and writing than they do speaking and listening, have been so oblivious to the social and psychological implications of their craft. Has the inclination towards a mainly 'mentalist' social science, which an attachment to 'individualism' often encourages (so too can an overdose of 'culturalism'), led to a disregard of the 'historical', 'social' and 'material' factors that Vygotsky's environment encouraged him to explore, if sometimes in the over-determined way we have seen? In making this point we need of course to acknowledge the important contributions of the Toronto School, and of those they have influenced in various ways e.g. Innis (1950, 1951), Ong (1958, 1982), Havelock (1963, 1973,

1976), Carpenter (1973), McLuhan (1962), Goody and Watt (1963, 1968) and Olson (1976). On the linguistic side, we should also recognize that there has been an insistence on writing as a separate channel, a distinct register, another style, in the work of Vachek (1973) and of F. Smith (see 1975 for summary). However these linguists are mainly interested in problems of teaching and learning a particular orthography, that is, in how to write and how to read (in this case, in English) rather than in the more general problems of a sociological, psychological and linguistic kind. And while they both recognize the relative independence of the written register (which is no longer seen simply as a matter of coding and encoding sound), Smith is still concerned to emphasize the lack of difference between the visual and the spoken modes, both of which he refers back to a common deep structure of which they are phenomenological transformations.

Three dimensions of the written and the spoken

I will return to both the problem of the common deep structure and the related question of a minimalist interpretation of differences. But first let us look at the specific evidence from linguistic and psycho–lingustic sources. For if we can show an effect of writing on language itself, given its role in the 'higher psychological processes', we would have found an important influence upon ways individuals interact with the world. The data may be of little direct significance in themselves but evidence of such changes provides support for the effect, in the shorter or longer terms, of changes in the means and mode of communication, on ways of understanding the world in general. Since I am dealing mainly with the results of linguistic and psycho–linguistic research, I shall concentrate on the two main issues that have been of immediate concern to contributors to these fields, namely

(1) differences between the written and oral registers of the same language, and

(2) differences between the performance of individuals in the written and in the oral registers.

Neither of these issues is directly related to the one that concerns us most closely, namely, the differences between those languages that have been written and those that have not. It is one we will return to later but it should be said that little attention has been paid to this linguistically since the nineteenth century, although at the semantic and pragmatic levels the problem has been raised by anthropologists, at least in the specific context of their tribes (e.g. Goody, E. 1978, Rosaldo 1982). Even for the other two issues the available evidence is limited mainly because the significance of the question has not always been recognized.

The written and spoken registers compared

Most of the work on the differences between the written and the spoken registers has been done in English, occasionally on other European languages, so that some of the features uncovered by various authors are likely to be language specific, and others of more general distribution. I list first of all the lexical features:

Lexical features

1 the tendency to use longer words (Drieman 1962; Gibson *et al.* 1966; Devito 1965, 1967; Kaump 1940; Green 1958, but Bushnell 1930 found no difference)
2 increased nominalization as against a preference for verbalization in speech, a process that is connected with a certain type of abstraction (Devito 1967:359; Fielding and Coope 1976; Brown and Fraser 1978; Chafe 1980)
3 greater variety of vocabulary e.g. in the selection of adjectives (Drieman 1962; Gibson *et al.* 1966; Gruner *et al.* 1967)
4 more attributive adjectives (Akinnaso 1982)
5 fewer personal pronouns (Gruner *et al.* 1967)
6 greater use of words derived from Latin as distinct from Anglo-Saxon (Levin, Long and Schaffer 1981; Akinnaso 1982).

In addition there are a number of syntactic and pragmatic features which differentiate the two registers and I replace my earlier list (1980b) by the much more extensive inventory given by Akinnaso (1982:104):

Syntactic differences

1 preferential usage of elaborate syntactic and semantic struc-

tures, especially nominal constructions (noun groups, noun phrases, nominalizations, relative clauses, etc.) and complex verb structures[1]

2 preference for subordinate rather than coordinate constructions
3 preferential usage of subject–predicate constructions instead of reference–proposition
4 preferential usage of declaratives and subjunctives rather than imperatives, interrogatives, and exclamations
5 preferential usage of passive rather than active verb voice
6 preferential usage of definite articles rather than demonstrative modifiers and deictic terms
7 higher frequency of certain grammatical features, e.g. gerunds, participles, attributive adjectives, modal and perfective auxiliaries, etc.
8 the need to produce complete information or idea units and make all assumptions explicit
9 reliance on a more deliberate method of organizing ideas, using such expository concepts as 'thesis', 'topic sentence', and 'supporting evidence'
10 preferential elimination of false starts, repetitions, digressions, and other redundancies which characterize informal spontaneous speech.[2]

There are a number of features in these lists which confirm our more general discussion about the divergence between oral and written languages – a different problem from the divergence between language of oral and written registers of the same language which is what we are dealing with here. While we have no evidence on the generality of these features in other cultures, we do note that the following are associated with the written forms

1 the greater use of abstract terms
2 the greater choice of words
3 the less personalized (and hence less contextualized) usage
4 the greater explicitness
5 the greater elaboration (syntactical)
6 the greater formality
7 the greater reliance on a dead language.

Grammar and rules

I have put these findings in a deliberately general way but in most cases they must be regarded as domain-specific. That is a question to which I will return. Meanwhile the increased formality of the written language can also be interpreted as providing evidence of a more explicit, indeed different concept of the rule, at least of grammatical rules. For example, an enquiry by Huddleston (1971) compares a rather limited range of material in English, namely the use of relative clauses in scientific texts on the one hand and in the oral discourse of university-educated individuals on the other (see also Quirk 1968; Crystal and Davy 1969). He found that internal and non-restricted clauses, which can be seen as elaborate interruptions of the flow of speech, are more common in the written texts. So too is the avoidance of the relative pronoun at the end of the sentence, a point which leads Huddleston to comment that "the influence of the prescriptive grammarian is clearly greater in the more carefully constructed written language". The comment is illuminating for it indicates the connection between the construction of 'grammars' and the existence of a written register, as well as suggesting the feedback of those formalized statements of 'rules' formulated by grammarians on the basis of their study of the written (and to a lesser extent, the spoken) language.[3] Take the use of prepositions at the end of the sentence, in, for example, "the throne she sat on". This usage is perfectly possible in spoken English. But 'grammatical' English, that is, written English, has in the past attempted to reject it outright and a rule was formulated (possibly by the eighteenth-century poet, Dryden) whereby no sentence should end in this way. This 'rule', on which Churchill commented ironically in a well-known but possibly apochryphal instruction to civil servants, is followed in formal documents of all kinds (Gower 1973:131). Like the avoidance of the split infinitive, it has fed back into the speech of the learned or the pedantic, those who spend much of their time with the written word and with worrying about its formalities. In other words there is a hierarchical differentiation of speech into proper and colloquial forms.

Whether this 'rule' about pronouns originated in an implicit trend to be found in some types of formal speech or whether it was

an importation of the grammarians from outside (from grammarians of Latin, for example) is not immediately relevant. Its very
existence demonstrates the influence of the written over the spoken
word, representing partly an intrinsic tendency to frame decontex-
tualised statements in over-generalized terms, and partly the role of
the teacher as scribe, and partly the distribution of power, including
power over the communicative process. But it also shows a shift not
so much in the notion of a 'rule' as in the process by which a
specific behavioural feature develops from an implicit tendency to
an explicit 'rule', a 'rule' that once formulated then proceeds to
govern formal action in a stronger normative way than heretofore.

   In the process of turning an unconscious tendency into a
conscious rule, the grammarians are doing two things. First, by
over-generalizing and decontextualizing, they are shifting from a
statistical to a 'mechanical' rule. Secondly they are giving that rule
a different normative pull, emphasizing the difference between
what some would describe as behaviour and social action (the latter
being oriented towards specific goals in the manner Weber and
Parsons have seen as being a critical feature of human social
interaction). This operation represents a shift of emphasis not only
in the notion of a rule but also (at least in some areas of interaction) from behaviour which has an implicit direction (and which in
many cases can be seen as a tendency) to behaviour oriented
towards more explicitly stated goals. This process is not simply one
of making the implicit explicit, of an increasing awareness of what
one is doing; the very formulation in writing, even where the rule
was a rule and not simply a trend, gives it a reflexive, feedback
quality, a normative pull, that it did not previously have.

Individual performance in the two registers

On the second of our two questions concerning the differences in
the linguistic behaviour of individuals depending upon which
register, oral or written, they are using, psycho–linguistic studies
begin to shed some light. A paper by Portnoy (1973) summarizes
previous investigations as well as analyzing the author's own
empirical results.

   Before discussing these investigations let me add a general

caveat. The samples in these various studies were relatively homogeneous, being mainly drawn from well-educated individuals, that is, respondents possessing great familiarity with the written mode; the exception to the rule both of homogeneity and of advanced education is the comparative work by Simmons on deaf and hearing children aged from eight to fifteen (though see also the study by Bushnell 1930). In other words these enquiries can throw little light on the influence of differences in literate attainment on oral behaviour. Nevertheless some interesting points emerge on which there is a considerable measure of agreement. Portnoy found that oral and written samples varied systematically with respect to word diversity and word redundancy; the written samples showed more diversity and the oral more redundancy. Indeed increased word diversity in written samples had earlier been reported by a series of investigators working with college students. With respect to the general characteristics of words, the shorter are generally found in oral discourse, the longer in written language. Sentence characteristics tend to reverse the trend in that the oral sentences are longer, that is, in one respect more complex, and they contain more imperative, interrogative and exclamatory sentences but fewer declarative ones. This finding seems to run in the same direction as that which shows written texts as being shorter (Drieman 1962).

Portnoy also tested for the comprehensibility of the oral utterances and the written texts of particular individuals. For this purpose she used a 'cloze' procedure involving the elimination of every fifth word from passages composed orally and in writing (other 'cloze' procedures use existing texts and different intervals). After a certain delay the passages were fed back to the individuals who had provided them, as well as to other respondents, all being required to fill in the blank spaces. The degree of fit between the later response and the earlier text, assessed both grammatically and semantically, provides a measure of the comprehensibility of the original. Taking the two samples as a whole, there was no significant difference in performance. However, examining each pair of responses for each respondent, significant differences in comprehensibility and in other respects were found between the way people used these two registers. From their responses it was possible to group these individuals into Speakers and Writers. The

Speakers used shorter words in line with the general tendency of oral communication, where comprehensibility is often a matter of repetition or redundancy; the Writers tended to use longer words in speech as well as in writing. Such a finding is not only in keeping with the general difference between registers but it also demonstrates a feedback of written upon oral performance.

A striking example of the same process comes from the work of Reder on the Vai language (Scribner and Cole 1981). He notes that literate men speak differently from men, and especially women, who cannot read the written language. This finding is the more significant in view of the relatively short history of Vai writing and the relatively low level of its use. Literates made greater use of the medial consonant 'l', preferring, for example, *kalo* to *kao* for 'moon', thus preserving an archaic form which was recorded in the syllabic script but tended to be foreshortened. This usage he attributes to speech being mediated by the internal representation of the Vai script (1981:198). At the same time Vai literates made a greater use of indefinite forms, perhaps as a result of the greater decontextualization of writing (p. 199). He comments: "In oral face-to-face settings, abundant non verbal cues and a common physical environment help establish a referential framework not usually available for written communication. Written language thus may need to draw more on abstract terms of reference than speech, including more use of indefinite noun forms" (p. 194). This fact he relates to the differences in the use of referential functions, just as the first was due to the different (visual) mediating mechanism, the result being to set apart not only the speech of literates from non-literates but also the spoken and the written language of literates themselves, the latter being the most marked case of difference (p. 196 ff.).

The evidence seems to be supported by the finding of Scribner and Cole on the rebus reading and writing tasks to which reference was made in chapter 10; prior experience in constructing meaning from graphic symbols is helpful in the semantic interpretation of others, that is, in making sense of sound and symbol (1981:174). The ability to read Vai script alters the way people 'read' other things. But above all, Reder stresses, the evidence shows that the capacity to read changes those internal representations of language that mediate speech. This is a remarkable contention since it indicates that by providing a visual component to language, writing alters not only the external models or maps (for example, the lists and tables) but also the internal ones, that is to say, it alters them in ways that feed back to the structure of speech and of perception.

The Vai study suggests that even when a language has a reasonably well adapted, recently formed phonetic script, the written register nevertheless differs from the oral in certain consistent ways connected with referential functions and with the preservation of old forms, and that the same differences are also found between the speech of those who read and of those who cannot. In other words there is some diglossia even in such relatively marginal cases, a finding that is significant for the understanding of educational achievement in general since the children of literates will have an advantage in learning the script, because their speech is likely to be closer to the written form, or at least their comprehension of the more convoluted speech of literates will be greater.

In the Vai case we find consistent differences not only between the speech (and obviously the writing) of literates and non-literates, but also between that of non-literate men and women, the former being closer to their literate counterparts. This results from the fact, Reder suggests, that the social segregation of the sexes means that non-literate men are more influenced by the speech patterns of the literates who are males.

This process of visual (literate) feedback on the oral is likely to manifest itself elsewhere in a class phenomenon. The Vai case of the internal 'l' has parallels in English. In French the word *herbe* means both grass and herb. The 'h' is silent, as it is in American English, undoubtedly because that was how it was pronounced at the time of colonization. But in eighteenth-century England school teachers decided that because the 'h' was written, it should be pronounced. On the other hand, in lower class colloquial forms the 'h' is, as grammarians would say, 'dropped', although in fact it is educated middle-class speech that has resurrected it, quite artificially. Having been adopted by the oral from the written, it came to act as a powerful and emotive discriminator between social classes.

Divergences between the written and oral registers

I have introduced the evidence about the linguistic aspect of the Vai study because, as with the application of the grammatical rules, it not only connects with the work on cognition but raises wider sociological and historical issues associated with the three aspects of the interface we are dealing with, namely, the difference between languages in societies with and without writing, the differences between the spoken and written registers in a single language and differences in individual performance in the two registers. Without this wider perspective, experimental evidence is bound to lead to minimalist interpretations that seem out of step with experience.

There are two, perhaps three, related issues. First, there is the historical and cultural link between the cognitive processes and the new linguistic operations that writing permits. Secondly, there is the nature of the divergence between oral and written registers, which takes two forms, that of dialect formation and diglossia, and that of 'class' or group differences in speech, such as those between men and women.

I begin by reverting to the assumption, made explicitly in the work of F. Smith and implicitly by many others that the differences between the oral and written registers are a matter of variations on an identical deep structure. The notion of a deep structure has been variously formulated. But the difficulty in the present context is that such a view seems to lead to a static conception of the role of language, written and oral, in social interaction.

Indeed as a linguistic theory it even raises problems for language transcription. Take Jones' discussion of the phoneme. "Viewed 'psychologically' a phoneme is a speech sound pictured in one's mind and 'aimed at' in the process of talking. The actual concrete sound (phone) employed in any speech utterance may be pictured sound or it may be another sound having some affinity to it ... " Following an early usage, he refers to one as the 'psychophonic' (representing only phonemes) and the other as 'physiophonic' (representing the sounds actually uttered) (1957:7). Placing a structuralist gloss on this remark in the context of his analysis of Eskimo orthography, Gagné comments "If we accept the distinction between *code* and *message* (speech) or between *psychophonic level* and *physiophonic level* (speech), and that the speech continuum of a given language is only an imperfect realization of the well-ordered inner reality – the code – and especially of the phonemic structure containing all the necessary elements that permute and combine in opposition to each other to express meaning, it would seem logical that an orthography whose main purpose is to symbolize the same meaning in visible form, should as much as possible be a reflection of the phonemic structure of the code" (1960).

This statement brings out very clearly a major problem of structuralist analysis. The assumption that the spoken word in the form of a message is an attempt to realize a code, can be interpreted either on a personal or on a group basis. The gap between a personal code and its realization looks like a failure (an imperfect realization) on the speaker's part. But the idea of a fixed code for a group runs up against even greater difficulties, partly because the boundaries are bound to be arbitrary to a high degree. One solution is to turn the whole notion on its head, get rid of the idea of a fixed generative code as partaking of the fallacy of misplaced concreteness, and look upon the code, at least in phonemic terms, as an abstraction derived from the message, and not the other way round. Without going this far, it is necessary to appreciate the hypothetical status of the code. Only by understanding the degree of arbitrariness in the choices we make for any system of writing can we appreciate the problems of teaching that skill. The difficulty of speakers of non-standard English is not that their speech differs from a fixed code which one can uncover by analytic procedures but that it differs from class or regional forms, the initial choice of which, while not exactly arbitrary, was largely a function of power. And it is a difficulty that arises in an acute form only in choosing one dialect out of many for the purposes of constructing a system of writing.

So while the mind is in no sense a *tabula rasa*, its basic processes of treating information can and must be influenced by the many changes in the means and modes of communication. An acceptance of this proposition affects the social, psychological and linguistic levels of analysis. Neither the spoken nor the written language are simply manifestations of some abstract linguistic ability that lies for ever hidden in the depths, unchanging, sempiternal. We accept a broadly 'functional' view of cognitive processes (if in that characterization we can include dysfunctional elements). Changes in the means of communication, changes that are external to the actor at least in the Durkheimian sense, alter the range of possibilities open to man, internal as well as external, increasing not his abilities but his capacities and the skills needed to take advantage of these.

Cross-word puzzles

The point may be illustrated by means of an apparently trivial example. In the train journey from the outskirts to the centre of many capital cities, a considerable number of commuters spend the first half-hour of each day engaged in an attempt to solve the cross-word puzzles published in their morning newspaper. A special kind of ability and motivation is required for such activity, the kind of ability that is summarized in the phrase a 'cross-word puzzle mind', referring to someone who has a particular skill at certain forms of detective work involving language. From the standpoint of an immediate calculation of means–ends relations, such activity is pointless, invented for its own sake, a 'game'. But pointless as it may be in the short term, except to pass the time in a manner that gives one a reward in the form of a self-congratulatory pat-on-the-back for one's skills (and sometimes public commendation or a prize), the game leads to a heightened consciousness of linguistic behaviour (in the field of semantics as well as of spelling).

The activity itself is entirely dependent upon writing, and in the present form on alphabetic writing. But it was not invented to amuse the contemporary commuter, being found early on in the history of writing. According to Zandee (1966), the oldest example comes from Ancient Egypt. A more general form of manipulation of linguistic signs is the acrostic, a set of verses (or words) whose initial letters form a word, phrase or even a sentence. The acrostic constituted a common feature of Egyptian texts as well as forming an important element in the Old Testament (Clère 1938; Demsky 1977). Abecedarian poems are found in Hebrew and acrostics more generally play a part in the writings of early Greek fathers, Roman playwrights and Elizabethan poets as well as being responsible for the fish symbol (ICHTHUS, Jesus Christus) in Christian iconography.

The example of the cross-word is less trivial than it first appears, not only because of its long history but because it promotes a kind of problem-solving which is remarkably close to many definitions of the 'cognitive process' itself, for example, that of Bruner's "going beyond the information given" (1974) or that of Glick (1975), the extraction and organization of information. More especially it is puzzle-solving (rather than debate) that the historian of science, Kuhn, sees as critical to normal scientific activity (1962:6–7). Puzzle-solving activity is of course found in oral societies, though it should be added that in the simpler cultures problem-solving was perhaps of less importance than problem-avoidance. But this particular form of the activity, the cross-word, depénds upon writing and the practice of finding a solution to its problems may promote problem-solving and achievement orientation in other spheres of life.

The cross-word is based on a matrix of columns and rows, the elements of which (the letters) add up in various directions. The numerical counterpart is the magic square, which substitutes numbers for letters in a manner common to much cabalistic, astrological and magical work that emanated from the Middle East after the development of writing and which still commands a large and enthusiastic following. Playing with numbers in this way is not simply an offshoot of developments in mathematics; like the cross-word puzzle the magic square can be a promoter of the abstract manipulation of quantities, at least from the standpoint of long-term cultural change. Substitute words for letters as the elements of the matrix and we get a table, that God-sent instrument of much early written activity, bureaucratic and intellectual, an instrument that still serves anthropologists, psychologists, seekers after knowledge of all kinds, to organize and formalize their information into classificatory frameworks, into systems of verbatim recall, into plans for future action.

Other grapho-linquistic techniques of cognitive operation

We have then certain techniques of cognitive operation – I use the term in a wider way than the many psychologists who tend to reserve the term for purely internal processes – which are critically dependent upon the provision of a graphic counterpart of language and of 'bits' of language. Let me formalize these particular forms of graphic encounter with language, even at the cost of slightly modifying current usage. First there is the separated WORD, letter, or number, which can be thought of as a logogram enclosed in a box or rubric. As I have noted, it is significant that there is no LoDagaa term for 'word', only for a 'bit of speech' (*yelbir*) of any undetermined length; the same is true of Vai (although it now has a syllabic system of writing), the term *koali kule* being translated by Scribner and Cole as "a piece of speech" (1981:143). The formal separation of words is of first importance for the study of language; implicit separation there is in oral cultures, but not the explicit divisions on which much linguistic analysis depends.

Secondly there is the LIST, a single column (or a row) of linguistic, numerical or other graphemic entries (e.g. iconograms), which are sometimes numbered or lettered consecutively. Lists like words have beginnings and ends, and whatever they list, they 'decontextualize' in a significant sense. This is particularly true when the lists, for example, of trees and bushes, are regarded as exclusive, since this binarism affects the system of categories.

Thirdly, there is the TABLE, usually a binary type of list. Fourthly, and hardly separable, is the MATRIX with its plurality of columns and rows. This series is based on form or shape. Its constituents could also be differentiated in other ways, by function or by type of entry; for example, a cross-word puzzle is a matrix with letters as the units, semantic lists consist of words, bureaucratic lists combine words and numbers, mathematical tables comprise numbers alone.

This series of spatial layouts filled with linguistic items abstracted from the sentence (decontextualized) is found early on in the history of writing, and indeed dominates its production. So that what is significant about the use of language in early writing systems is that much of it displays a very different syntactical structure from spoken discourse.

Lists and categories

We find, for example, a large number of lexical lists, of trees, roles, classes of various kinds, which possess several characteristics that make them differ from the categories that usually emerge in oral communication. First, they consist of isolated lexemes abstracted from the flow of speech, and indeed from almost any 'context of action' except that of writing itself. Secondly, they are formalized versions of classificatory systems that are to some degree implicit in language use but go beyond those classificatory systems in important ways. In particular they take category items out of the sentence structure, and group them by similarities, sometimes even providing them with unpronounced (i.e. written, not spoken) class indicators. Thus the categories are given a formal shape, a specific beginning and a definite end, into which each item has to fit, at least for school purposes. Moreover the boxes tend to be exclusive. Fruits end here; vegetables begin there; the tomato has to be placed in one box or table rather than another, setting aside (in this learning situation) the flexibility of oral usage which has a greater toleration of ambiguity and anomaly, a greater contextualization. But the very absence of such toleration may raise interesting questions in the mind (and the pen) of the person forced to choose between placing an item in one box rather than another. As is the case with other written procedures, the notion of 'contradiction' is sharpened.

The empty-box

The cross-word puzzle emphasizes yet another feature of these matrices since it presents the clues separately and asks us to deduce the entry itself, insisting upon the completion of all the empty boxes so that a fit is obtained between spatial layout and verbal form. A similar problem may be set those who construct or complete any table. So powerful are these elementary forms of what the creators of computer software call 'spread sheets' that anyone composing a

	1	2
A		
B		

matrix is almost forced to fill all the gaps, to leave no 'empty box'. The table abhors a vacuum. Such a situation may prove a very powerful instrument for research as when scientists seek to fill the gap in the atomic table by searching around for another element; on the other hand it may equally lead to tabulated nonsense as when a constructor of, for example, a four-square diagram of the kind shown above has only three items in a series, yet insists on the insertion of a fourth at any price. As with the classification of the tomato this process may at times be generative but it may well lead down a blind alley. However the fact that the result is recorded in writing enables us to test its implications over time, in the light of other, newer information or inferences. We can reject at a later stage a format or formula that has been generative at an earlier one.

Reordering information

We have seen that, while all writing adds a visual–spatial dimension to language (which hitherto had only an audio–temporal one), the formalized graphic arrangements in matrices provide precise spatial locations for (principally) nouns and numbers. At the same time they not only extract, codify and summarize a great deal of information otherwise embedded in the flux of experience, but they also make it possible to manipulate, reorganize and reformulate this information in a manner that is virtually inconceivable in the purely oral context. One example of the way this process works is given in discussing formal operations among the Vai (chapter 9), where an examination of the manuscripts of Ansumana Sonie showed how he was able to reorder information to make it more accessible, to reclassify the actions he was recording, and to rework the categories being used.

Arithmetical operations

The results of this 'external' activity (the making and manipulation of tabulated information) are frequently internalized by being placed in the long term memory, from whence they are retrieved for oral presentation. Oral arithmetic is of this kind, based as it is upon the multiplication tables. Both the table and its contents are products of the visual rather than the aural mode, for as an activity anything but the simplest multiplication (as distinct from successive addition) seems dependent upon the existence of a graphic system. Just as the electronic calculator has made oral multiplication partially obsolescent, so the arithmetic table improved upon earlier processes of calculation. In oral societies multiplication is virtually non-existent. And addition itself is based upon counting a set of objects or, more abstractly, by direct visual representation (as with the abacus, though this instrument seems to be found in societies with rather than without writing); counting the individual items is sometimes replaced by the cognitive process that has been called subitising, a kind of visual estimating of items of six and below, limits that seem to be set by structural features of the human brain (Kaufman *et al.* 1949; Miller 1956).

Apart from counting procedures, there is perhaps another form of 'subitising' in which Africans often engage and which may promote skills of rapid counting, again by the use of external 'cognitive' aids. These procedures are central to the game known to the Asante as *warri*. It is played with a 'board' that has two sets of cups, one commanded by each player, in which are placed a number of beans, cowries or other tokens. Each player takes a turn at redistributing the contents of (initially) one cup. The versions are many, but the essential feature of the game is so to distribute a cupful of cowries in consecutive cups that one ends up at a certain point and gains control of the opponent's tokens. Picking up and playing is done very rapidly, requiring the player to make a quick, informed guess, both as to how many tokens there are in a particular cup and as to how far round the board they will take him.

All board games are based on some kind of a matrix on which counters are moved. The more developed forms are to be found in societies with writing, especially in North India, the Far East and the Middle East where they promote a certain type of problem-solving and operational skill. In Africa *warri* is an exception to this distribution but as a game, it seems to increase the capacity to count tokens both rapidly and accurately, a particularly useful activity in cowry economies.

I have been pointing to a series of instruments of cognitive operation that are at once inside the mind and outside on paper. One is not the sole cause of the other; there is an interaction between mental model and graphic model. The graphic model, especially when representing language, advances the potentiality of cognitive operation.

The syllogism

Apart from this method of reorganizing concepts and numbers in tabular form, there is another set of 'external' procedures dealing with logic, inference, contradiction, argument and proof, with establishing the 'truth'. The main tool of 'traditional', formal logic is the syllogism, which presents information in variations of the form of

> All A are B
> C is A
> Therefore C is B

> All men are mortal
> Socrates is a man
> Therefore Socrates is mortal.

Jevons (1870) defined this procedure as "an act of thought by which from two given propositions we proceed to a third proposition, the truth of which necessarily follows from the truth of these given propositions". It is intrinsic to 'traditional' logic, as Aristotle laid it out in the *Organon*, which was the study of the general conditions of valid inference. Inferences were either inductive, from the particular to the general, or deductive, from universal to particular, a prime example of which was the syllogism; when combined, they produced a train of reasoning. While the syllogism is described by Jevons as an act of thought, it can also be viewed as an act of graphic representation, in the sense that laying out an argument in this way is hardly a characteristic feature of oral discourse but, quite apart from its use of abstract linguistic elements (A, B, C, etc.), is one whose formal presentation depends upon the written word.

One negative form of syllogism is known by the Latin name of *modus tollens*:

> if A,
> B,
> but not B;
> therefore not A.

As we have seen in chapter 2, Lloyd (1979) considers this powerful form of argument to be an important element in the development by the Greeks of rigorous notions of 'proof' which were critical for the rejection of 'magic' in favour of 'science'. This development was accomplished by a shift from specific to general scepticism, which I would regard as largely a matter of a shift to *recorded*, cumulative scepticism. As with other procedures involving proof and inference, this technique does seem to have been emerging in the earlier literate cultures of Mesopotamia; its development and formalization was a Greek achievement, based again on the use of writing for analytic presentation.

Writing and diglossia

The discussion of lists and logical procedures calls attention to the limitations of psycho–linguistic tests that begin by examining oral and written performance by taking equivalent tasks. For example, in these tasks the written sentence is more likely to be complete than the oral one. But there are many usages in the early literate period which demonstrated writing's ability to disregard syntactical structures, by isolating words, syllables, then letters. There are a large range of linguistic genres, among which are the essay, the novel, the letter itself, which have no real equivalent in oral discourse. Both the type and nature of the genres found in the different registers obviously vary. But the gap between them also exists at the level of linguistic usage. For example, Reder's observation that Vai literacy encouraged conservatism among readers suggests that writing may not only place some brake on linguistic change in that register but also widen the gap between the speech of Writers and Speakers. Von Humboldt (1863) long ago pointed out that written language tends to preserve certain phonological features that become infrequent in or vanish from colloquial speech. The same point is made by Landsberger for Ancient Mesopotamia and by Baines (1983) for Ancient Egypt. Such conservation is an almost inevitable consequence of the use of writing. For the written word would have a very limited circulation if it was simply used to transcribe each idiosyncratic usage or dialect variation. The written language has to reach back in time; otherwise one is denied access to the past cultural heritage, which is the very resource writing has succeeded in preserving. Equally the investment in learning a system of writing has a greater pay-off the less it is restricted in space and time; that is to say, the more it can restrict linguistic change and dialect formation, the more people it can include under its umbrella.

But if writing tends to restrict forms of linguistic change, it clearly does not altogether damp down the quasi-spontaneous development of oral variants. Hence there tends to be an increasing divergence of the written from the spoken word, a gap which, in the introduction and body of *The Lyrical Ballads* (1798), led Wordsworth and Coleridge to press for the written language to be adapted more closely to the spoken tongue. A more radical separation of written and spoken languages developed in Ancient Egypt, eventually bursting out in a sudden dramatic change bringing the two closer together once more. Again the conserving nature of writing leads to revolution rather than reform since it inhibits gradual adaptation. The politics of language becomes more conscious, more explicit, because of the absence of implicit adjustments in the written form.

It is of critical importance for practical and theoretical purposes to recognize that the written and oral registers in a particular society may take a further step and use quite different languages.

An extreme case of the gap between the two occurred in medieval England where Latin was used mainly for writing and English and French mainly for speaking, depending upon what stratum you belonged to. The resulting interaction was highly complex. "Although medieval vernacular literary texts often reflect oral diction, in business documents by contrast not only the style and register but even the language itself might change in the process of transforming the spoken into the written word. A statement made in court in English or French, for example, might be written down in Latin, or conversely a Latin charter might be read out in English or French" (Clanchy 1979:160). The author of this study of literacy in medieval England goes on to observe that "written language was not usually derived directly from the speech of the majority of the people but from tradition, political authority and social status" (p. 173).

Such a divergence between the written and the oral obviously created problems. Learning to read meant learning to read Latin and that meant learning Latin, that is, learning a 'dead' language. The activity was totally different from one in which people learn to read their own native language. On the other hand, as I discovered in the course of observing adult literacy campaigns in northern Ghana prior to independence, teaching motivated adults to read their own language presents no great problems. However, the learner learns little if nothing is then available for him to read except a few children's stories. What these highly motivated students wanted to read and write was English, not their maternal LoDagaa. For English was (and remains) the main language of instruction even in the local primary schools, and was used by all newspapers, in all public notices and in most political activities.

In other words the situation of extreme diglossia is not uncommon. It existed in Ancient Mesopotamia under the Akkadians so that access could be maintained to past documents written in Sumerian. It exists widely in Africa, not only as a relic of colonial rule but because the adoption of a metropolitan language for written and much oral communication avoids having to choose one local language among many, which would create overwhelming political and cultural problems; nothing is so closely identified with one's personality as one's language. In addition, there is the desire to have access to international knowledge through the possibility of communicating in a language of major circulation, the same kind of motive that leads to the widespread acceptance of English as a medium of international intercourse even in more developed circumstances.

Access to past literature and to other peoples was one positive aspect of the use of Latin in Norman England; it brought the country into touch with the scholarship of the rest of Catholic Europe. A similar advantage has been attributed to the Chinese logographic script; it holds a diverse country together precisely because it does not exclusively represent the sounds of any one specific local dialect or language.

In any of these situations of written–oral diglossia, children (and adults) experience difficulties in learning to read because they have to learn another language. In the perspective of world history the extreme case is not all that uncommon. But the same problems arise to a lesser extent in all learning of reading and writing since a single written language obviously cannot correspond to the whole variety of dialects to be found in a particular country, although of course the same script can be used to record them all. Either one dialect has to be chosen among many for this purpose (as was the case with the South Midlands dialect in England in Chaucerian times) or else a 'neutral' written language has to be constructed which does not privilege a particular region or a particular group. The choice of the South Midlands dialect of English gave an immediate advantage to the south and a corresponding cost to Scots; under these conditions, Scots becomes a 'dialect', Southern English a 'language'. Equally in France, the language of the south, *lenga d'oc*, came to be known as the *patois*, even in recent times, by the actors themselves, in contrast to *la langue d'oïl*, which was *le français*, *la langue/le language*, the national tongue itself. However, it was the language of Occitaine that had the earliest claim to high literacy, giving rise to a tradition of considerable dimensions and in which women too composed as troubadours (Bogin 1976). Yet it was the *langue d'oïl* of the North that came to dominate; political and religious considerations gradually became translated into a linguistic domination that has been modified only in a marginal way by recent regional movements. These movements have been closely linked to the language question and at one level represent resistance to the effective standardization throughout the country of a single language in the written channel.

A different example of the effects of standardization is that of contemporary China. After some fifty years of debate, the Committee for the Reform of Writing decided in 1958 to introduce a system of alphabetic transcription called *pinyin* using twenty-six Roman letters. In elementary manuals for children the alphabetic form is placed side by side with the characters, thus producing an accepted pronounciation for each logogram. The eventual result could be to make redundant one function of the traditional script, which provided a common visual system of transcription for the country's different languages and dialects, by encouraging the use of a common language (*putonghua*), an essential aim of the linguistic policies of the Republic (Alleton 1978).[4] Thus in different ways, the traditional and modern scripts have the important effect of unifying the linguistic diversity within the political unit. So too in early modern Europe, alphabetization combined with printing served as a potentially unifying force in many states by imposing a standard form of linguistic communication, which in turn influenced the spoken word by offering high-prestige models.

While the choice of one dialect as the model for the written form will privilege groups that are already in most cases privileged (and possibly further depress others that were already depressed), the 'neutral' alternative does not, if our contention is correct, make much difference in the medium and longer run. The feedback of the written on the oral, of which linguistic research provides ample evidence, means that the speech of the literate elite will inevitably draw nearer to the written forms (whatever the origin of these latter), and hence facilitate the learning of the written language by their children. It is an aspect of the reproduction of the elite which is further reinforced by the content of their communications in the home and with their peers.

Class and register

If there are systematic differences between the registers which are reflected in the speech of individuals and which have cognitive implications, then performance in both speech and writing will be linked to the nature of the class structure. For the relation between these differences in performance raises a question that has been implicit in much of our discussion, that is, the link between reading skills and class (or family background), which is critical for educational policy.

It would be obviously wrong to assume that every person from a more 'oral' household will do worse at learning to read than those from households where more emphasis is given to literate skills. The diglossic situation can be overcome by individuals who are good at learning another (foreign or semi-foreign) language. If that is learned in another context and from other teachers than those who produced the natural language, the results may be very different in terms of verbal performance (both in speech and writing). We have seen from Portnoy's work that Writers are not necessarily Speakers, nor Speakers Writers. Because of the different functions of the registers, and the different developmental and social contexts in which we learn to speak and to read, a facility or infelicity with words, verbal ability or inability, is not necessarily transferable. Gray, the eighteenth-century poet, was said to write like an angel and speak like a fool. Some students who seem inarticulate in seminars may write excellent answers in examinations. Had one been judging from speech alone, their linguistic performance would have been considered to be a prime example of Bernstein's 'restricted code' (1964), often found in individuals from urban working-class homes. Their restricted code in speech is not simply a matter of a pattern of communication brought about by the intimidating context of the seminar; the same restricted vocabulary, the repetitive use of words and simplified grammar can be observed in relaxed as well as in formal situations; meanwhile the same individuals who display a restricted code in speech, may employ a very elaborate one in writing.

What does this say about the relation of speech to writing? What does it say about the relation of class to codes? To take the last point first, while urban working-class speech may be more restricted (on a series of simple criteria such as word diversity) than that of the middle class, this restriction may be connected to two rather contradictory factors. In the first place, it may result from a deliberate limitation of verbal interaction in a group situation where the use of a complex word is held to be fancy, intellectual, unmanly. Communication in an army barracks, for example, often involves the deliberate suppression of diversity in word, dress and action, while semantically empty, all-purpose adjectives such as 'bloody' are used to convey emphasis; the schoolchild's superlatives (super, fantastic, etc.) do the same job for many of us, and one might adapt the well-known phrases of Bernstein and Malinowski to speak of 'a restricted code of emphatic communion'. In the second place, while some contexts of verbal utterance may restrict the exploitation of linguistic resources, the evidence quoted earlier suggests that writing encourages elaboration; and indeed a dyglossic situation may in itself promote a range of usage. For example, we have noted that various authors have commented upon the divergence of written from oral forms in Ancient Mesopotamia; in Ancient Egypt and elsewhere the written register systematically prevents 'archaic' forms from sliding into oblivion. In this and in many other ways it creates an elaborated code that combines both past and present.

Thus on the one hand a restricted code may represent a deliberate limitation on the total range of linguistic expression in certain contexts (for example, group conversation) as distinct from its more comprehensive exploitation in others (for example, the address to the union meeting). Such restriction is not necessarily limited to one class nor does it necessarily represent anyone's total linguistic behaviour. On the other hand, though providing a channel of mobility as well as confirming higher status, education in literate forms is clearly related to the system of stratification. Those who have an advantage do not easily let go; literates encourage literate behaviour, consciously or unconsciously.[5] Since the greater elaboration of the written register is likely to affect the oral style of those who spend a high proportion of their time in reading and writing, not only on rhetorical occasions but in ordinary discourse as well. Nevertheless, since performance in these different registers may differ substantially as between individuals, we have to be careful about their allocation to a single category.

This discussion raises a general point about the nature of 'restricted codes' or 'non-standard' speech. Let me summarize the argument. Before typing individuals according to these terms and relating such typing to class, one needs to bear in mind that individuals are not limited to operating in the same code for different registers (or even for different contexts), and that performance in the written register may be at odds with performance in the spoken one. Since in most cultures with writing, upper ('class') speech is closer to the written register (they may be the only ones to write or to employ writers), it is plainly more difficult for those accustomed to so-called non-standard English to learn how to read and write. Contrary to the views of Chomsky and other linguists, the problem of teaching reading is not simply one of "bringing into consciousness a system that plays a basic role in the spoken language itself" (1970:4); it is a question of learning a variety of language that may be significantly different from, say, Lowlands Scots or Birmingham English. Such a task is perfectly possible; everyone has to face it in some degree. But for some segments of the population it may be quite different from learning to read one's maternal tongue and closer to that of those school-children in West Africa who have to do their lessons in Arabic or English, that is, in non-maternal languages. As we have seen, the reasons why children whose maternal tongue is of limited circulation have to work in these other languages are similar to those that force English children to learn to read a special type of language, and they are reasons which, given the nature of literate culture, are not easy to set aside.

Bernstein's distinction between 'restricted' and 'elaborated' codes, characterizing working class and middle class children respectively, is seen by Kay as a matter of the increasing autonomy of the linguistic channel; the "richer speech style" or code is "precise and logically explicit" (1977:3). He associates this autonomy with the difference between local and world languages, and the suggested mechanisms are increasing specialization (which involves lexical specialization) and the introduction of writing. The lexical elaboration of world languages is paralleled by the lexical usage of the upper and middle classes who employ them, and has to be contrasted with the languages of local cultures or of subordinate classes. And lexical elaboration entails (according to recent theories) grammatical structure, for "lexical items are inextricably intermeshed in the semantic and transformational structure of language" (Kay 1977:4).

In any case lexical elaboration is not simply a matter of using more words, but a question of the nature of the increase as well as of different uses of the same words. If such elaboration is associated with the increasing autonomy of the linguistic channel, then one of the prime movers in this trend has to be the use of writing. For written language is partly cut off from the context that face-to-face communication gives to speech, a context that uses multiple channels, not only the purely linguistic one, and which is therefore more contextualized, less abstract, less formal, in content as in form.

But is the difference between lower and upper speech only a matter of the latter having adopted the more autonomous mode? Surely there is also a 'hierarchical backlash' which means that, for example, the adopted or transformed speech of an immigrant community coming into a subordinate situation (as slaves, for example) might be less elaborate than their original African language at home. If so, can we not talk of actual impoverishment, of underdevelopment (while recognizing the problems of measurement and the errors of those who have failed to treat dialect differences in their own right) in a sense more concrete than the notion of relative deprivation alone would suggest? In other words relative deprivation may actually restrict speech forms.

In discussing the relation between oral and written behaviour in the same and different individuals belonging to a single 'speech community', it hardly needs repeating that oral behaviour is learned earlier, in a familial setting and informally, whereas writing is learnt later, and usually in the more formal setting of the school; though not required in any absolute sense, the teaching of reading and writing often involves a more authoritarian situation and a more rigid set of procedures than the transmission of spoken language. Moreover, while the latter is critical to the human condition, the former is in a sense optional.

I remarked earlier that little systematic work had been done on the first issue I raised, namely the relation between oral and written languages (for example, between Hopi and English), as distinct from the difference between written and oral registers of the same language and individual performance in these registers.

A tentative link between these fields is provided by the work of certain writers concerned with problems of orthography, and specifically with the teaching of English both as a foreign language (e.g. Pulgram 1951, 1965; Vachek 1973) and to native speakers themselves. The overall situation in its empirical and theoretical aspects, has been reviewed by F. Smith (1975) who has tried to integrate relevant findings with the work of Chomsky and Halle. He starts from an assumption we have been concerned to stress, that writing is not simply a matter of recording sound, that is, speech. In English, he argues, there is a lack of correspondence even at the level of spelling; but he perceives a correspondence at a 'deeper', 'underlying' level, for "English orthography is more closely related to underlying aspects of language involving meaning than to the sound pattern of any one dialect" (1975:347). Looking at evidence from linguists and psychologists (Wardhaugh 1969; Joos 1962; Miller 1951, ch. 4), he sees no evidence of differences in the grammatical structure or lexicon of written and oral registers, only of different proportions of occurrence and degrees of complexity (1975:348), leading him to conclude that, while rejecting "the more superficial proposition that writing is speech written down", nevertheless "speech and writing are variants or alternative forms of the same language".

That is to say, Smith is led by the argument of Chomsky and Halle to claim that since English orthography is related to "an underlying abstract level of language and not to sound", "differences in spoken dialect should not be relevant to reading" (1975:352). English orthography is the optimal system for all dialects and it is an "egregious error to assume that written language is somehow a closer representation of a particular ... standard dialect than of any other". In apparent modification of this brave assertion he notes that, if anything, written language should be regarded as "dialect in its own right". If this is so, then surely one dialect can resemble a second more closely than a third, and the dialect of written English is likely to resemble the speech of clerical rather than of manual workers, not necessarily because of closeness of representation (it has been argued that classical Chinese never was a spoken language) but because of feedback, whether syntactical, lexical or stylistic, of the written on the oral register.

While Smith recognizes the 'independence' of text from utterance, his particular use of the model of deep and surface structure treats the former as a constant (among variable dialects) and as dominating, in a vectorial sense, the surface. This rationalist position, which fails to take account of the historical situation, turns language into an entity of dubious status and fails to allow for any feedback from external changes either over the short or over the longer term.

12

Recapitulations

The views regarding the nature of the difference between the oral and the written and the attempt to see these as manifestations of a common deep structure bear some resemblance to the ideas of those psychologists who see abilities as constant and skills as variable. While human nature is by definition the same, and in that sense human abilities, nevertheless human capacities are enhanced by employing various instruments of a material and intellectual kind; any alternative assumption has serious limitations both for research and policy.

Take the example of cognitive processes in general. Glick (1975) has suggested that these can be thought of as:

1 the extraction and organization of empirical information by means of concept behaviour, systems of classification, which are partly dependent upon specific languages, and partly on the world out there (Rosch 1977)
2 the formation of plans for behaviour (Miller, Gallanter and Pibram 1960)
3 the elaboration of more general theories about the world (Werner and Kaplan 1963).

In each of these areas there is substantial if unsystematic evidence to indicate that writing affects cognitive processes in important ways, as we have seen in the discussion of conceptual listing, administrative lists, and the development of more regular and systematic modes of proof and argument.

These brief comments suggest how the material we have examined on the differences between written and oral languages or registers, limited as it is, displays some striking similarities to another difference which has been talked about in vague cultural terms. This is the difference between what Lévi-Strauss refers to as the domesticated and the savage, what others refer to as primitive and advanced, or as simple and complex, hot and cold. Some major differences touched upon in this discussion can reasonably be attributed to the advent of writing and the subsequent developments – the formalization of discourse, the extension of some forms of abstraction, of logic (e.g. the syllogism) and of rationality, not in the sense that common usage usually espouses but in a more restricted fashion that refers to the analysis of formal propositions in ways that seem to depend upon visual inspection and material manipulation.

The different implications of oral and written communication for cognitive development may also have important physiological correlates, arising out of the hemispheric differences in the brain which influence the processing of sensory material. Laterality studies have shown that the left hemisphere is superior in the recognition of oral materials, while the right is specialized for the recognition of non-verbal shapes, patterns and nonsense figures (Cohen 1973:349; White 1969); the hemispheric preferences for nominal as against physical analysis emerge in a preference for serial as against parallel processing of linguistic stimuli that can be performed either verbally or visuo–spatially (Cohen 1973:355). We may note in passing that lateralization appears to be a specifically human trait (animals are randomly left or right-handed) and probably connected with the development of language; moreover as far as I am aware the only demonstrable sex-differences in cognitive processes among humans have to do with differences in lateralization that affect visuo–spatial ordering and verbal ability. The profound social, psychological, and possibly physiological effects of language on cognitive processes need little stressing; that other changes in the system of interpersonal communication may have parallel effects should occasion no surprise.

Let me illustrate this with a remark on reading rather than writing, for it is of more general relevance, particularly in the era when the printed word supplements the written. Travelling in a commuter train one has had the experience of observing over three quarters of the individuals present engaged in the same pattern of linguistic communication, with the same set of absent actors, ignoring all those who were physically present. They were reading the one available evening newspaper. This kind of activity involves the shift from the largely interactional, contextual use of language, and, while writing may emphasize maximal elaboration, reading may encourage self-reflection upon a text rather than participation in an utterance. The full implications of such a change for cognitive processes have hardly begun to be assessed. Some of the implications are emerging from cross-cultural research in the sphere of education. In his review of psychological work on cognitive development, Glick acknowledges the need to break down the global variables of schooling. When we do so we find that a candidate for the effective factor is "training and reading" (1975:627), while the work of Gibson *et al.* (1962) has shown how achievement in this area alters the way in which 'form discriminations' are made, and may increase the relevance of 'form' when there are alternative systems of classification. Another important finding is that of Greenfield *et al.* (1966) where the authors argue for the importance of training in the written language to increase the use of the hierarchical devices that a language contains. For writing, they maintain, must take language out of the "immediate referential context". Concepts are then more easily manipulated, more easily turned upside down. The individual is "freed from the immediate contexts of the things thought about" (Glick 1975:634). Here once again, external factors play an important role in internal processes. For example, the particular activity in which my commuters were engaged clearly depended not merely upon writing, but upon the existence of the printing press; it could not have happened with script alone. In this way the example serves as an illustration of how developments in the technology of the intellect (and specifically in graphic systems) affect cognitive processes. Which is not, of course, to deny that other factors such as class, ideology or position in the sibling group do not also have a part to play; indeed it is the attempt to uncover and weigh these different influences on human situations that is a central task of the social sciences. The 'decontextualization', 'impersonalization' and 'complexity' are to be linked not only with literacy in itself, but with communication in class or caste societies, where the experiential context of speakers and listeners cannot be assumed to be identical or even similar, making it necessary for linguistic acts to be made more explicit if they are to understand one another. Both writing and class are linked to historically specific situations, and seem to have similar influences upon the processes of communication.

Let me turn to other general themes in this account that seem to require some further emphasis. A perpetual trend of complex, written cultures is the search for, and to some extent identification with, the simpler cultures of the past. One has only to recall the attraction of 'savage' cultures for the eighteenth-century Rousseau, the lure of the medieval period for the nineteenth-century Carlyle and the whole Gothic revival, the continuing opposition in European thought between the tribal, Germanic versus the urban, Roman traditions and its association with the growth of nationalism, an opposition that at the same time represents the vernacular versus the Latin, and the oral versus the written. A modern version of the same theme lies behind the search for the natural, the untouched, the oral, influencing the growth of oral history, the interest in the oral tradition (especially folksong), and the attraction of anthropology, and representing in some of its guises the apotheosis of the oral and the renunciation of the written as the real source of truth. We have to be careful not to set up oral cultures as a more satisfying version of our own, corrupted civilization, and on the other hand not to see that civilization, the culture of cities, a written culture, as the cure for all barbarisms. It is just such an intermediary position we have tried to maintain between the written and the oral.

On a more specific level, my concern with the reproduction of the utterance (especially of standardized oral forms) touches upon the nature of these cultures, especially the relative fixity or creativity of their traditions, and the way individuals within them act and think. In playing down the role of verbatim memory in oral cultures, I am setting aside certain widespread assumptions of those who have drawn what is at once a parallel and a contrast between an idealized oral culture and the situation in literate societies. For example, E. A. Havelock sees 'contrived speech' (what I have called standardized oral forms) as being a way of storing information, the regularity of the rhythm acting as a mnemonic (1971:26). Poetry is said to serve the purpose of the genetic code in animals and of the book in literate societies; it is literacy, he claims, that has robbed us of the capacity to memorize (p. 44). In Greece, before the coming of the alphabet, knowledge was preserved and transcribed through poetry, which was first written down by Homer, Hesiod and others, a doctrine he sees as upheld by the passage from Aristophanes' play, *Frogs*

> Consider from the beginning
> How the master-poets have been the poets of utility;
> Orpheus published our rituals and the prohibition against homicide
> Musaeus published medical cures and oracles, Hesiod
> Works of tillage, seasons of harvest and ploughing; as for divine Homer
> Surely his honour and glory accrued simply from this, that he gave needful instruction
> In matters of battle order, valorous deeds, arms and men
> (1030–1036)

The master-poets are, then, poets of utility. But it is difficult to see why or how useful information was transmitted in this way. Indeed the very notion of instruction does not seem altogether appropriate even in the case of agriculture, for here the information is directed by and to the literate – the writers and readers (who don't know), rather than the farmers and the doers (who do). Much less would the archaic details of battles be of much practical value to later warriors. Above all it is difficult to see Homer or Hesiod being memorized exactly (in such a way as to secure the accurate transmission of information) without the use of written aids. My suggestions on this topic have been forcefully underlined in a recent psychological study by Hunter who maintains that "the human accomplishment of lengthy verbatim recall arises as an adaptation to written text and does not arise in cultural settings where text is unknown" (1985:20). By lengthy verbatim recall (LVR) he refers to the repetition of a sequence of fifty words or longer.

The absence of verbatim recall necessarily means variation, at least in long oral forms. One can interpret the ensuing versions as variations on a theme, which some see as deriving from a common deep structure. But for a composition like the Bagre, for example, this assumption tends to divert attention away from an analysis of the nature of the relations between the 'surface' meaning of different recitations, relations which are from one standpoint historical and which, in the extreme case, can turn out to be of a syntagmatic rather than a paradigmatic kind; the ends of such a chain may have only the most general elements in common, though each particular part resembles the next. Where recitation has a ceremony as its subject, as in the White Bagre, or where there is a tight narrative structure, the variants may be held in check by points of reference, external in one case, sequential in the other. But that is much more difficult when there is a strong philosophical, discursive or conceptual element, as in the Black Bagre, since there are fewer constraints on the creative imagination.

The notion that what is quintessential about a series of variants (or a homologous set) is the common component may also lead one astray. With written literature the assumption seems highly questionable; the elements that are common to *Hamlet* and *The Revenger's Tragedy* are not necessarily the most central to an understanding of the Shakespearean play, or even of the earlier model. To set aside the differences in favour of a common theme is one thing, but to ignore the fact that the central thematic content itself may have changed (in a way not necessarily involving the broad narrative framework) is quite another.

The same belief persists in other scholarly enquiries. But to assume that persistence means centrality is clearly mistaken for many areas of social life. The persistence of particular features and the variation in others may reflect the changing nature of fashion. Equally, the lack of response to changing circumstance (indicating a loose entailment) may indicate that the features with which one is dealing are of little importance to the whole.

The common elements in the Bagre, White or Black, are certainly not unimportant. On the other hand we cannot assume that what disappears between, say, versions A and F in a syntagmatic chain (or even in a chain of quasi-randomly recorded versions) is either without 'structural' relevance or simply substitutable by what has come after. Meaning develops and declines, usually between the versions of different speakers rather than between the variants of one.

The latter point needs expanding. These syntagmatic relations of which we spoke are not simply sequential; when the set of Bagre versions we have collected is broken down, they represent:

1 versions by the same speaker on different occasions
2 versions by different speakers on the same occasion
3 versions by different speakers on different occasions.

On the measures we adopted in various tests, the versions by the same speaker on different occasions were closer to one another than any other. So commonsense would suggest, but here it is given numerical support. While the versions by the same individual did differ, a speaker clearly 'stored' a version that he had produced (or reproduced) early on, partly by means of a sequence of 'topics' (which would include narrative segments), and partly by phrases (formulas), always working through the rhythm and formal syntax of recitation. Every performance produced its own variants, but those of the same speaker were closer to one another.

Similar kinds of problem arise in connection with the interpretation of Ifa divination where we have a large corpus of 'verses' that are handed down to diviners in the course of their initiation. According to Bascom, it would take years to determine their number; "those which are known vary not only from one diviner to another but also from one part of Yoruba territory to another" (1969:121). Some commentators have claimed the total to be of the order of a half a million, but 4,000 seems a more likely figure. What we do not know, however, is the average number known by an individual diviner, or indeed whether any one person could ever get to know the lot. It would seem from Bascom's description that the local variations make this impossible. In other words the 4,000 verses form a corpus from the statistical standpoint but not from that of an individual Yoruba. And even if it was in his head, constituting the framework of a cognitive system for one such man, or even for the totality of the divining fraternity, it would be difficult to see it as an intrinsic part of the thought of all Yoruba, since great care was taken to prevent the 'secrets' from spreading. Knowledge, ritual knowledge, was distributed in a deliberately uneven and restricted fashion, but in any case could not really be considered as a single corpus, knowable by one individual.

The same is true of the Bagre. The problems arise from the very nature of the way myth is transmitted. Any long standardized form has to be passed on in a manner that is potentially creative; the act of transmission is an act of creation and vice versa. And the question of the relation between the variants so produced cannot be decided on the basis of prior assumption, but is a matter for empirical enquiry.

Moreover, prior assumptions about a common structure lead to a static view of the process of transmission and creation. Support for an alternative view comes from Stanner's insightful analysis of aboriginal Australian religion, which I quote at length because of its informed authority. Writing of the Kunmanggur myth, he maintains that there is no 'univocal version' of this or any aboriginal myth.

One is not dealing with dogmata or creeds, so there is no question of an authoritative or doctrinal form. Narrators may, and do, start or finish at somewhat different points; omit or include details; vary the emphases; describe events differently and attribute them to different causes and persons. Certainly, there is a sort of standard nub or core, a story with a plot, that all observe broadly. But, in my opinion, there is no accepted or enforced consensus, as in a formulated creed. I began my studies with a presupposition, drawn I know not whence, that for intellectual reasons there must be a consensus, a consistency of all versions in all parts. With short and evidently unimportant myths, a high consistency between versions could be obtained. But I failed to do so with the long and elaborate myths. These tax the aboriginal memory by reason of their complexity, but the complexity is not the cause of the variation, which seems due rather to the fact that the formula of the nub or core-story allows a wide field in which free imagination can play. The moving shapes of actual life appear to be drawn on to exemplify the formula, and the elements of the core appear also to be open to commutation. Variations of such kinds may be noted in versions of the myth given by individual persons among the Murinbata and also among the tribes of the same cultural region. I did not perceive for a long time the possibility that the variations might be as significant as the postulated consensus; that there might be one or more meaningful structures of variation. Experience eventually convinced me that the variations do indeed have inspirations and a logic of their own. When one is disabused of the misleading notion of a dogmatic version, variable only because of the frailty of human memory or from similar causes, one is compelled to consider the possibility that what keeps a myth 'alive' is not only the intrinsic interest or relevance of its story and symbolism: the dramatic potential is also involved. Every myth deals with persons, events and situations that, being less than fully described, are variably open to development by men of force, intellect or insight. Under such development, motive can be attributed, character suggested, and events and situations elucidated – or commutated – in a formative way without any actual breach of a tradition. By the same token, elisions can occur. So that unless one is able to compare versions of a myth given by the same individuals, or at least people of the same intimate group, at sufficient intervals, one cannot say with surety much about the status of a version recorded on a particular occasion. (1966:84–5)

What is remarkable about this statement is that Stanner began, as I myself did, with the assumption that there must be a consensus, "a consistency of all versions in all parts". But he is led to assert, against Strehlow's view of central Australian myths, that "Mytho-poeic thought is probably a *continuous* function of aboriginal mentality, especially of the more gifted and imaginative minds, which are not few". While in the north, there is "painstaking adherence to traditions", "the traditions themselves are a con-tinuous inspiration" – men are not "simply living on the spiritual capital of olden times" (1966:85). Versions vary with person and occasion; "Listeners rarely interupt other's narrations to protest or disagree"; there is no canon. Indeed where a narrative element is not dominant, as in the Bagre, even major themes may vary, so that the "standard nub or core" can be seen as either fluid or ever-shrinking. Only on one point would I wish to modify and expand Stanner's remarks, on the implied division between mythopoeic and other forms of 'thought' or mentality. In my view the 'problem of myth-variation', of the creativity of many recitations of 'a' myth, relates to the difference between oral and written communication; this is indicated not only in the reference to aboriginal memory (writing is an alternative method of storage and transmission), but also in both our presuppositions of consistency which were based upon written models. The use of a term like mythopoeic has primarily a signposting function; the significant features referred to in this way are products of oral communication, a fact that carries implications for 'mentality' or 'modes of thought' as these terms are often understood. Or to put it another way, writing is a mechanism that permits us to change the format of our creative endeavours, the shape of our knowledge, our understanding of the world, and our activities within it.

Let us look at the question of what happens to myths of the kind of Kunmanggur or Bagre when they get written down. One version recorded on a particular occasion (and about whose status, as Stanner observes, one can say very little) tends to become the model by which others are judged. In the Bagre case, the production of variants has not ceased but these are often now seen against the background of my written version. Not only seen, but judged, for the written version acquires a truth value that no single oral version possesses. The written version may have been wrongly transcribed, wrongly presented, but if not, the gap between this and contemporary oral forms tends to be explained in terms of truth and falsity, with the written being endowed with truth partly because of the high status of that channel (the language of the sacred books) but also because it is older, having been recited by those who are now ancestors.

The more general implications of this discussion could lead us into the empiricist–rationalist argument about the pre-existing structure of the mind as against an externalist view of the origin of knowledge. It is an area I would wish to avoid. The terms of the debate seem of doubtful value in the present context, which certainly has little to do with materialism versus mentalism. To stress the importance of changes in the technology of the intellect is not deny the role of mental processes either in the mediation or in the origin of those innovations, since that 'technology' includes features such as the syllogism.

The fundamental significance of the spoken language for human interaction is acknowledged by all; the extent to which writing may intervene in art and life is less widely appreciated, and differs from person to person, culture to culture. Today, not an unusual day, I have spent the time typing on a typewriter, dictating responses to my mail, reading newspapers, books, papers and a dissertation, drafting memoranda. Virtually the only oral communication I have had has been on the telephone, voice-to-voice but not face-to-face. Not all these activities depend upon an ability to read and write, but most do. They involve a type of interaction that is markedly different from oral discourse. Most of them require other actors, as authors or readers, but indirectly and in ways that are necessarily more reflective than speaking. I may consider a letter before writing it, alter phrases, even tear it up. The process and context of creation (and of reception) is very different. Indeed I may simply write for myself, trying to put down on paper the kind of commentary of the inner voice that accompanies all my acts, a self-commentary. But once again the process of writing down is more deliberate, like dictating an utterance and turning it into a text. It is at once more reflective and at the same time permits me to reorganize the order of things, to work out the meaning of things, to explicate more formally. And while formal operations may lead to copying, to stagnation, they may also help to break through the crust of customary thinking by bringing out 'contradictions', 'illogicalities', 'non-sequiturs', categorical ambiguities and so on, which are more likely to be glossed over in speech. Cognitively as well as sociologically, writing underpins 'civilization', the culture of cities.

Notes

1 The historical development of writing

1 I am using many of these words and phrases (e.g. non-significant) as if they were hedged by single inverted commas, for they are employed in a more restricted manner than in common speech. In describing a pattern as non-significant, I do not imply that it has no meaning for the creator or the perceiver; it may of course arouse approval or other emotions and be interpreted in a variety of ways; the distinction I make between meaning and significance corresponds to Ekman's characterization of certain gestures (emblems) as having a precise and generalized meaning, specifiable in words (1976); it also relates at some remove to notions of intention, purpose and understanding.

2 Leroi-Gourhan comments that all true pictography is recent, mostly dating from after the period of contact with literate societies. The point is well taken for many graphic systems, which have been subjected to direct or to stimulus diffusion. But for America, the achievements of the Maya and other societies suggest that pictographs, as distinct from pictograms, may well have been present at an earlier period.

3 On an important extension of the argument to the Indus civilization, see Shengde 1985.

4 In this passage I have accepted a generally held position derived from Bühler (1898). There is another view. Raymond Allchin, in a personal communication, comments: "There is a powerful argument against the idea that the Brahmi script was derived from a Semitic borrowing. The whole structure and conception of the script is quite different and must, in my view, have had an independent genesis. When an attempt was made to adapt the Aramaic script to writing an Indian language (i.e. in the Kharosthi script), the Aramaic character was retained and continued to dominate the script for many centuries. Yet in the attempt there is a clear Brahmi influence discernable; therefore, I have always thought, the Brahmi script must have been there before the arrival of the Aramaic. In recent years I have been leaning towards the view that the Brahmi script had an independent Indian evolution, probably emerging from the breakdown of the old Harappan script perhaps in the first half of the second millennium BC. But while we have no surviving inscrip-

tions datable to anything before the beginning of the third century BC, this remains hypothetical". It should be added that the Greek script was also used in parts of Central and South Asia at an early date. Inscriptions are reported from Persepolis at the end of the sixth, beginning of the fifth, century BC and in Swat in Pakistan to a period earlier than that of the Indo-Greeks of the second century BC (G. P. Carratelli, 1966, Greek inscriptions of the Middle East, *East and West* 16:31–6). The general area of northwestern Pakistan known as Gandhāra had long been a meeting place of Indian and Mediterranean influences and was subject to Achaemenian Iran in the sixth and fifth centuries BC, before being conquered by Alexander in the fourth century.

3 Africa, Greece and oral poetry

1 Our knowledge of the recitations of Africa has been greatly advanced by two important series of printed works, which have not always received the public attention they deserve. In English, there is the *Oxford Library of African Literature*, edited by G. Lienhardt, and the late W. Whiteley and E. E. Evans-Pritchard; in French there is *Classiques Africains* under the editorship of E. de Dampierre.

2 A similar but not identical point has been made by Adam Parry when he noted that "unlettered culture in Yugoslavia has been a rural, one might almost say, backwoods phenomenon, existing alongside a literary urban culture" (1966:212).

3 In unpublished dissertations R. Beye (1958) and J. H. N. Austin (1965) argue the importance of the catalogue style as an informing principle in the *Iliad* and the *Odyssey* (A. Parry 1966:208).

4 A. Parry quotes Whitman as arguing that the monumental purpose of the large epic was profoundly served by anything that bestowed fixity of form, e.g. writing, and Wade-Gery that "the alphabet was adopted for the recording of hexameter poetry" (p. 215).

5 I have discussed the impact of literacy on a neighbouring non-literate society in northern Ghana (1968b), though I have no evidence of any 'literary' influence in the case of the Bagre.

6 The term *kubris* seems to signify not only the Law of the Land but also the unknown material on which those laws are written. The word later came to mean public documents of all kinds, a parallel development to that which occured with the Roman *tabulae*.

4 Oral composition and oral transmission: the case of the Vedas

1 Great stress was laid on detailed accuracy and the slightest mistake in chanting a certain sāman was sufficient to produce the madness of the reciter (Staal 1961:34).

2 For an alternative view, see p. 64.

3 See, for example, the text quoted by Staal from the Vedāntaparibhāṣā: "And thus in the initial period of creation Paramesvara created the Veda with the same sequence as the sequence of the Veda existent in earlier creation, but not a Veda of a kind different from that" (Staal 1961:1).

4 Buddhists and Jains also placed a great premium on the memorization of scriptures, but the act of copying a manuscript (even of a heretic) could be counted as a good deed (Oliver 1979:61).

5 The impact of Islamic writing on oral cultures

1 Some other features are associated with Islam – the stress on sandals, handed down from father to son (p. 62), and the taboo of one group on the wearing of Turkish slippers (p. 124) – a definition of one's role in opposition to Islamic culture.

2 The importance of Islam in the area is brought out in the excellent film which Germaine Dieterlen and Jean Rouch have made of the 1969 performance of the Dogon *sigi* ceremony. The final shot shows the mosque in the background and the serpent masks in the foreground.

3 My collaborator, J. A. Braimah, was elected to the Kpembe chiefship and became Yagbumwura, the paramount of Gonja, in February 1983.

4 The religious status of the ruling estate in Gonja is a matter for discussion, not to my mind a very profitable one. It would perhaps be more appropriate to call it partially Muslim, but it still ranked as non-literate, with one notable exception in recent years.

5 In commenting upon two studies of Ifa divination, Morton-Williams (1966:407) writes: "The sixteen columns of the set of *odu* signs are identical with the signs used in a system of geomancy originating in antiquity in the Near East. The procedure survived to be acquired as a form of astronomical geomancy in Mediaeval Europe and continued later (see, for instance, Franz Hartmann's *The Principles of Astrological Geomancy: the Art of Divining by Punctuation According to Cornelius Agrippa and Others*, London, 1889 and 1913). It was also accepted by the Arabs, and several authors have surmised that not only Ifa and related forms in West Africa but also *Sikidi* divination in Madagascar were developed locally as variations on the system as diffused by the Arabs into Muslim Africa . . . Indications of an Arabic origin for the basic procedure of Ifa divination are given in the names Ifa, which may derive from the Arabic *al-fa'l*, pl. *fu'ul* and *af'ul* (auspice) and Orunmila, possibly the Yoruba vocalization of Arabic *al-raml* . . . 'divination by sand'."

6 I have discussed this view at greater length in other places, namely 1957, 1961 and 1975.

7 The attendance of the chiefs of Tuluwe at Kpembe in August 1894 is evidence of the latter (Braimah and Goody 1967:132); the events leading up to the Kong war and the invasion of Samory's forces are examples of the former.

8 Wa, Dagomba, Nanumba, Asante, Banda and Bouna.

8 Memory and learning in oral and literate cultures: the reproduction of the Bagre

1 These discussions are reviewed by Cole and Scribner (1977), to whom I am indebted for oral as well as written assistance.
2 See M. Gilbert, *Jewish History Atlas*, London, 1969; E. E. Evans-Pritchard, *The Nuer*, Oxford, 1940.
3 In this attempt to see the Bagre in relation to certain general intellectual discussions, I am indebted to many individuals with whom I have collaborated and to institutions that have supported the research. First among these is S. W. D. K. Gandah, with whom I have worked on the collection, translation and annotation of various versions of the Bagre over many years of hard and patient work. My more immediate debts are to the École des hautes études en sciences sociales and to the Van Leer Foundation respectively for their hospitality and support from March to June, and June to September 1975. On the subject of oral 'literature' in Africa, I am grateful for conversations with Pierre Smith of the CNRS, Paris; on the psychological side, I have to thank the other Van Leer Fellows, M. Cole, R. Case, D. Olson and W. Rohwer, Jnr. On re-reading this chapter and on looking again at Finnegan's discussion of these questions in her book, *Oral Literature in Africa*, I find she has anticipated many of the points made here; she assesses the flexibility of oral composition, and observes that it is the existence of writing that may lead to "the concept of a correct version, which can be copied or learnt in exact form" (1970:106–7). Even where strong emphasis is placed upon exactness, as in the case of the Ifa verses, variation is considerable (Bascom 1969).

9 Writing and formal operations: a case study among the Vai

1 This paper was written with Michael Cole and Sylvia Scribner. The research on which it is based was made possible by a grant from the Ford Foundation to Scribner and Cole, and Fellowships to Goody and Cole from the Van Leer Foundation, Jerusalem. Our thanks to Mohamed Nyei for making possible the interviews on which this paper is based.
2 E. N. Goody, *Contexts of Kinship*, Cambridge, 1972.
3 The Vai word is *kɔŋpiŋ*, which derives the English 'company' and is a term widely used for a 'voluntary' or non-kinship association in West Africa. See P. Hill, *The Migrant Cocoa-Farmers of Southern Ghana, a study in rural capitalism*, Cambridge, 1970.
4 For a brief description of local practice, see the articles by J. Goody and I. Wilks in *Literacy in Traditional Societies* (ed. J. Goody), Cambridge, 1968.
5 See Koelle (1854) for an account of the early history of the Vai script. Current practices in the use and teaching of the script have been

investigated by M. Smith whom we thank for helpful comments on the paper.

6 Field notes, June 1975.

7 Dollars have been used as currency in Liberia for many years, including the period covered by these books. However, sterling was in common use when Sonie first entered business and continued as currency for much longer in neighbouring Sierra Leone.

8 What is known as a 'clan' by English-speaking Vai is a territorial unit, the sub-division of a chiefdom.

9 Accounts of funeral contributions among the LoDagaa are given in J. Goody, *Death, Property and the Ancestors*, Stanford University Press, 1962; accounts of contributions to the Bagre association of the same people are found in J. Goody, *The Myth of the Bagre*, Oxford, 1972. See also chapter 6 above.

10 See Scribner and Cole, 1976, for a brief description of other types of activity involving Vai literacy.

11 Language and writing

1 As Steven Levinson has pointed out to me, sentence complexity is difficult to define, a fact that lies behind the inconsistency between this observation and that of Portnoy. Both, however, seem to me reconcilable. It is a question of a more adequate definition of the variables.

2 Sentences are rarely left hanging in the air. Of course, the written language systematically extracts lexemes (especially nouns) from the context of the sentence, as in a dictionary.

3 Bourdieu's criticism of the notion of 'rule' (1977) is relevant here.

4 One interesting current use of a logographic script from Taiwan indicates its strengths, apart from the avoidance of certain reading difficulties. The island is inhabited by people speaking a variety of non-mutually intelligible Chinese languages, as well of course as those of the indigenous population. Television programmes are often supplemented by subtitles in Chinese script which are intelligible to all readers, no matter which language they speak. A broadly comparable use of Chinese characters (*kanji*) is made in Japan to sort out the ambiguities arising from the use of the syllabic script (*kana*), which is problematical because of the number of homophones.

5 It could be said that literacy institutionalizes a criterion of achievement which appears to (and to some extent does) replace ascription. But in fact, family circumstance plays a notable part in such achievement and hence disguises a certain perpetuation of the *status quo*.

Bibliography

Adams, R. McC. 1966. *The Evolution of Urban Society*. Chicago
Akinnaso, F. N. 1981. The consequences of literacy in pragmatic and theoretical perspectives. *Anthropology and Education Quarterly* 12:163–200
   1982. On the differences between spoken and written language. *Language and Speech* 25:97–125
Albright, W. F. 1949. *The Archaeology of Palestine*. London
Alleton, V. 1978. La transcription alphabétique du chinois: forme et pédagogie du *pinyin* en République Populaire de Chine. *Cahiers de Linguistique d'Orientalisme et de Slavistique*, Univ. de Provence 10:9–21
Bâ, A. H. and Dieterlen, G. 1961. *Koumen: texte initiatique des pasteurs peul*. Paris
Bâ, A. H. and Kesteloot, L. (eds.) 1969. *Kaïdara*. Paris.
Bâ, A. H., *et al.* 1974. *L'éclat de la grande étoile suivi du Bain rituel*. Paris
Baines, J. 1983. Literacy and ancient Egyptian society. *Man* N.S. 18:572–99
Bartlett, F. C. 1932. *Remembering*. Cambridge
Bascom, W. 1969. *Ifa Divination: communication between gods and men*. Bloomington, Indiana
Bernstein, B. 1964. Elaborated and restricted modes: their social origins and some consequences. In J. Gumpertz and D. Hymes (eds.), *The Ethnography of Communication, American Anthropologist*, 66:6, pt.2
Biebuyck, D. and Mateene, K. C. (eds.) 1971. *The Mwindo Epic: from the Banyanga, Congo Republic* (first edn. 1969). Berkeley, California
Binger, L. G. 1892. *Du Niger au Golfe de Guinée: par le pays de Kong et le Mossi*. Paris
Bloch, M. (ed.) 1975. *Political Language and Oratory in Traditional Society*. London
Bloomfield, L. 1933. *Language*. New York
Boas, F. 1927. *Primitive Art*. Oslo
Boelaert, E. 1949. Nsong'â Lianja, l'épopée nationale des Nkundó. *Aequatoria* 12:2–76

1957. Lianja-verhalen, I. Ekɔfɔ-versie. *Annales du Musée Royal du Congo Belge*. vol. 17

1958. Lianja-verhalen, II. De voorouders van Lianja. *Annales du Musée Royal du Congo Belge*, vol. 19

Bogin, M. 1976. *The Women Troubadors*. New York

Bottéro, J. 1977. Les noms de Marduk, l'écriture et la 'logique' en Mésopotamie ancienne. In *Ancient Near Eastern Studies in Memory of J. J. Finkelstein*, Connecticut Academy of Arts and Sciences, Memoir 19, 5–27

1982. Le 'Code' de Hammu-rabi. *Annali della Scuola Normale Superiore di Pisa* 12:409–44

Boulding, K. E. 1961. *The Image*. Ann Arbor, Mich.

Bourdieu, P. 1977. *Outline of a Theory of Practice* (transl. R. Nice). Cambridge

Boyer, P. 1983. Barricades mysterieuses et piège à pensée: introduction à l'analyse des épopées fang, '*mvet ekan*'. Doctoral thesis, University of Paris, X

Braimah, J. A. n.d. *Gonja Drums*. Bureau of Ghana Languages, Accra

Braimah, J. A. and Goody, J. 1967. *Salaga: the struggle for power*. London

Brice, W. C. and Grumach, E. 1962. Studies in the structure of some ancient scripts: the writing system of the Proto-Elamite Account Tablets of Susa. *Bulletin of the John Rylands Library* 45:15–57

Brough, J. 1953. Some Indian theories of meaning. *Trans. Philol. Soc.* 161–76

Brown, P. and Fraser, C. 1978. Nominal and verbal language styles. Ms. Social and Political Sciences Committee, University of Cambridge

Brown, R. W. 1958. *Words and Things*. Glencoe, Ill.

Bruner, J. S. 1966. *Studies in Cognitive Growth*. New York

1974. *Beyond the Information Given: studies in the psychology of knowing*. London

Bryden, M. P. and Allard, F. 1974. Dichotic listening and the development of linguistic processes. In M. Kinsbourne (ed.), *Hemispheric Asymmetry of Function*. London

Bühler, J. G. 1898. *On the Origin of the Indian Brāhma Alphabet* (second edn, Strassburg)

Bushnell, P. P. 1930. *An Analytic Contrast of Oral with Written English*. Bureau of Publications, Teachers College. Columbia University

Butel, P. and Mandon, G. 1977. Alphabétisation et scholarisation en Aquitaine au XVIIIe et au début du XIXe siècle. In F. Furet and J. Ouzouf, *Lire et Écrire*. Paris

Camara, S. 1976. *Gens de la parole; essai sur la condition et le rôle des griots dans la société Malinké*. Paris

Carpenter, E. 1973. *Oh, What a Blow that Phantom gave Me!* New York

Carpenter, R. 1933. The antiquity of the Greek alphabet. *Am.J. Arch.* 37:8–29

Carraher, T. and D. 1981. Do Piagetian stages describe the reasoning of unschooled children? *The Quarterly Newsletter of the Laboratory of Comparative Human Cognition* 3:61–68

Chadwick, H. M. 1912. *The Heroic Age*. Cambridge

Chadwick, H. M. and N. K. 1932–40. *The Growth of Literature*, 3 vols. Cambridge

Chadwick, J. 1976. *The Mycenaean World*. Cambridge

Chafe, W. 1980. The deployment of consciousness in the production of a narrative. In W. L. Chafe (ed.), *The Pear Stories: cognitive, cultural, and linguistic aspects of narrative production*. Norwood, New Jersey

Chomsky, N. 1968. *Language and Mind*. New York

1970. Phonology and reading. In H. Levin and J. P. Williams (eds.), *Basic Studies in Reading*. New York

Chomsky, N. and Halle, M. 1968. *The Sound Pattern of English*. New York

Clanchy, M. T. 1979. *From Memory to Written Record*. London

Clark, J. G. D. 1977. *World Prehistory* (third edn). Cambridge

Clark, J. P. 1977. *The Ozidi Saga: collected and translated from the Ijo of Okabou Ojobolo*. Ibadan

Clère, J. J. 1938. Acrostiches et mots croisés des Anciens Egyptiens. *Chronique d'Egypte* 25:35–58

Cohen, G. 1973. Hemispheric differences in serial versus parallel processing. *J. Experimental Psychology* 97:349–56

Coldstream, J. N. 1977. *Geometric Greece*. London

Cole, M. and Scribner, S. 1974. *Culture and Thought*. New York

1977. Cross-cultural studies in memory and cognition. In R. V. Kail, Jnr. and J. W. Hagen (eds.), *Perspectives on the Development of Memory and Cognition*. Hillsdale, New Jersey

Compére, M-M. 1977. École et alphabétisation en Languedoc aux XVIIe et XVIIe siècles. In F. Furet and J. Ouzouf, *Lire et Écrire*. Paris

Coupez, A. and Kamanzi, T. 1970. *Littérature de Cour au Rwanda*. Oxford

Cox, M. 1893. *Cinderella* (Folklore Society Monograph series, No.31). London

Cross, F. M. 1967. The origin and early evolution of the alphabet. *Eretz-Israel* 8:8–24

1974. Leaves from an epigraphist's notebook: the oldest Phoenician inscription from the Western Mediterranean. *The Catholic Biblical Quarterly* 36:490–3

Crystal, D. and Davy, D. 1969. *Investigating English Style*. London

Dasen, P. R. 1972. Cross-cultural Piagetian research: a summary. *J. Cross-cultural Psychol.* 3:29–39

Debray, R. 1980. *Le Scribe: genèse du politique*. Paris

Demsky, A. 1977. A proto-Canaanite Abecedary dating from the Period of the Judges and its implications for the history of the alphabet. *Tel Aviv* 4:14–27

De Dampierre, E. (ed.) 1953–. *Classiques Africains*. Paris

De Rop, A. 1964. Lianja, l'épopée des Mɔngɔ. *Académie Royale des Sciences d'Outremer* 30:1

De Saussure, F. 1960. *Course in General Linguistics*. London (first French edn 1916)

Devito, J. A. 1965. Comprehension factors in oral and written discourse of skilled communicators. *Speech Monographs* 32:124–8

1967. Levels of abstraction in spoken and written English. *J. of Communication* 17:354–61

Dewdney, S. 1975. *Scrolls of the Southern Ojibway*. Toronto

Diringer, D. 1948. *The Alphabet, a Key to the History of Mankind*. London

1962. *Writing*. London

Djilas, M. 1957. *The New Class: an analysis of the Communist system*. London

Drieman, G. H. J. 1962. Differences between written and spoken language. *Acta Psychologia* 20:36–57, 78–100

Driver, G. R. 1948. *Semitic Writing*. London

Douglas, M. 1966. *Purity and Danger*. London

Dumestre, G. and Kesteloot, L. 1975. *La Prise de Dionkoloni*. Paris

Dupuis, J. 1824. *Journal of a Residence in Ashantee*. London

Dow, S. 1956. Review of works on Homer. *Classical Weekly* 49:116–9

Ebin, V. 1978. The Aowin priestesses: vessels of the gods. Ph.D. dissertation, University of Cambridge

Ekman, P. 1976. Movements with precise meanings. *J. of Communication* 26:14–16

Erbs, A. 1975. *Approche de la religion des Birifor*. Paris

Evans-Pritchard, E. E. 1937. *Magic, Witchcraft and Oracles among the Azande*. Oxford

1940. *The Nuer*. Oxford

Fairservis Jnr., W. A. 1983. The script of the Indus Valley civilization. *Scientific American* 248:44–52

Falk, D. 1984. The petrified brain. *Natural History* 93:36–9

Fallers, L. A. n.d. *Bantu Bureaucracy*. Cambridge

Febvre, L. and Martin, H. J. 1958. *L'Apparition du livre*. Paris

Fielding, G. and Coope, E. 1976. *Medium of communication, orientation to interaction, and conversational style*. (Paper presented at the Social Psychology Section, Conference of the British Psychological Society)

Finnegan, R. 1970. *Oral Literature in Africa*. Oxford

1973. The Great Divide. In R. Finnegan and R. Horton (eds.), *Modes of Thought*. London

1977. *Oral Poetry: its nature, significance and social context*. Cambridge

Flint, M. S. 1954. *Revised Eskimo Grammar Book* (Canadian Eastern Arctic) (original ed. E. J. Peck, *Grammar Book*, Little Whale River, 1883). Toronto

Fox, J. A. and Justeson, J. S. 1985. Evidence for the languages of the Classic Maya. In L. Campbell and J. S. Justeson (eds.), *Phoneticism in Mayan Hieroglyphic Writing*. Albany, New York

Gagné, R. C. 1960. On the importance of the phonemic principle in the design of an orthography. *Arctic* 13, reprinted in R.C. Gagné, *Tentative Standard Orthography for Canadian Eskimos*, Welfare Division, Ministry of Northern Affairs and National Resources. Ottawa (1961)

Gardiner, A. H. 1916. The Egyptian origin of the Semitic alphabet. *Journal of Egyptian Archaeology* 3:1–16

   1947. *Ancient Egyptian Onamastica*. London

Gelb, I. J. 1952. *A Study of Writing*. Chicago (rev. edn 1963)

   1974. Writing, forms of. *Encyclopaedia Brittanica*, vol. 19 (fifteenth edn). Chicago

Gellner, E. 1978. Notes towards a theory of ideology. *L'Homme* 18:69–82

Gibson, E. J., Gibson, J. J., Pick, A. D. and Osser, H. 1962. A developmental study of the discrimination of letter-like forms. *J. Comp. and Phys. Psych.* 55:897–906

Gibson, J. W. *et al.* 1966. A quantitative analysis of differences and similarities in written and spoken messages. *Speech Monographs* 33:444–51

Gilbert, M. 1969. *Jewish History Atlas*. London

Glick, J. 1975. Cognitive development in cross-cultural perspective. In F. D. Horowitz (ed.), *Review of Child Development Research*, 4. Chicago

Gluckman, M. 1944. The logic of African science and witchcraft. *J. Rhodes-Livingstone Inst.* 1:61–71

   1949–50. Social beliefs and individual thinking in primitive society. *Memoirs and Proceedings of Manchester Literary and Philosophic Society* 91:73–98

   1955. *The Judicial Process among the Barotse of Northern Rhodesia*. Manchester

Gombrich, E. H. J. 1968. *Art and Illusion: a study in the psychology of pictorial art* (third edn). London

Goody, E. N. 1972. *Contexts of Kinship*. Cambridge

   1978. Towards a theory of questions. In E. N. Goody (ed.), *Questions and Politeness: strategies in social interaction*. Cambridge

Goody, J. 1954. *The Ethnography of the Northern Territories of the Gold Coast, West of the White Volta*. Colonial Office, London, (mimeo)

   1957. Anomie in Ashanti? *Africa* 27:356–365

   1961. Religion and ritual: the definitional problem. *British Journal of Sociology* 12:142–163

   1962. *Death. Property and the Ancestors*. Stanford

   1964. The Mande and the Akan Hinterland. In J. Vansina *et al.* (eds.), *The Historian in Tropical Africa*. London

   1968a. Time: social organization. *International Encyclopedia of the Social Sciences*, vol.16. New York

   1968b. (ed.) *Literacy in Traditional Societies*. Cambridge

   1970. Marriage policy and incorporation in northern Ghana. In

R. Cohen and J. Middleton (eds.), *From Tribe to Nation in Africa*, San Francisco. Reprinted in J. Goody, *Comparative Studies in Kinship*. Stanford, 1969

1971a. *Technology. Tradition and the State in Africa*. London

1971b. The impact of Islamic writing on the oral cultures of West Africa. *Cah. d'Et. Afr.* 11:455–66

1972. *The Myth of the Bagre*. Oxford

1975. Religion, social change and the sociology of conversion. In J. Goody (ed.), *Changing Social Structure in Ghana*. London

1977a. Tradizione orale e ricostruzione del passato nel Ghana del Nord. *Quaderni Storici* 35:481–92

1977b. *The Domestication of the Savage Mind*. Cambridge

1977c. Mémoire et apprentissage dans les sociétés avec et sans écriture: la transmission du Bagré. *L'Homme* 17:29–52

1980a. Rice burning and the Green Revolution in northern Ghana. *J. Dev. Studies* 16:136–55

1980b. Thought and writing. In E. Gellner (ed.), *Soviet and Western Anthropology*. London

1982. *Cooking, Cuisine and Class*. Cambridge

1986a. *The Logic of Writing and the Organization of Society*. Cambridge

1986b. Religion, writing and revolt in Bahia. *Visible Language* 20:316–43

Goody, J. and Duly, C. 1981. Studies in the Use of Computers in Social Anthropology (Report to the S.S.R.C.)

Goody, J. and Gandah, S.W.D.K. (eds.) 1981. *Une Récitation du Bagré*. Paris

Goody, J. and Watt, I. P. 1963. The consequences of literacy. *Comparative Studies in Society and History* 5:304–45. Reprinted in J. Goody (ed.), 1968, *Literacy in Traditional Societies*. Cambridge

Gordon, E. I. 1959. *Sumerian Proverbs: glimpses of everyday life in Ancient Mesopotamia*. Philadelphia

Gough, K. 1968. Implications of literacy in traditional China and India. In J. Goody (ed.), *Literacy in Traditional Societies*. Cambridge

Gower, E. 1973. *The Complete Plain Words* (rev. B. Fraser, second edn). H.M.S.O., London

Gray, J. 1964. *The Canaanites*. London

Green, J. R. 1958. A comparison of oral and written language; a quantitative analysis of the structure and vocabulary of a group of college students. Unpubl. Ph.D diss., New York University

Green, M. W. 1981. The construction and implementation of the cuneiform writing system. *Visible Language* 15:345–72

Greenfield, P. M. 1972. Oral or written language: the consequences for cognitive development in Africa, the United States and England. *Language and Speech* 15:169–78

Greenfield, P. M., Reich, L. C. and Olver, R. R. 1966. On culture and equivalence. II. In J. S. Bruner *et al.* (eds.), *Studies in Cognitive Growth*. New York

Greimas, A. J. 1966. *Sémantique structurale*. Paris

Griaule, M. 1965. *Conversations with Ogotemmêli: an introduction to Dogon religious ideas*. (Fr. edn 1948) London

Gruner, C. R. *et al.* 1967. A quantitative analysis of selected characteristics of oral and written vocabularies. *J. of Communication* 17:152–8

Gurney, O. R. 1952. *The Hittites*. London

Hainsworth, J. B. 1970. The criticism of an oral Homer. *J. Hellenic Studies* 90:90–8

Hammel, E. A. 1972. *The Myth of Structural Analysis: Lévi-Strauss and the Three Bears*. Reading, Mass.

Hartman, F. 1889. *The Principles of Astrological Geomancy: the art of divining by punctuation according to Cornelius Agrippa and others*. London

Hatta, T. 1977. Recognition of Japanese *Kanji* in the left and right visual fields. *Neuropsychologia* 15:685–8
    1981. Differential processing of Kanji and Kana stimuli in Japanese people: some implications from Stroop-test results. *Neuropsychologia* 19:87–94

Havelock, E. A. 1963. *Preface to Plato*. Cambridge, Mass
    1973. *Prologue to Greek Literacy*, Lectures in Memory of Louise Taft Semple. University of Cincinnati Classical Studies, vol. 2. Cincinnati
    1976. *Origins of Western Literacy*. Monograph Series, No.14. The Ontario Institute for Studies in Education

Hawkins, J. A. 1979. The origin and dissemination of writing in Western Asia. In P.R.S. Moorey (ed.), *Origins of Civilization*, pp. 128–66. Oxford

Hill, P. 1970. *The Migrant Cocoa-Farmers of Southern Ghana, a study in rural capitalism*. Cambridge

Hiskett, M. 1957. Material relating to the state of learning among the Fulani before their Jihād. *Bull. S.O.A.S.* 19:550–78

Hockett, C. F. 1960. The origin of speech. *Sci. Am.* 203:88–106

Hodgkin, T. 1966. The Islamic literary tradition in Ghana. In I. M. Lewis (ed.), *Islam in Tropical Africa*. London

Horton, R. 1967. African traditional thought and western science. *Africa* 37:50–71, 155–187

Huddleston, R. D. 1971. *The Sentence in Written English*. Cambridge

Hunter, I. M. L. 1985. Lengthy verbatim recall: the role of text. In A. Ellis (ed.), *Progress in the Psychology of Language*, vol. 1. Erlbaum Associates, London

Innes, G. 1973. Stability and change in *griots'* narrations. *African Language Studies* 14:105–18

Innis, H. 1950. *Empire and Communication*. Oxford
    1951. *The Bias of Communication*. Toronto

James, T. G. H. 1979. *An Introduction to Ancient Egypt* (rev. edn). London

Jeffrey, L. H. 1961. *The Local Scripts of Archaic Greece: a study of the origin of the Greek alphabet and its development from the eighth to the fifth centuries BC*. Oxford

Jeorger, M. 1977 L'alphabétisation dans l'ancien diocèse de Rouen au XVIIe et au XVIIIe siècles. In F. Furet and J. Ouzouf (eds.), *Lire et Écrire*. Paris

Jevons, F. R. 1870. *Elementary Lessons in Logic: deductive and inductive*. London

Johnson-Laird, P. 1983. *Mental Models*. London

Jones, D. 1943. Differences between spoken and written language. *Journal of Education* 70:207–8

  1957. *The History and Meaning of the Term 'Phoneme'*. Int. Phonetic Ass., London

Joos, M. 1962. The five clocks. *International J. of American Linguistics*, Monograph No. 28

Kaufman, E. L., Lord, M. W., Reese, T. W. and Volkmann, J. 1949. The discrimination of visual number. *Am. J. Psych.* 62:498–525

Kaump, E. A. 1940. An analysis of the structural differences between oral and written language of one hundred secondary school students. Unpubl. Ph.D. diss., University of Wisconsin

Kay, P. 1977. Language evolution and speech style. In B. G. Blount and M. Sanchez (eds.), *Sociocultural Dimensions of Language Change*. New York

Keith, A. 1948. *A New Theory of Human Evolution*. London

Kinnier Wilson, J. V. 1974. *Indo-sumerian: a new approach to the problems of the Indus script*. Oxford

Kirk, G. 1962. *The Songs of Homer*. Cambridge

  1976. *Homer and the Oral Tradition*. Cambridge

Koelle, S. W. 1854. *Outline of a Grammar of the Vai Language, together with a Vai-English vocabulary and an account of the Vai mode of syllabic writing*. London

Kramer, F. W. 1970. *Literature among the Cuna Indians*. Göteberg

Kramer, S. N. 1956. *From the Tablets of Sumer*. Indian Hills, Colorado

Kuhn, T. 1962. *The Structure of Scientific Revolutions*. Chicago

Labov, W. 1970. The logic of non-standard English. In F. Williams (ed.), *Language and Poverty*. Chicago

Labouret, H. 1932. *Les Tribus du rameau Lobi*. Paris

Lavelle, L. 1947. *La Parole et l'écriture*. Paris

Leach, E. 1976. *Culture and Communication: the logic by which symbols are constructed*. Cambridge

Le Brun, A. and Vallat, F. 1978. L'origine de l'écriture à Suse. *Cahiers de la délégation archéologique française en Iran* 8:15–18

Lenneberg, F. H. 1953. Cognition in ethnolinguistics. *Language* 29:463–71. Reprinted in P. Adams (ed.), *Language in Thinking* (Penguin Modern Psychology Readings), 1972. London

Leroi-Gourhan, A. 1964. *Le Geste et la parole*. Paris

Lévi-Strauss, C. 1964. *Le Cru et le cuit.* Paris
   1965. Le triangle culinaire. *L'Arc* 26:17–29. Engl. trans. P. Brooks, *Partisan Review* 1966. 33:586–95
Levin, H. *et. al.* 1981. The formality of the Latinate lexicon in English. *Language and Speech* 24:161–71
Levtzion, N. 1966. Early nineteenth century Arabic manuscripts from Kumasi. *Transactions of the Historical Society of Ghana* 8:99–119
Levy, J. and Trevarthen, C. 1976. Metacontrol of hemispheric function in human split-brain patients. *J. Exp. Psychol.: Human, Perception, Performance* 2:299–312
Lévy-Bruhl, L. 1910. *Les Fonctions mentales dans les sociétés inférieures.* (Eng. transl. 1926). Paris
Lewis, I. M. 1966. Introduction. In I. M. Lewis (ed.), *Islam in Tropical Africa.* London
Lieberman, P. *et al.* (1972). *The Speech of Primates.* The Hague
Lieberman, S. J. 1980. Of clay pebbles, hollow clay balls, and writing: a Sumerian view. *Am. J. Arch.* 84:339–58
Lienhardt, G., Whiteley, W. and Evans-Pritchard, E. E. (eds.), *Oxford Library of African Literature.* Oxford
Lloyd, G. E. R. 1966. *Polarity and Analogy.* Cambridge
   1979. *Magic, Reason and Experience: studies in the origins and development of Greek science.* Cambridge
Lord, A. B. 1960. *The Singer of Tales.* Cambridge, Mass.
   1967. The influence of a fixed text. In *To Honor Roman Jakobson*, vol. 2 (Janua Linguarum, Series Maior, 32). Paris and the Hague
Lord, A. B. (ed.) 1974. The wedding of Smailagić Meho, by Avdo Međedović, *Serbocroatian Heroic Songs Collected by Milman Parry*, vol. 3. Cambridge, Mass.
Luria, A. R. 1973. *The Working Brain: an introduction to neuropsychology.* London
   1976. *Cognitive Development.* Cambridge, Mass.
MacIntyre, A. 1967. *A Short History of Ethics.* London
MacLeod, R. C. 1930. *The Island Clans during Six Centuries.* Inverness
Macqueen, J. G. 1975. *The Hittites and their Contemporaries in Asia Minor.* London
Mallery, G. 1886. *Pictographs of the North American Indians – a preliminary paper.* Fourth Annual Report of the Bureau of Ethnology to the Secretary of the Smithsonian Institution, 1882–83. Washington
   1893. *Picture-writing of the American Indians.* Tenth Annual Report of the Bureau of Ethnology to the Secretary of the Smithsonian Institution, 1888–89. Washington (Reprinted Dover Publications, New York, 1972, 2 vols.)
Marcel, T. *et al.* 1974. Literality and reading proficiency. *Neuropsychologia* 12:131–9
Marcus, J. 1976. The origins of Mesoamerican writing. *Ann. Rev. Anthrop.* 5:35–67

1980. Zapotec writing. *Sci. Am.* 242:50–78

Matthiae, P. 1979. *Ebla in the Period of the Amorite Dynasties and the History of Recent Archaeological Discoveries at Tell Mardikh.* Malibu, California

1980. *Ebla: an empire rediscovered.* London (Italian edn 1977)

Maxwell, K. B. 1983. *Bemba Myth and Ritual: the impact of literacy on an oral culture.* New York

McCarter, P. K. 1975. *The Antiquity of the Greek Alphabet and the Early Scripts.* Missoula, Montana

McLuhan, M. 1962. *The Gutenberg Galaxy.* Toronto

Mehta, V. 1984. *Daddyji-Mamaji.* London

Meillassoux, C. *et al.* 1967. *Légende de la dispersion des Kusa: épopée soninké.* Dakar

Miller, G. A. 1951. *Language and Communication.* New York

1956. The magical number seven, plus or minus: some limits on our capacity for processing information. *Psychol. Rev.* 63:81–97

Miller, G. A., Gallanter, E. and Pibram, K. 1960. *Plans and the Structure of Behavior.* New York

Morton-Williams, P. 1966. Two studies of Ifa divination. Introduction: the modes of divination. *Africa* 26:406–8

Mulder, J. W. F. and Hervey, S. G. J. 1972. *Theory of the Linguistic Sign* (Janua Linguarum, Series Minor, 136). The Hague

Murra, J. 1980. *The Economic Organization of the Inka State.* Greenwich, Conn.

Nadel, S. F. 1951. *The Foundations of Social Anthropology.* London

Nagler, N. N. 1967. Towards a generative view of the oral formula. *Trans. and Proc. Am. Philological Association* 98:269–311

Narveh, J. 1973. Some Semitic epigraphical considerations on the antiquity of the Greek alphabet. *Am. J. Arch.* 77:1–8

Needham, J. 1956. *Science and Civilization in China* Vol. 2, *History of Scientific Thought.* Cambridge

Neisser, U. 1976. *Cognition and Reality: principles and implications of cognitive psychology.* San Francisco

Neugebauer, O. 1969. *The Exact Sciences in Antiquity* (second edn). New York

Niane, D. T. 1965. *Sundiata: an epic of old Mali* (transl. G. D. Pickett). London

Nordenskiöld, E. 1938. *An Historical and Ethnological Study of the Cuna Indians.* Göteborg

Norman, D. A. 1969. *Memory and Attention.* New York

Norris, H. T. 1972. *Saharan Myth and Saga.* Oxford

Oates, J. 1980. The emergence of cities in the Near East. In A. Sherratt (ed.), *The Cambridge Encyclopaedia of Archaeology.* Cambridge

Ojemann, G. A. 1983. Brain organization for language from the perspective of electrical simulation mapping. *The Behavioral and Brain Sciences* 6:189–230

Oliver, C. F. 1979. Some aspects of literacy in Ancient India. *The Quarterly Newsletter of the Laboratory of Comparative Human Cognition* 1:57–62

Olson, D. R. 1975. Review of *Towards a Literate Society*, J. B. Caroll and J. Chall (eds.), *Proceedings of the National Academy of Education* 2:109–78

    1976. From utterance to text: the bias of language in speech and writing. In H. Fisher and R. Diez-Gurerro (eds.), *Language and Logic in Personality and Society*. New York

Ong, W. J. 1974. *Ramus Method, and the Decay of Dialogue* (first published 1958). New York

    1982. *Orality and Literacy: the technologizing of the word*. London

Opie, I. and P. 1959. *The Lore and Language of Schoolchildren*. Oxford

Oppenheim, A. L. 1964. *Ancient Mesopotamia*. Chicago

Page, D. 1973 *Folktales in Homer's Odyssey*. Cambridge, Mass.

Parpola, A. 1970. *Further Progress in the Indus Script Decipherment*. Copenhagen

Parry, A. 1966. Have we Homer's Iliad? *Yale Classical Studies* 20:177–216

Parry, M. 1930. Studies in the epic technique of oral verse-making. I. Homer and Homeric style. *Harvard Studies in Classical Philology* 41:73–147

    1932. Studies in the epic technique of oral verse-making. II. The Homeric language as the language of an oral poetry. *Harvard Studies in Classical Philology* 43:1–50

    1971. *The Making of Homeric Verse* (A. Parry, ed.). Oxford

Parsons, T. 1937. *The Structure of Social Action*. New York

    1951. *The Social System*. Glencoe, Ill.

Pepper, H., De Wolf, P. and P. (eds.) 1972. *Un Mvet de Zwè Nguéma, chant épique fang*. Paris

Pettinato, G. 1981. *The Archives of Ebla: an empire inscribed in clay*. New York

Piaget, J. 1966. *The Child's Conception of Physical Causality* (Engl. transl.). London

Portnoy, S. 1973. A comparison of oral and written behaviour. In K. Salzinger and R. S. Feldman (eds.), *Studies in Verbal Behaviour: an empirical approach*. New York

Powell, M. A. 1981. Three problems in the history of cuneiform writing: origins, direction of script, literacy. *Visible Language* 15:419–40

Pulgram, E. 1951. Phoneme and grapheme: a parallel. *Word* 7:15–20

    1965. Graphic and phonetic systems: figures and signs. *Word* 21:208–24

Quinton, A. 1967. Knowledge and belief. *The Encyclopaedia of Philosophy* 4:345–52. New York

Quirk, R. 1968. Relative clauses in educated spoken English. In *Essays on the English Language*. London

Rawski, E. S. 1979. *Education and Popular Literacy in Ch'ing China*. Ann Arbor, Mich.

Ray, J. D. 1978. The world of North Saqqara. *World Archaeology* 10:149–57

Reder, S. 1981. The written and spoken word: influence of Vai literacy on Vai speech. In S. Scribner, and M. Cole (eds.), *The Psychology of Literacy*. Cambridge, Mass.

Renou, L. 1947. *Les Écoles vediques et la formation du Veda*. Paris
   1954. *The Civilization of Ancient India*. Calcutta (French edn 1950).

Rosaldo, M. Z. 1982. Things we do with words: Ilongot speech acts and speech act theory in philosophy. *Language and Society* 11:203–37

Rosch, E. 1977. Human categorization. In N. Warren (ed.), *Studies in Cross-cultural Psychology*, vol. 1. London

Rosemont Jnr., H. 1974. On representing abstractions in Archaic Chinese. *Philosophy East and West* 24: 71–88

Rosenmeyer, T. G. 1965. The formula in early Greek poetry. *Arion* 4:295–308

Russo, J. A. 1967. Review of A. Hoekstra, *Homeric Modifications of Formulaic Prototypes* (Amsterdam 1965). *Am. J. Philology* 88:340–6

Salzinger, R. S. and Feldman, R. S. (eds.), 1973. *Studies in Verbal Behavior: an empirical approach*. New York

Sasanuma, S. *et al.* 1977. Tachistoscopic recognition of *Kana* and *Kanji* words. *Neuropsychologia* 15:547–53

Schmandt-Besserat, D. 1977. An archaic recording system and the origin of writing. *Syro-Mesopotamian Studies* 1/2:1–32
   1978. The earliest precursor of writing. *Sci. Am.* 238:38–47
   1981. From tokens to tablets: a revaluation of the so-called "numerical tablets". *Visible Language* 15:321–44

Scribner, S. 1969. *Cognitive Consequences of Literacy*. Albert Einstein College of Medicine (mimeo)

Scribner, S. and Cole, M. 1973. Cognitive consequences of formal and informal education. *Science* 182:553–9
   1974. Research program on Vai literacy and its cognitive consequences. *IACCP Cross-Cultural Psychology Newsletter* 8:2–4
   1976. Literacy as practice and social milieu. (Paper presented at International Congress of Psychology, Paris)
   1981. *The Psychology of Literacy*. Cambridge, Mass.

Schapera, I. 1955. The sin of Cain. *J. R. Anthrop. Inst.* 85:33–44

Seydou, C. (ed.) 1972. *Silâmaka et Poullôri*. Paris

Shengde, M. J. 1985. The inscribed calculi and the invention of writing: the Indus view. *J. Econ. Soc. Hist. Orient.* 28:50–80

Sherzer, J. 1983. *Kuna Ways of Speaking*. Austin, Texas

Simmons, A. A. 1962. A comparison of the type-token ratio of spoken and written language of deaf and hearing children. *The Volta Review* 417–421

Skoyles. J. R. 1984. Alphabet and the Western mind. *Nature* 309:409–410

Smith, E. 1975. The relations between the spoken and the written language. In E. and L. Lenneberg (eds.), *Foundations of Language*, vol.2. London

Smith, P. 1975. *Le Récit populaire au Ruanda* (Classiques Africains). Paris

Smith, R. 1966. On the White Yajurveda vaṃśa. *East and West* 16:112–25

Smout, T. C. 1969. *A History of the Scottish People 1560–1830*. London

Southall, A. 1956. *Alur Society: a study in processes and types of domination*. Cambridge

Staal, J. F. 1961. *Nambudiri Veda Recitation* (Disputationes Rheno-Trajectinae, 5). The Hague

Stanner, W. E. 1959–63. *On Aboriginal Religion*. Oceania Monograph No. 11. Sidney (1966)

Stebbing, L. S. 1939. *Thinking to Some Purpose*. Harmondsworth

Stone, L. 1969. Literacy and education in England 1640–1900. *Past and Present* 42:69–139

Street, B. 1985. *Literacy in Theory and Practice*. Cambridge

Thomas, K. 1971. *Religion and the Decline of Magic*. London

Todorov, T. 1970. *Introduction à la littérature fantastique*. Paris

Trimingham, J. S. 1959. *Islam in West Africa*. Oxford

Tsao, Y. C. *et al.*, 1979. Stroop interference in the left and right visual fields. *Brain and Language* 8:367–71

Tseng, O. J. L. and Wang, W. S. Y. 1984. Search for common neurocognitive mechanism for language and movements. *Am J. Physiol.* 246:R904–R911

Turner, V. 1966. *The Ritual Process: structure and antistructure*. London

Ucko, P. J. and Rosenfeld. A. 1967. *Palaeolithic Cave Art*. London

Vachek. J. 1939. Zum problem der geschriebenen Sprache. *Travaux du Cercle Linguistique de Prague* 8:94–104

   1959. Two chapters on written English. *Brno studies in English* 1:7–38

   1973. *Written Language: general problems and problems of English* (Janua Linguarum, Series Critica, 14). The Hague

Vansina, J. 1965. *Oral Tradition*. London (first Belgian edn. 1961)

Ventris, M. and Chadwick, J. 1956. *Documents in Mycenaean Greek*. Cambridge

Vieillard, G. 1931. Récits peuls du Macina et du Kounari. *Bulletin du comité d'études historiques et scientifiques de l'Afrique Occidentale Française* 14:137–56

Von Humboldt, W. 1971. [1863] *Linguistic Variability and Intellectual Development*. Coral Gables, Fla.

Vygotsky, L. S. 1934. *Thought and Language* (Engl. transl. 1962). Cambridge, Mass.

   1978. *Mind and Society: the development of higher psychological processes* (Engl. transl.). Cambridge. Mass.

Wang, W. S. Y. 1981. Language structure and optimal orthography. In O. J. L. Tseng and H. Singer (eds.), *Perception of Print: reading research in experimental psychology*, pp. 223–36. Hillsdale, New Jersey

Wardhaugh, R. 1969. *Reading: a linguistic perspective*. New York

Warnock, G. J. 1971. *The Object of Morality*. London

Werner, H. and Kaplan. B. 1963. *Symbol Formation*. New York

White, M. J. 1969. Laterality differences in perception: a review. *Psychological Bulletin* 72:387–405

Whorf, B. L. 1956. *Language, Thought and Reality* (ed. J. B. Carroll). Cambridge, Mass.

Wilbert, J. W. (ed.) 1978. *Folk Literature of the Gê Indians*, vol. 1. University of California, Los Angeles

Wilks, I. 1963. The growth of Islamic learning in Ghana. *J. Hist. Soc. Nigeria* 2:409–17

  1968. The transmission of Islamic learning in the Western Sudan. In J. Goody (ed.), *Literacy in Traditional Societies*. Cambridge

Williams, B. 1972. *Morality: an introduction to ethics*. New York (1976, Cambridge)

Williams, R. (ed.) 1981. *Contact: human communication and its history*. London

Wilson, B. (ed.) 1970. *Rationality*. Oxford

Wiseman, D. J. 1970. Books in the Ancient Near East and in the Old Testament. In P. R. Ackroyd and C. E. Evans (eds.), *The Cambridge History of the Bible*, vol. 1, *From the Beginnings to Jerome*. Cambridge

Wordsworth, W. and Coleridge, S. T. 1793. Introduction. In W. Wordsworth and S. T. Coleridge (eds.), *The Lyrical Ballads*. London

Yates, F. 1966. *The Art of Memory*. London

Zandee, J. 1966. An Egyptian cross-word puzzle. *Ex Oriente Lux*, Leiden

Zuidema, T. 1982. Bureaucracy and systematic knowledge in Andean civilisation. In G. A. Collier, R. L. Rosaldo and J. D. Wirth (eds.), *The Inca and the Aztec States, 1400–1800: anthropology and history*. New York

Zurif, E. B. and Sait, P. E. 1970. The role of syntax in dichotic listening. *Neuropsychologia* 8:239

Index

abcedaries, 61
Abyssinia, 98
accounts, 36
acrostics, 272–3
Afeg, 48
  Afeg Tablet, 45
Africa 139, 140, 141, 155
  diglossia, 281
  epic poetry, absence of, 100–1
  literature, relationship of society to, 97
  Nsibidi script, 139
  oral tradition, 79, 80
  orally transmitted religion, 130–1
  see also East Africa, West Africa
aoidoi, 158
Akkadian, 43, 72–3, 74, 92
  diglossia, 281
alphabets, 40–53, 97, 106
  China, contemporary, 283
  chronological order of development, 42, 61–3
  consonantal, 44, 46, 62–3, 64, 65
  origin of, 40–1, 61–3, 125
  Roman, ordering of letters, 64
Arabic, 98, 120, 125, 194
  ability of literates, 235
  literacy in West Africa, 215
  script, 126
  use by Vai in West Africa, 194–5, 224
Aramaic script, 43, 45, 63
argument
  in literate and non-literate societies, 72
  oral reproduction of, 178
  role of, in Greek achievement, 64–5, 70, 72

Aristotle
  logic, 278
  Poetics, 106
Asante, 97, 136, 154, 277
  Arabic manuscripts, content, 130
Asia, Central
  literacy, relationship to reasoning, 220–1
astrology
  the zodiac, 128
astronomy, 121, 132
  as force in development of science, 74
  role of writing in, 239–40
Australian *Churinga*, 74–5
Azande, 68

Baal Myth, 45
Babylonia, 65, 74, 76, 132, 145
  schools, 183
  script, 42
Bagre, myth of the, xiii, 79, 80–1, 89, 96, 99, 101, 103–4, 109, 149, 150, 157, 169–70, 294, 295, 298
  Black, 89, 91, 95, 152, 170, 171, 234
  First, 149, 150
  Funeral, 151
  Lawra, 150
  recitation of, 81, 88, 103–4, 150, 151, 156, 168–71, 223, 295
  recording, 94–6, 172; written, effect of, 298–9
  transmission, 111, 296–7
  variability in, 103, 104, 156, 170, 295–6, 299
  White, 87, 88, 91, 168, 170, 171, 172, 295
  written versions, truth value of, 299

321